PENGUIN BOOKS

LIGHT THE DARK

Joe Fassler is a writer based in Brooklyn. He regularly interviews authors for *The Atlantic*'s "By Heart" series. He is a graduate of the Iowa Writers' Workshop, and his fiction has appeared in *Boston Review, Electric Literature,* and elsewhere. In 2011, his reporting for TheAtlantic.com was a finalist for a James Beard Foundation Award in Journalism. He is currently a senior editor at *The New Food Economy.*

Doug McLean is an artist and illustrator based in the Boston area. He has an MFA in visual arts from Rutgers University and has been contributing drawings for the "By Heart" series since 2013.

Light the Dark

Writers *on* Creativity, Inspiration, *and the* Artistic Process

Edited by

Joe Fassler

Illustrations by

Doug McLean

PENGUIN BOOKS

PENGUIN BOOKS

An imprint of Penguin Random House LLC
375 Hudson Street
New York, New York 10014
penguin.com

The contributions by Junot Díaz, Ayana Mathis, Leslie Jamison,
Hanya Yanagihara, Eileen Myles, Marilynne Robinson, and Neil
Gaiman are published for the first time in this volume. The other
essays appeared in the "Big Heart" series on TheAtlantic.com,
some in different form and/or under different titles.

Illustrations by Doug McLean

LIBRARY OF CONGRESS CATALOGING-IN-PUBLICATION DATA
Names: Fassler, Joe, editor.
Title: Light the dark : writers on creativity, inspiration, and the artistic
process / edited by Joe Fassler ; illustrations by Doug Maclean.
Description: New York : Penguin Books, 2017.
Identifiers: LCCN 2017003038 (print) | LCCN 2017020729 (ebook) |
ISBN 9781524704643 (ebook) | ISBN 9780143130840 (paperback)
Subjects: LCSH: Creation (Literary, artistic, etc.) | BISAC: LANGUAGE
ARTS & DISCIPLINES / Composition & Creative Writing.
Classification: LCC BF408 (ebook) | LCC BF408 L53 2017 (print) |
DDC 153.35—dc23
LC record available at https://lccn.loc.gov/2017003038

Printed in the United States of America
1 3 5 7 9 10 8 6 4 2

Set in Dante

Contents

JOE FASSLER *Preface* ix

AIMEE BENDER *Light the Dark* 1

SHERMAN ALEXIE *Leaving the Reservation
of the Mind* 7

ELIZABETH GILBERT *In Praise of Stubborn Gladness* 15

STEPHEN KING *You've Been Here Before* 23

AMY TAN *Pixel by Pixel* 31

JUNOT DÍAZ *A Friend of the Mind* 39

WILLIAM GIBSON *The Handshake* 47

KHALED HOSSEINI *Everything I Meant to Say* 55

ANDRE DUBUS III *Do Not Think, Dream* 61

MARY GAITSKILL *I Don't Know You Anymore* 69

MICHAEL CHABON *To Infinity and Beyond* 75

WALTER MOSLEY *How I Awoke* 83

JIM CRACE *Stealing Plums and Counting Stones*   87

EDWIDGE DANTICAT *All Immigrants Are Artists*   93

BILLY COLLINS *Into the Deep Heart's Core*   99

KATHRYN HARRISON *Please Stop Thinking*   109

DAVID MITCHELL *Neglect Everything Else*   115

ROXANE GAY *Dreaming in Drag*   123

TOM PERROTTA *Ordinary People*   127

AYANA MATHIS *Against Unreality*   137

JIM SHEPARD *No One Ever Changes*   145

KARL OVE KNAUSGAARD *Lose Yourself*   149

LESLIE JAMISON *On Commonness*   157

JONATHAN LETHEM *Letting the Leopards In*   165

JESSE BALL *The Edge of Sense*   173

ANGELA FLOURNOY *A Place to Call My Own*   179

LEV GROSSMAN *Into the Wardrobe, into the Self*   185

YIYUN LI *Strangers on a Train*   193

MAGGIE SHIPSTEAD *Time Passes*   199

JEFF TWEEDY *Translating the Subconscious*   205

NELL ZINK *The Long Game*   213

CHARLES SIMIC *Lifting the Blanket*   219

VIET THANH NGUYEN *Follow This Voice*   227

EMMA DONOGHUE *You and Me*   233

CLAIRE MESSUD *Words on Paper Will Outlast Us*   239

JANE SMILEY *Nobody Asked You to Write That Novel*   247

JONATHAN FRANZEN *My Favorite Curmudgeon*   257

HANYA YANAGIHARA *Writing for Right Now*   267

BEN MARCUS *Recommended Dosage*   273

MARK HADDON *Music for Misfits*   281

AZAR NAFISI *Enough About Me*   287

T. C. BOYLE *How Stories Say Goodbye*   295

ETHAN CANIN *Rehearsals for Death*   303

EILEEN MYLES *Happy Accidents*   311

MARILYNNE ROBINSON *The Brain Is Larger
    Than the Sea*   319

NEIL GAIMAN *Random Joy*   325

Acknowledgments   333

I read a book one day and my whole life was changed.
—ORHAN PAMUK, *The New Life*

Preface

I'll be honest: This preface didn't write itself. I struggled with these words, the ones you're reading now. And that surprised me, even though I've learned that writing is rarely easy, because I really thought this would be a breeze.

After all, the goal was straightforward. I only needed to introduce this collection, which grows out of "By Heart," an online series I created for *The Atlantic* in 2013. I've been explaining the approach for years: I ask working artists (many of them writers) to choose a favorite passage from literature, the lines that have hit them hardest over the course of a lifetime's reading. Each person looks closely at his or her selection, explains its personal impact, and makes a case for why it matters. Taken together, these pieces offer a rare glimpse into the creative mind at work—how artists learn to think, how they find inspiration, and how they get things done.

But it turned out to be harder than I expected to settle on a single frame. These pieces—which start as phone or coffee table conversations, then become transcripts that I edit and send back to the writer to polish and complete—are part memoir, part literary criticism, part

craft class, part open studio. They take on an array of big topics: identity, adversity, ethics, aesthetics. Not to mention that each writer draws
from a private well of experience, and their interests vary widely. Over
the course of more than 150 interviews for *The Atlantic*, as well as brand-
new ones for this book, I've felt like a perpetual student—of creative
writing and literature, sure, but also of sociology, psychology, and political science. Every week I have private office hours with a different brilliant teacher. But though each writer had been asked the same simple
question, no single thesis seemed to capture the richness of their responses. Trying to find one was as hard—almost—as choosing a single
favorite line from all the passages you cherish.

Then something happened. It's an experience these writers often describe having, I've noticed, when things become difficult: I found the
way forward between the covers of another book.

This time, it was Nobel laureate Orhan Pamuk's novel *The New Life*,
which begins with this incredible first sentence: "I read a book one day
and my whole life was changed." What a way to start! Pamuk counters
the expectations we bring to a story's first pages—*go ahead, dazzle me*—
with a fictionalized experience of ecstatic reading. The narrator's head,
as he reads, seems to float off his shoulders. The pages themselves
shine with penetrating light. And that's when he realizes: He'll never
be the same, not after this.

I'd picked the novel almost randomly from my shelf, and read these
words in disbelief—it was as if they'd been written for me. Because
they're exactly what this book is about, and as I read them I suddenly
understood the approach that I needed to take here.

At the core of each of these pieces is a moment of transformative
reading—an encounter with a short, artful sequence of words that hits
with life-altering force. Whether the crucial encounter happened decades ago or just last week, each contributor tells some version of the
same story: *I read something, and I wasn't the same afterward*. It might seem
fantastical, at first, the way Pamuk's narrator looks down on luminous
pages while his head floats near the ceiling. But the authors in this

collection, like everyone who's felt themselves transfigured by a work of art, know it's not too far from real-life experience. Aimee Bender explains how lines by Wallace Stevens made her heart race and mind sparkle, like she'd downed a few strong espressos. A passage in *Anna Karenina* made Mary Gaitskill physically rise to her feet, the words too intense to take sitting down. David Mitchell calls a cherished James Wright poem a "skull melter," a coinage I love: It conjures a sense of intense light and heat, and also of the cage of the head dissolving away, allowing the mind, the self, to blend freely with the world outside. It really *can* feel like that, stumbling on the right words at the right time. This book seeks to put that indescribable experience into concrete language.

But what do we mean, really, when we say *this book changed my life*? And what's happening in those heightened minutes of engagement, as our heads seem to fill with helium, as our feet pull from the floor? After years of interviewing writers, I think I've found the simplest way to say it: It's about problem-solving. It's akin to what scientists call "the aha! moment"—the instant when the solution to some complex problem becomes clear. These accounts reckon with that strange, heightened sensation, the feeling of a momentous realization sinking in. Then, they chart the unpredictable path ideas take from genesis to maturity, mapping the way creative epiphanies come into being, grow, and take enduring shape.

Some of these pieces describe creative breakthroughs—moments when another book points the way forward, like what happened to me with Pamuk and this preface. In the snaking cadences of Portuguese novelist António Lobo Antunes, for instance, Viet Thanh Nguyen found the voice he needed to begin a novel about the Vietnam War— the book that became his Pulitzer Prize–winning debut. As these writers describe overcoming artistic challenges, you'll also find insight into craft: master classes on beginnings and endings, plot and character, sound and rhythm, finding inspiration, beating writer's block. But none of this, I should say, belongs to the general, cheerless genre of "writing advice." It's something far more useful, and it extends into any creative activity: Specific individuals share how they solved specific problems, day by day, and book by book.

Some of these breakthroughs take place on a far more personal level—these writers describe reaching fundamental insights about who they are and how they want to live. Toni Morrison's *Beloved* taught an angry Rutgers student named Junot Díaz that his identity had been shattered by injustice, but also that great art could provide a kind of glue. And it took an Adrian C. Louis poem for Sherman Alexie to understand that literature wasn't just Joyce Kilmer and John Keats: It was also on the Spokane reservation where he grew up, waiting for him. Not that everyone reaches such clarity, not all the time. Sometimes, it's just the feeling that a book has enlarged you somehow, providing you not so much with answers as with better, clearer questions. As Pamuk's protagonist describes it:

> This was the kind of light within which I could recast myself; I could lose my way in this light; I already sensed in the light the shadows of an existence I had yet to know and embrace. . . . My whole life was changing as I read the new words on each new page.

These writers inhabited one world when they turned the page. By the time they flipped it again, they inhabited another universe entirely. Something about the way the words were written aged them in an instant and provided a glimpse of who they would now have to become.

The Wallace Stevens poem Aimee Bender discusses, "Final Soliloquy of the Interior Paramour," is about the power of the imagination to break down barriers. It's about the ability we all share to enliven our world through imagination and creativity. In Stevens's telling, that power is no less than god-like: "We say God and the imagination are one . . . / How high that highest candle lights the dark." That's the experience told and retold in this book, the moment when the high candle of the mind beams incandescent, bringing clarity to what had been obscure, mysterious, overlooked, and forgotten—lighting up the dark.

Isn't that what you're looking for, too? The kind of encounter described in these pieces—when a few words take off the top of your skull and let the light shine in? I'm guessing that's why you hold this book in your hands, even now. A life can change in a paragraph, in a turn of phrase, in a single well-used word. This book maps the way to many of those moments. Let it re-create the experience of wandering through a well-curated bookstore, everything secondhand. Feel yourself fill with the anticipation that this time, maybe, the passage you stumble on will draw a vivid line, that clear before and after. Can you smell the yellowing pages, softened by years of thumbs? Can you feel your fingers brush these spines? Take something down. Each one has been chosen for a reason. And if it changes your life, too, you're not alone.

JOE FASSLER

Light the Dark

How high that highest candle lights the dark.
—WALLACE STEVENS,
"Final Soliloquy of the Interior Paramour"

AIMEE BENDER

Light the Dark

I FIRST HEARD "Final Soliloquy of the Interior Paramour" at a funeral. A large funeral, and a very sad one. A poet read it to the people gathered, and I found it moving, and helpful, but in a kind of inexplicable way. It's something of an oblique poem. It concerns mystery, and its language is itself mysterious. Yet there was something in it that I sensed, even listening for the first time, about a community coming together to support this family and pay tribute to this life.

The poet knew Stevens's poem very well—it was like it had metabolized in her. She'd absorbed it fully in a way that helped us absorb it, too. I felt that magical alchemy of poetry, the way it acknowledges things we can't fully understand. I felt very sad about the death that had happened, but there was a healing line from this poet to the people sitting around.

Right away, I knew I'd want to look that poem up and spend more time with it. One line—"We say God and the imagination are one"—stuck with me especially. There's something beautifully enigmatic about that line: It contains what feels so expansive and mysterious about the imagination to me. I love the way it treats the imagination with an almost-religious reverence.

A friend of mine, the *Tin House* editor Cheston Knapp, wrote an essay once where he recalled memorizing a Frost poem as a younger man—he was making fun of himself, calling out the pretentiousness of this. And it's funny, because I found myself thinking: *I want to do that.* Not in a showy way. I don't want to perform a poem. I just like the idea of having the words accessible in my mind. I love poetry, and I wanted to carry Stevens's poem with me. To live with it. I'd never been required to memorize anything before—the days of learning poems by heart in school are gone—and suddenly, I wanted to.

It took a while for me to learn the words, which I'd repeat to myself while driving in L.A. Trying to speak a poem over and over, you learn to pay attention to all its nooks and crannies: I had to ask myself, is it "a" or "the"? Is the phrase "miraculous influence," or something else? You have to slow down so intensely to read a poem and take it all in. As I tried to digest it, chew over all its details, I started to feel the way the lines flowed into one another. I started to understand it through its shape.

Here's what surprised me: When I had it all memorized, I felt *elated.* I had a physical response to holding all those words in my mind together. A real buzz—that was shocking to me. But it also makes sense because it was the same thing that happened to me at the funeral: Hearing the poem aloud, it had this certain physical magic that I recognized. Speaking it aloud, the same powerful feeling came through. When I spoke the poem, just as when I heard it, I could feel something happening within.

The poem's meaning shifted for me, too. The line I'd liked so much at first, "We say God and the imagination are one," began to seem darker. I started to feel it was acknowledging human limitation, addressing the way we invent things to comfort ourselves. That's when the next line rose up, a line I'd completely overlooked when reading on the page: "How high that highest candle lights the dark."

This image is expansion and limit all at once. Stevens has just told us that our largest, most expansive thoughts are still contained within us, that our sense of God or something larger exists only within our minds. We feel there's something larger but, no—that's in our minds. Yet this idea turns again with "how high that highest candle lights the dark": Even within our human limitations, how beautiful we can be. It's still just a little candle, but how high: our beauty, our capacity for thought and feeling, for togetherness. Our humanness is vast and ripe and gorgeous, and, as Stevens says at the end of the poem, "being there together is enough." Even though he's struggling with the nature of what we imagine, the poem ultimately enters a place where connection is possible between people. Ultimately, I think it's a hopeful poem in that way.

Part of the reason the memorization appealed to me is I felt like I want these lines available to me at certain times of my life—if something is difficult, or something is joyous, I want to feel like I have access to words that will help me think about and express what I'm feeling. And the more the better. We can be so vague in our memory of books. Paragraphs that we loved become slippery, then gone. Memorization was a way for me to force myself to be more precise, and to forge a more permanent relationship to the words. It allowed a certain kind of magical construction to get in my mind and simmer there. The work of tinkering with the language that exquisite, that well-wrought, is so exciting—it reminds you what art can do. I had a physical reaction. I felt caffeinated. And that feeling lasted for a long time.

Granted, I'm someone who loves words. I've always loved poetry—so it's suited to me. But I still was shocked by the poem's palpable effect on me. I think we're biologically impacted by language. It can be deeply, deeply nourishing. And I don't mean that as a metaphor. It can feel like something cellular gets fed. When language is treated beautifully and interestingly, it can feel good for the body: It's nourishing, it's rejuvenating. This is not the way we typically think about literature, which we tend to talk about as taking place inside the head—even if it's the emotional part of the head. To feel energized by Stevens was a singular experience that reminded me how words register in our physical bodies, too. It felt like concrete proof that literature is important.

I was talking once to David Wilson, who curates the Museum of

Jurassic Technology. He said, "I don't know why not knowing where a story is going is nourishing, but it is." I love that—because it's true. When I don't know where a story is going, I feel better—I physically feel better, after not knowing and then being surprised. Language, when it's that worked-through, is such a gift. The human being needs language, and the human being needs language to be treated well—not just with easy, throwaway sentences. Skimming and reading constantly and reading lightly is not enough. Slow down: It's good for the brain. Memorizing Stevens *forced* me to slow down. It was nice to realize, *I can turn off the radio as I drive. I can say these poems aloud, and see what they do.*

I draw this same physical nourishment from my own work, too, at times. If I write something that I'm happy about, it means the language is clicking in some way that will sustain me for weeks. Sometimes, one good paragraph can keep me going through weeks of bad paragraphs, all the writing that feels like walking through sludge.

And it's interesting that the writing I tend to think of as "good" is good because it's mysterious. It tends to happen when I get out of the way—when I let it go a little bit, I surprise myself. I feel most pleased with my language when I don't understand it completely. When it sustains hope that there's more to write about, that there's an open door for me to explore. That's when the writing gets really fun. I feel like it's all about waiting for a kind of discovery that takes place on the sentence level. That's the thing that drives me.

Language is the ticket to plot and character, after all, because both are built out of language. If you write a page a day for thirty days, and you pick the parts where the language is working, plot and character will start to emerge organically. For me, plot and character emerge directly from the word—as opposed to having a lightbulb about a character or event. I just don't work like that. Though I know some writers do, I can't. I'll think, oh, I have an insight about the character, and when I'll sit down to write, it feels extremely imposed and lasts for two minutes. I find I can write for two lines and then I have nothing else to say. For me, the only way to find something comes through the sentence level, and sticking with the sentences that give a subtle feeling that there's something more to say. This means I've hit on something unconscious enough to write about—something with enough unknown in there to be brought out. On some level I can sense that, and it keeps me going.

That's why I love Stevens's poem, too—it sits between these great mysteries that he's articulated without dispelling them completely. Some of those mysteries clarify, but they're not all going to clarify. I think a good poem will always stay a little mysterious. The best writing does. The words that click into place, wrap around something mysterious. They create a shape around which something lives—and they give hints about what that thing is, but do not reveal it fully. That's the thing I want to do in my own writing: present words that act as a vessel for something more mysterious. I know it's working when I feel like there's something hovering beneath the verbal, that mysterious emotional place that Stevens wrote about.

Language is limited, it's a faulty tool. But how high it lights the dark.

O Uncle Adrian! I'm in the reservation of my mind.

—ADRIAN C. LOUIS,
"Elegy for the Forgotten Oldsmobile"

SHERMAN ALEXIE

Leaving the Reservation of the Mind

IN 1987, I dropped out of Gonzaga and followed a high school girlfriend to Washington State University (it's called Wazoo). And by complete chance, I enrolled in a poetry workshop that changed my life. On the first day, the teacher, Alex Kuo, gave me an anthology of contemporary Native poetry called *Songs from This Earth on Turtle's Back*. There were poems by Adrian C. Louis, a Paiute Indian, and one in particular called "Elegy for the Forgotten Oldsmobile." If I hadn't found this poem, I don't think I ever would have found my way as a writer. I would have been a high school English teacher who coached basketball. My life would have taken a completely different path.

It was this line, in particular:

O Uncle Adrian! I'm in the reservation of my mind.

I'd thought about medicine. I'd thought about law. I'd thought about business. But that line made me want to drop everything and be a poet. It was that earthshaking. I was a reservation Indian. I had *no options*. Being a writer wasn't anywhere near the menu. So, it wasn't a lightning bolt—it was an atomic bomb. I read it and thought, "This is what I want to do."

The line captured that sense of being tribal, being from a reservation—and the fact that you could never leave. I was the first person in my family ever to go to college, leaving the reservation, leaving my tribe, feeling excited about going but also feeling like I'd betrayed the tribe. And knowing that no matter where I ended up, or what I did, I would always be there. Some large part of me would always be there, on the reservation.

At the same time, I'd never seen myself in a work of literature. I loved books, always, but I didn't know Indians *wrote* books or poems. And then to see myself so fully understood in one line of a poem, as though that one line of a poem written by someone else was my autobiography . . . It was like understanding human language for the first time. It was like hearing the first words ever spoken by a human being, and understanding for the first time the immense communicative power of language.

I had never intellectualized this feeling that I'd had my entire life. And then, to hear the thing aloud. To see it in print. These are the kind of emotions that nobody puts words to, at least not where I'm from. So an intellectual and emotional awakening were fused in this one line. They came together and slapped me upside the head.

I'd written stuff before, but it was always modeled after greeting cards or the standard suspects: Joyce Kilmer, a Keats poem. The classics that every high school kid reads. But as soon as I saw that poem, I knew I could write about myself—my emotional state, the narrative of my emotional life. When I wrote before, I was always wearing a mask—I always adopted a pose. I was always putting on a white guy mask. And all of a sudden, I could actually use my real face.

Immediately, I started writing poems. The poems I wrote were about things that actually happened. I didn't think an Indian's life was important enough to write about until Louis gave me permission to do it. My first poem was called "Good Times," after a Lucille Clifton poem. My poem's original title was "In the HUD House," but I changed it later. It's in my first book, *The Business of Fancydancing*, and it's probably the only one I still have memorized.

Bang. It was right there. It was waiting for me. People talk about "that moment when you just know"—I don't think that many people actually have that moment. But I did. And from then on, there was never a Plan B.

I started publishing with the micro-presses, twenty-six years ago. I was published in journals that were photocopied and hand-stapled. With print runs of a hundred or less. With names like *Tray Full of Lab Mice* and *Giants Play Well in the Drizzle*. I was finding acceptance in those kinds of journals: None of the other Indian writers had really ever *sent* them anything. So when this Indian voice, which they'd never heard before, came in by mail—well, I got published quickly in those journals. The first five or six submissions I sent out were accepted. I ended up in the journals with Bukowski a lot. It was those kinds of places. There was a similar ring to our work—his was much rowdier, but it was the same notion of a desperate life.

I graduated from college and couldn't find a damn job. So I ended up back on the res. And I was on the res—no job, no money, no hope. Those were the days when you wrote letters, so I reached out to Adrian Louis, whose work meant so much to me. I sent him this ranting, raving letter, and he wrote back. There was a $50 bill taped to the paper that said, "Keep writing your poems." So I did.

I wrote some of these poems and stories on a typewriter I borrowed from my girlfriend in the unfinished basement of my reservation HUD house. With typewriter ribbons that I bought with the $50 that Adrian Louis sent to me. It was the most important $50 of my career, certainly.

Then the Brooklyn-based small press Hanging Loose published me. Logically, it should have peaked there. A Native American writer writing mostly about the reservation: I should have stayed "small press." I should have stayed on the reservation inside the literary world. But I got lucky. I was part of an omnibus review of Native literature on the front page of the *New York Times Book Review*. And that only because the editor, Richard Nicholls, was in the slush room—where all the review copies come flying in, pile up, and nobody looks at them—and saw the cover of my book and liked it.

So, it's a line that sits with me all the time. I know I've mentioned it many times before. But until I started talking about it in-depth, it had become rote for me, I think. And it's making me reexamine it again; it's coming to life again by thinking about it so much. What does it mean for me now?

When I was younger, my reaction was much more personal. It became a personal statement for me. And now I think it's a philosophy. I feel like I could start a church with that line. The number one tenet of that church? No cedar flutes. Also, no references to talking animals. And a concerted effort to get everyone off the res. What would be the symbol of my church? It'd be a broken circle. And that would be a positive sign. That break in the circle would really be an explosion of possibility. Indians always praise circles. But they actually are chain-links.

Now I am actively and publicly advocating for Native kids to leave the reservation as soon as they can. The reservation system was created by the U.S. military. It was an act of *war*. Why do we make them sacred now, even though most reservations are really third-world, horrible banana republics? I think "I'm in the reservation of my mind" has an incredibly destructive connotation for me now. It's apocalyptic, when I think about it. The human journey has always been about movement. And a century ago, when we moved onto the reservation, my tribe stopped moving. All the innovation we've done since then has been just modeling after Europeans. I mean, our greatest successes are casinos! So, "I'm in the reservation of my mind" addresses this lack of innovation, the Native imagination being shackled and curtailed, as well as the failure to celebrate the innovations that have happened.

That line "I'm in the reservation of my mind" also suggests to me the marginalization of Native literature. You know, approximately 70 percent of Natives live off the reservation. But you wouldn't guess that judging by our literature. Almost all of it is reservation-centric. So our entire literature is in the reservation of its mind. That line doesn't just describe Adrian's poetic world, the world inside that poem, and it doesn't just describe the effect it had on me: I think it describes the entire literary Native world.

Joy Harjo, who's a Creek Indian poet and a jazz musician, was once asked by a white reporter why she played the saxophone, since it's not an Indian instrument.

And she said: "It is when *I* play it."

If "I'm in the reservation of my mind" is the question, then "It is when I play it" is the answer. It's an internal condition, and we spend too much time defining ourselves by the external. There is always this implication that in order to be Indian you *must* be from the reservation. It's not true and it's a notion that limits us—it forces us to define our entire life experiences in terms of how they do or do not relate to the reservation.

The line also calls to mind the way we tend to revisit our prisons. And we always go back. This is not only true for reservation Indians, of course. I have white friends who grew up very comfortably, but who hate their families, and yet they go back every Thanksgiving and Christmas. Every year, they're ruined until February. I'm always telling them, "You know, you don't have to go. You can come to my house." Why are they addicted to being demeaned and devalued by the people who are supposed to love them? So you can see the broader applicability: *I'm in the suburb of my mind. I'm in the farm town of my mind. I'm in the childhood bedroom of my mind.*

I think every writer stands in the doorway of their prison. Half in, half out. The very act of storytelling is a return to the prison of what torments us and keeps us captive, and writers are repeat offenders. You go through this whole journey with your prison, revisiting it in your mind. Hopefully, you get to a point when you realize there was beauty in your prison, too. Maybe, when you get to that point, "I'm in the reservation of my mind" can also be a beautiful thing. It's on the res, after all, where I learned to tell stories.

You know, for many years, I felt very insecure about being a writer—it wasn't Indian enough. And then, one day, I was on stage and it occurred to me: *Wait. I travel the world telling stories. How Indian is that?* I'm doing the traditional thing—I'm doing the oldest thing known to humans! Before fire and the wheel, we had stories. Why did I ever let Indians who managed casinos make me feel bad about storytelling?

So there is power in this. I get to pick and choose what the prison means to me, float in between the prison bars, return in my mind when and how I want to. We're all cursed to haunt and revisit the people and places that confine us. But when you can pick and choose the terms of that confinement, you, and not your prison, hold the power.

We must risk delight. We can do without pleasure,
but not delight. Not enjoyment. We must have
the stubbornness to accept our gladness in the ruthless
furnace of this world.

—JACK GILBERT, "A Brief for the Defense"

ELIZABETH GILBERT

In Praise of
Stubborn Gladness

IN 2006, I taught creative writing at the University of Tennessee at Knoxville—a rotating chair that brought a new visiting writer each year. I was amused to learn that the writer before me had also been named Gilbert, a fact that caught my eye. (I started jokingly calling the position The Gilbert Chair.) The man had been a poet named Jack Gilbert, whom I'd never heard of. I started asking around about him. It turned out that he'd made quite an impression on the students, and the things I heard about him fascinated me. Jack Gilbert hadn't taught them much about the business of poetry, or how to get published. Instead, he just tried to inspire them to have brave, full lives.

One of the graduate students told me he grabbed her arm one day, as she was leaving class.

"Do you have the courage to be a poet?" he said. "The jewels that are hiding inside you are begging you to say yes!"

Because he said these kinds of things, the students were all very taken with him.

So I found one of Jack Gilbert's books and started to read. I fell in love with him completely—with his poems, but also with his unusual biography. He became the poet laureate of my life, and has been ever since then, for what he wrote and how he wrote and how he regarded his vocation.

Jack Gilbert was born in Pittsburgh in the 1920s. He worked in steel mills and then went out to become a poet. In the 1960s, he published his first book—which was nominated for a Pulitzer, and won the Yale Prize. Here was this charismatic, incredibly handsome, beautiful, and captivating person—in other words, everything you want your young poet to be. He became pretty famous for a poet, photographed for *Vogue* and so on, and could have easily banked on that for a long time. Instead, he disappeared.

He went to live in Europe for twenty years: He lived on mountaintops in Greece, lived in Denmark, went to Italy, had love affairs, never published but just kept writing. He scraped by as best he could, and allowed himself to be completely forgotten. He was completely uninterested in fame, even bored by it. All he wanted to do was focus on his poetry and publish, oh, every twenty years. He did just two major interviews in his life, a brilliant one for the *Paris Review*, and another one with the famous editor Gordon Lish. Lish asked him how isolation had affected his career. Gilbert laughed and said, "I suppose it's been fatal, but I don't really care!"

Gilbert's work is Whitmanesque—it's grandiose, romantic, and very passionate. He's only interested in the big mysteries: God, sex, love, suffering, redemption. He doesn't dabble in anything short of that. And he lived a life that didn't dabble in anything short of that.

He wrote what may be my very favorite poem, "A Brief for the Defense," late in his life; there's maturity in it no youth could ever muster. It feels like something that should be in Ecclesiastes—it's biblical in its wisdom and scope. The poem takes on the central trauma of human consciousness, which is: What are we supposed to do with all this suffering? And how are we supposed to live?

The first lines of the poem are:

Sorrow everywhere. Slaughter everywhere. If babies
are not starving someplace, they are starving
somewhere else. With flies in their nostrils.

So it begins with an admission of how devastating the world is, how unfair and how sad. He goes on to say what he's seen from a life of watching very carefully: women at the fountain in a famine-stricken town, "laughing together between / the suffering they have known and the awfulness / in their future." He describes the "terrible streets" of Calcutta, caged prostitutes in Bombay laughing. So there's this human capacity for joy and endurance, even when things are at their worst. A joy that occurs not despite our suffering, but within it.

When it comes to developing a worldview, we tend to face this false division: Either you are a realist who says the world is terrible, or a naïve optimist who says the world is wonderful and turns a blind eye. Gilbert takes this middle way, and I think it's a far better way: He says the world is terrible *and* wonderful, and your obligation is to joy. That's why the poem is called "A Brief for the Defense"—it's defending joy. A real, mature, sincere joy—not a cheaply earned, ignorant joy. He's not talking about building a fortress of pleasure against the assault of the world. He's talking about the miraculousness of moments of wonder and how it seems to be worth it, after all. And one line from this poem is the most important piece of writing I've ever read for myself:

> We must risk delight. We can do without pleasure,
> but not delight. Not enjoyment. We must have
> the stubbornness to accept our gladness in the ruthless
> furnace of this world.

This defines exactly what I want to strive to be—a person who holds onto "stubborn gladness," even when we dwell in darkness. I want to be able to contain both of them within me at the same time, remain able to cultivate joy and wonder even at life's bleakest.

Sometimes you are lucky enough to meet people who can do this. When I was a diner waitress in Philadelphia in the early '90s, there was a homeless guy who used to come in and sit at the counter, who we all grew fond of and used to feed. He was brilliant, erudite, and well-read, and corrected me when I was a cheeky idiot twenty-two-year-old and called James Jones, who wrote the beautiful novel *From Here to Eternity*, "a one-hit wonder." Which is an idiot thing for a twenty-two-year-old to say. He said, "Hey, kid, you can talk like that after you've made *one* masterpiece."

He had trained as a concert pianist when he was younger, and he lost his finger in an accident when he was well on his way to becoming famous. With this missing finger on one hand, of course, he would never become a concert pianist. He'd grown up in this very wealthy, very brittle family, and had never experienced much tenderness until he went to the hospital with his crushed finger. He told me: "I'll tell you something, kid. The nurses were so kind to me, they were so warm to me, and they were so sweet in a way I had never known before." I remember him holding up his hand then, showing me the missing finger, and saying, "It was worth it!"

That's the "stubborn gladness" Jack Gilbert was talking about. When you weigh the sorrows against these tiny moments of grace—on the balance, it is still worth it to be a human being.

I don't think you can write that poem as a young person. I don't even know if you can write that poem as an old person who hasn't been paying close attention. And that's a fundamental feature of Jack Gilbert—a commitment to paying attention, to not wanting to miss it, and not wanting to turn an eye from it. He has another poem that's a conversation between him and the gods, who offer him a chance to be famous if he would just give up his weird life. But he doesn't settle for that. He says:

> Let me fall
> in love one last time, I beg them.
> Teach me mortality, frighten me
> into the present.

Give me something real, he's asking, and he's not fooling around. Who makes a prayer that includes the words "frighten me"? That's a bold thing to ask for. It's not "frighten" me in the sense of bungee jumping or surfing—it's wanting to stand on the edge of the abyss and look in, look in carefully with an alert gaze. It's a commitment to literature, and a commitment to living.

I saw the same quality in my great-aunt Lolly, who has not had an easy life—but she's the most stubbornly glad person I've ever met. When she was eighty-five, I visited her and she said to me, "Guess what? Guess what I have, Liz?"

"What," I said.

"I have cancer," she said, and this big grin spread across her face. "Isn't that *interesting*?"

And that's part of stubborn gladness, too: to regard things, even the hardest things, as—at their base—interesting. It's hard to say that without sounding like a Pollyanna, but the people who you know who can really do this are not innocents. You see it, too, in Steve Jobs's last words: *Oh wow. Oh wow. Oh wow.*

Full-on wonder, even at the moment of death.

Jack Gilbert addresses this experience directly in "A Brief for the Defense": "If the locomotive of the Lord runs us down," he writes, "we should give thanks that the end had magnitude." That's another one I always lean on. At least it was magnificent—you lived and died, that's *magnificent*. To be able to summon some sort of wonder and gratitude for the fact you got to live and die is the highest calling. It is the best way to go through life—it beats almost any other model of thinking I've ever encountered. I like it better than anything.

As someone who struggles with anxiety and cowardice, as we all do, I'm profoundly inspired by this full-on commitment to wonder, to wonder as a response to anguish or difficulty. It makes everything a puzzle, right? A catastrophe is nothing but a puzzle with the volume of drama turned up very high. For now, I'm best with stubborn gladness when taking on the challenges in my writing life. Because writing can be a very dramatic pursuit, full of catastrophes and disasters and emotion and attempts that fail. My path as a writer became much more smooth when I learned, when things aren't going well, to regard my struggles as curious, not tragic.

So, *How do we get through this puzzle? That's funny, I thought I could write this book and I can't,* instead of, *I have to drink a bottle of gin before eleven to numb myself at how horrifying this is.* You could almost call it a spiritual practice I've cultivated over the years. I really worked to create that kind of relationship—so that it's not a chaotic fight. I don't go up against my writing and come out bloody-knuckled. I don't wrestle with the muse. I don't argue. I try to get away from self-hatred, and competition, all those things that mark and mar so many writers' careers and lives. I try to remain stubborn in my gladness.

We have this very German, romantic idea that if you're not in pain, and if you're not causing pain by making your art, then you're not really doing it right. I've always questioned that. That's one thing that's drawn me to Jack Gilbert—especially when I learned about his relationship to the Beats, who he felt were talented, but blowing it. They weren't reverent enough toward the work, he thought, to want to live clean, sober, disciplined lives in respectful awe of what they were doing. I think this comes from a romantic view—I mean, listen to the language we use to talk about creative process: "Open up your vein and bleed." "Kill your darlings." I always want to weep when people speak about a project and say: "I think I finally broke its back." That is a really fucked-up relationship you have with your work! You're trying to crack its spine? No wonder you're so stressed out! You've made this into a battlefield! We should know enough about the world to realize that anything that you fight fights you back.

I actually have this bright young writer who I really love and who I'm semi-mentoring. When he told me that he'd finished his book, he related his triumph in terms of sex and death: "I love my book. I feel like I killed it. And now it's so hot—I'm going to put this thing out into the world, so everybody can fuck it!"

Okay, he's twenty-five. But I've been to other parts of the world where it is not the assumption that we must beat our art into submission. Indonesian artists say you should begin and end your work with a prayer of gratitude—it's a more reverent kind of collaboration. I respond to that attitude better. I think it's what people have been doing for a lot longer than German Romanticism, which still has its claws in us. I like the idea of collaborating with something respectfully, rather than trying to break it and kill it.

But to write this way, to live this way, takes courage. I have an uncle who's a great reader of poetry, and I shared Jack Gilbert's work with him. He said he didn't like him, and I asked why. My uncle said, "I like the poems, but I don't like the way the poems make me feel I haven't lived a brave or interesting enough life." That's the pain and pleasure of reading Gilbert. He offers an uncompromising challenge to his readers: Make the very most of your life, no less. In this, he holds up a model of something I would so love to be. Sometimes I brush up against it sideways, and then skirt away from it again—because I long for security and affirmation more than I long for the purity of a life spent in examination of the poetic mysteries.

"Do you have the *courage* to be a poet?" Gilbert asked the graduate student, after all. We need courage to take ourselves seriously, to look closely and without flinching, to regard the things that frighten us in life and art with wonder. We tend to surround ourselves with the things that make us feel safe, but can then wall us in. We're aspirational, we're ambitious, we're insecure, we want comforts. Live bravely when you're young, we say. And maybe again when you retire, if you play your cards right.

Jack Gilbert refused that argument: *No, I'm just going to live that way every single day of my life, thanks.* And he did, by all accounts.

This is what happened.

—Douglas Fairbairn, *Shoot*

STEPHEN KING

You've Been Here Before

THERE ARE ALL sorts of theories and ideas about what constitutes a good opening line. It's a tricky thing, and tough to talk about because I don't think conceptually while I work on a first draft—I just write. To get scientific about it is a little like trying to catch moonbeams in a jar.

But there's one thing I'm sure about. An opening line should invite the reader to begin the story. It should say: Listen. Come in here. You want to know about this.

How can a writer extend an appealing invitation—one that's difficult, even, to refuse?

We've all heard the advice writing teachers give: Open a book in the middle of a dramatic or compelling situation, because right away you engage the reader's interest. This is what we call a "hook," and it's true, to a point. This sentence from James M. Cain's *The Postman Always Rings Twice* certainly plunges you into a specific time and place, just as something is happening:

They threw me off the hay truck about noon.

Suddenly, you're right inside the story—the speaker takes a lift on a hay truck and gets found out. But Cain pulls off so much more than a loaded setting—and the best writers do. This sentence tells you more than you think it tells you. Nobody's riding on the hay truck because they bought a ticket. He's basically a drifter, someone on the outskirts, someone who's going to steal and filch to get by. So you know a lot about him from the beginning, more than maybe registers in your conscious mind, and you start to get curious.

This opening accomplishes something else: It's a quick introduction to the writer's style, another thing good first sentences tend to do. In "They threw me off the hay truck about noon," we can see right away that we're not going to indulge in a lot of foofaraw. There's not going to be much floridity in the language, no persiflage. The narrative vehicle is simple, lean (not to mention that the book you're holding is just 128 pages long). What a beautiful thing—fast, clean, and deadly, like a bullet. We're intrigued by the promise that we're just going to zoom.

Of course, it's a little do-or-die here for the writer. A really bad first line can convince me *not* to buy a book—because, god, I've got *plenty* of books already—and an unappealing style in the first moments is reason enough to scurry off. I'll never forget the botched opening lines of A. E. van Vogt—a Canadian science fiction writer, long dead, who liked to effuse a little bit. His book *Slan* was actually the basis of the *Alien* films—they basically stole them to do that, and ended up paying his estate some money—but he was just a terrible, terrible writer. His short story "Black Destroyer" begins:

On and on Coeurl prowled!

You read that, and you think—my god! Can I really put up with even five more pages of this? It's just *panting*!

So an intriguing context is important, and so is style. But for me, a good opening sentence really begins with voice. You hear people talk about "voice" a lot, when I think they really just mean "style." Voice is more than that. People come to books looking for something. But they don't come for the story, or even for the characters. They certainly don't come for the genre. I think readers come for the *voice*.

A novel's voice is something like a singer's—think of singers like Mick Jagger and Bob Dylan, who have no musical training but are instantly recognizable. When people pick up a Rolling Stones record, it's because they want access to that distinctive quality. They know that voice, they love that voice, and something in them connects profoundly with it. Well, it's the same way with books. Anyone who's read a lot of John Sandford, for example, knows that wry, sarcastic amusing *voice* that's his and his alone. Or Elmore Leonard—my god, his writing is like a fingerprint. You'd recognize him anywhere. An appealing voice achieves an intimate connection—a bond much stronger than the kind forged, intellectually, through crafted writing.

With really good books, a powerful sense of voice is established in the first line. My favorite example is from Douglas Fairbairn's novel *Shoot*, which begins with a confrontation in the woods. There are two groups of hunters from different parts of town. One gets shot accidentally, and over time tensions escalate. Later in the book, they meet again in the woods to wage war—they reenact Vietnam, essentially. And the story begins this way:

This is what happened.

For me, this has always been the quintessential opening line. It's flat and clean as an affidavit. It establishes just what kind of speaker we're dealing with: someone willing to say, *I will tell you the truth. I'll tell you the facts. I'll cut through the bullshit and show you exactly what happened.* It suggests that there's an important story here, too, in a way that says to the reader: *and you want to know.*

A line like "This is what happened" doesn't actually *say* anything— there's *zero* action or context—but it doesn't matter. It's a voice, and an invitation, that's very difficult for me to refuse. It's like finding a good friend who has valuable information to share. Here's somebody, it says, who can provide entertainment, an escape, and maybe even a way of looking at the world that will open your eyes. In fiction, that's irresistible. It's why we read.

We've talked so much about the reader, but you can't forget that the opening line is important to the writer, too. To the person who's actually boots-on-the-ground. Because it's not just the reader's way in, it's the *writer*'s way in also, and you've got to find a doorway that fits us both. I think that's why my books tend to begin as first sentences—I'll write that opening sentence first, and when I get it right I'll start to think I really have something.

When I'm starting a book, I compose in bed before I go to sleep. I will lie there in the dark and think. I'll try to write a paragraph. An opening paragraph. And over a period of weeks and months and even years, I'll word and reword it until I'm happy with what I've got. If I can get that first paragraph right, I'll know I can do the book.

Because of this, I think, my first sentences stick with me. They were a doorway I went through. The opening line of *11/22/63* is "I have never been what you'd call a crying man." The opening line of *Salem's Lot* is "Almost everyone thought the man and the boy were father and son." See? I remember them! The opening line of *It* is "The terror, which would not end for another twenty-eight years—if it ever did end—began, so far as I know or can tell, with a boat made from a sheet of newspaper floating down a gutter swollen with rain." That's one that I worked over and over and over.

But I can tell you right now that the best first line I ever wrote—and I learned it from Cain, and learned it from Fairbairn—is the opening of *Needful Things*. It's the story about this guy who comes to town, and uses grudges and sleeping animosities among the townspeople to whip everyone up into a frenzy of neighbor against neighbor. And so the story starts off with an opening line, printed by itself on a page in 20-point type:

You've been here before.

All there by itself on one page, inviting the reader to keep reading. It suggests a familiar story; at the same time, the unusual presentation brings us outside the realm of the ordinary. And this, in a way, is a promise of the book that's going to come. The story of neighbor against neighbor is the oldest story in the world, and yet this telling is (I hope) strange and somehow different. Sometimes it's important to find that kind of line: one that encapsulates what's going to happen later without being a big thematic statement.

Still, I don't have a lot of books where that opening line is poetry or beautiful. Sometimes it's perfectly workman-like. You try to find something that's going to offer that crucial way in, any way in, whatever it is as long as it works. This approach is closer to what worked for my book *Doctor Sleep.* All I remember is wanting to leapfrog from the timeframe of *The Shining* into the present by talking about presidents, without using their names. The peanut farmer president, the actor president, the president who played the saxophone, and so on. The sentence is:

> On the second day of December in a year when a Georgia peanut farmer was doing business in the White House, one of Colorado's great resort hotels burned to the ground.

It's supposed to do three things. It sets you in time. It sets you in place. And it recalls the ending of the book—though I don't know it will do much good for people who only saw the movie, because the hotel doesn't burn in the movie. This isn't grand or elegant—it's a door-opener, it's a table-setter. I was able to take the motif—chronicle a series of important events quickly by linking them to presidential administrations—to set the stage and begin the story. There's nothing "big" here. It's just one of those grace notes you try to put in there so that the narrative has a feeling of balance, and it helped me find my way in.

Listen, you can't live on love, and you can't create a writing career based on first lines.

A book won't stand or fall on the very first line of prose—the story has got to be there, and that's the real work. And yet a really good first line can do so much to establish that crucial sense of voice—it's the first thing that acquaints you, that makes you eager, that starts to enlist you for the long haul. So there's incredible power in it, when you say, *Come in here. You want to know about this.* And someone begins to listen.

Not I, not any one else can travel that road for you,
You must travel it for yourself.

It is not far, it is within reach,
Perhaps you have been on it since you were born and did not
    know,
Perhaps it is everywhere on water and on land.

        —WALT WHITMAN, "Song of Myself"

AMY TAN

Pixel by Pixel

In my novel *The Valley of Amazement*, a character named Edward Ivory recites the following lines from Walt Whitman's "Song of Myself":

> Not I, not any one else can travel that road for you,
> You must travel it for yourself.

> It is not far, it is within reach,
> Perhaps you have been on it since you were born and did not know,
> Perhaps it is everywhere on water and on land.

I discovered this passage when I was writing the book, wondering how Edward, the son of a Western merchant, came to be in China. As I was working, I randomly took a book of poems off my shelf and found this passage facing me. The words just stared up at me from the page. And I realized: *This is what the character is about.* No, more than that: *This is what my writing is about. This is what my whole life is about.*

No one can travel your own road for you; you must travel it for yourself. My faith in this stems from my childhood. I grew up in a family with a system of religious beliefs handed down to me. In addition to being an engineer, my father was a Baptist minister. I attended church every Sunday. Sometimes, during the summer, I went to church every day—attended Bible study, choir practice, constant church activities. I tried so hard to be good. I tried so hard to hear Jesus. I tried so hard to get guidance from God. But I never could. I did my best to be a good Baptist, but I felt like a fraud.

Then, there was a year that I really tried to believe. My brother became ill with a brain tumor. The religious amperage was turned up in our house, and in the church: If we believed hard enough, he would be saved. But he didn't get better. Instead, my father also became ill. He, too, was discovered to have a brain tumor. So the amperage turned up even higher. And they both died.

That year, as I tried to be especially good, I was sent to a church counselor for reading a banned book. And while my father was dying— while I was being told that I was disappointing God, as well as my father—that person from the church molested me. It was the combination of these experiences, ultimately, that made me reject the beliefs that had been handed to me. I decided to set out on my own, to find a way of viewing the world that was distinctly my own.

And I had an unexpected ally in this. After my father died, my mother revealed all these beliefs I never knew she had. It turned out she was only pretending to be a good Baptist. My mother believed in curses, karma, good luck, bad luck, feng shui. Her amorphous set of beliefs showed me you can pick and choose the qualities of your philosophy, based on what works for you. You develop your own personal framework, based on what you've seen and known. You take the ideas you rely on for survival, and discard what weighs you down.

My mother's openness has remained inspiring to me. I strive to be a skeptic, in the best sense of that word: I question everything, and yet I'm open to everything. And I don't have immovable beliefs. My values shift and grow with my experiences—and as my context changes, so does what I believe.

I do close the door on methodology—I close the door on evangelism, for example. I close the door on humiliation as a means to extract something from someone. But while I might disagree with someone's approach, I don't think it's my right to judge any human need. As Whitman says, we are all alone in this fundamental sense. You'll have companions, but no one really knows what it's like to be you. So no one can tell you how you must understand the world, and you can't say what someone else must do or be.

Our uniqueness makes us special, makes perception valuable—but it can also make us lonely. This loneliness is different from being "alone": You can be lonely even surrounded by people. The feeling I'm talking about stems from the sense that we can never fully share the truth of who we are. I experienced this acutely at an early age. When I was six or seven, I used to read a thesaurus searching for the words that meant exactly what I felt. And I could never find them. I could see shades of meaning in the different ways something could be said; I could appreciate the difference, say, between the verbs "fall" and "catapult." But when I had a feeling like sadness, I couldn't find a word that meant everything that I felt inside of me. I always felt that words were inadequate, that I'd never been able to express myself—ever. Even now, it's so hard to express what I think and feel, the totality of what I've seen.

But this loneliness is the impetus for writing, because language is the best means we have to connect. I've found that the way to capture the truth of a character—and beyond that, to reflect the truth of how I feel—is to write microscopically. To focus on all the tiny details that, together, make sense of character. Each person's perspective is absolutely unique; my job is to unearth all the specific events and associations that form an individual consciousness. It's not enough to show how someone behaves in a single moment—I want to provide the whole history and context that informs each action.

Once, someone asked me to be on an honorary advisory committee with the ACLU. Now, I really admire the ACLU, and I value the important work they do. But I said, "You look at things universally, telescopically, macroscopically. I'm microscopic." I'm at that tiny end where stories begin. I wouldn't be able to say—it should *always* be this way, for *all* people. Generalizations are just not part of how I think. Stories begin with microscopic-level detail, in the particularities that make up each individual life. That's my territory.

As I write a story, I have to be open to all the possibilities of what these characters are thinking and doing and what might apply. For me, the best way to do this is writing longhand, the way I write the early drafts of a novel. Writing by hand helps me remain open to all those particular circumstances, all those little details that add up to the truth.

So much of my work through the beginning—and especially through the middle—of writing a story is establishing what the characters believe as they go on and face ever-changing situations and hardships. Whether they fall in love, or have a death that occurs, or think that they're dying—how do they respond, and what experiences shape the way they respond? I have to be open to their beliefs, whatever framework they might come up with to respond to the circumstances of their lives. As Whitman says, "Perhaps it is everywhere on water and on land": I don't try to confine myself to one particular road, but instead allow myself wide-ranging exploration.

There's so much chaos in my early drafts. As I try to open myself up to all possibilities, anarchy tends to reign. So how do I know when I'm moving in a productive direction? If anything might happen in a character's life, how do I determine which details will serve me well?

When I first started writing fiction, someone handed me a book called *Zen Mind, Beginner's Mind* by Shunryu Suzuki. It starts like this: "In the beginner's mind there are many possibilities, but in the expert's there are few." What I have to do is go back to my beginner's mind, trying as much as possible to get rid of all my assumptions, the usual pat thoughts, the confusions I have, the conclusions that cause me to contrive direction in the story. It's very dangerous to begin with your assumptions and conclusions—you close off possibilities. If I am patient and open, at some point, the wordless feeling I'm trying to express will drive the story to whatever the end point is.

So, I try to see as much as possible—in microscopic detail. I have an exercise that helps me with this, using old family photographs. I'll blow an image up as much as I can, and work through it pixel by pixel. This isn't the way we typically look at pictures—where we take in the whole gestalt, eyes focusing mostly on the central image. I'll start at, say, a corner, looking at every detail. And the strangest things happen: You end up noticing things you never would have noticed. Sometimes, I've discovered crucial, overlooked details that are important to my family's story. This process is a metaphor for the way I work—it's the same process of looking closely, looking carefully, looking in the unexpected places, and being receptive to what you find there.

As a result, I err on the side of going into too much detail when I do research and write. I abandon 95 percent of it. But I love it. It's part of my writing process. I never consider it a waste of time. I never know where I'm going when I write. It's the same reason I never come to conclusions about anything. Why I'd never have static beliefs. I'm constantly fluid in what I believe and what my conclusions are. Story-wise, of course, it has to lead somewhere narratively—otherwise we'd never turn in our books (and maybe I'll do that one day, just work on a book forever for myself, its process as my framework). But we have to turn it in—and at that point, you are guided by craft. You get to do your anarchy, try this and try that, try everything, and then apply craft. Trade in the longhand pages for the computer screen. That's the taskmaster, the person wielding the whip—you can't go anywhere you want to go. You sit in this room, and clean up this mess.

But so much of writing, for me, is about being open—open to new ideas, open to other frameworks, open to details I don't understand at first. I love that Whitman says "perhaps it is everywhere on water"—because water is a new pathway I just discovered. I used to be so afraid of water. I would never get in the ocean, or else I'd do it with great trepidation. It frightened me to be unable to see what lay beneath the water's surface. The ocean is so enormous, it seemed like anything could come along.

But I have marine biologist friends who discover species no one has ever seen before—and they inspired me to give the underwater world a chance. For my sixtieth birthday, I went to a remote island and spent the whole week just snorkeling and looking at as many things as I could. I even saw sharks! Everything about the ocean just became a playland, and I thought—how could I miss this world, this enormous world, bigger than the world we have on land? To me that was a metaphor for how in life, in work, there can be huge openings you don't even anticipate.

She is a friend of my mind. She gather me. man. The pieces I am, she gather them and give them back to me in all the right order. It's good, you know, when you got a woman who is a friend of your mind.

TONI MORRISON, *Beloved*

JUNOT DÍAZ

A Friend of the Mind

I READ TONI MORRISON for the first time when I was a student at Rutgers. I owe my university many things, and I'm indebted to my professors for a multitude of reasons, but if I had to narrow down the greatest gratitude of my university years, it would be reading Toni Morrison—specifically, reading *Beloved*. Perhaps more than any other text, *Beloved* made me the person I am. It's the book that altered my personal and creative DNA.

I was nineteen years old, and coming to terms with my experience as an immigrant, both as a person from the Dominican Republic, and as a person of African descent in a country that has very simplistic notions of what the African diaspora is. So I was reckoning with my personal history as well as the larger communal history of (to say it in the most synoptic terms) my people. I encountered *Beloved* in the middle of that transformation, in the middle of that historical, philosophical, ontological storm.

This is a novel about slavery. The horrific cataclysm we call slavery has transpired, and this postapocalyptic narrative is about trying to live with its aftereffects. That, of course, is also a description of the United States right now, and one reason this book continues to have such power is because it demonstrates the way those temporally distant circumstances are still intimately close to us. What is so vital about *Beloved*, and why it continues to shine inside of me, to burn like a star, is the argument it makes about the amnesia with which we view the institution of slavery.

For those of us of African descent, the reconstruction never ended. This idea that it was a discrete moment in history—something that you check off, and then progress past—is absurd. We're still attempting, all of us, whether you're of African descent or not, to pick up the pieces. But as a country we want to say that the past is the past, that no crime has been committed. We want to claim ourselves healthy without doing the hard, necessary work of healing. And this is why the ghosts of our past continue to possess us so violently.

The characters in this novel are possessed by this nightmare of our history the same way our society is possessed by a nightmare history we don't want to acknowledge. *Beloved*'s thesis is that, until a real and honest relationship with the past is achieved—until we've pierced the collective amnesia, overcome the level upon level of denial—it is impossible for us to have a future. The only time this book begins to talk about the future is when these characters have finally begun to come to terms with their past.

As Morrison writes at one point in the novel, "Freeing yourself was one thing; claiming ownership of that freed self was another." *Beloved*'s central question is: How do the people who have been shattered by this nightmare history—as individuals, as a community—assemble, reassemble, and reconstruct themselves in a meaningful way?

This question is addressed directly in the last pages of the penultimate chapter, in a final conversation between Sethe and Paul D, our protagonists, survivors of the brutal Sweet Home plantation (of America, in a way). After all that has happened to her, Sethe is at a breaking point—in total despair, unable to leave her bed. As he tries to encourage Sethe to keep going, and as he tries to articulate his own feelings about her, Paul D remembers the way his friend Sixo described the woman he loved. Sixo, who routinely risked his life on a thirty-mile journey, between the end of work Saturday and the start of Monday morning, just to see her for an hour. Of the Thirty-Mile Woman Sixo says:

> She is a friend of my mind. She gather me, man. The pieces I am, she gather them and give them back to me in all the right order. It's good, you know, when you got a woman who is a friend of your mind.

This reassembling, this act of creating a self from the shattered pieces, is not something one can take on individually—Sixo needed the Thirty-Mile Woman to help him do it. The passage reinforces the idea that any kind of healing, whether it's individual or communal, has to take place in collaboration with other people. Healing is relational. We like to think that one can heal oneself just by force of will, but my experience certainly aligns with the argument the passage makes: We need other people. We need relationships. We need to feel in communion.

But this passage not only describes the larger kind of philosophical work that is important to the text. It also describes what a monumental work of art does: takes the pieces of you, reassembles them, and hands them back to you in all the right order. Literature can also heal us relationally. If a relationship with a person, someone we know for just a short time, can forever alter our lives, then why not a book?

As a Dominican immigrant and person of African descent, it was not easy to find a "friend of my mind" in literature—to find someone who, somewhere and somehow, wasn't hostile to my existence. You'd be amazed how common an experience it was to read a book and realize that ultimately the text was not a friend, that it did not hold people like me in esteem, and in fact reflected many of the prejudices, many of the political and rhetorical violences, that afflict us as people and as communities. This was before I really dove into my college experience, before I started reading books by people of color. I was more or less reading in the mainstream, and the mainstream was very hostile to people like me. Book after book, text after text, I'd come across a joke that would turn my stomach or a passage that would stab me in the heart. I had tons of friends of color, I lived in a community of color, yet when I would read there would always be this dull pain that every now and then spiked into an agony—a realization that the writers and their texts I was consuming, they were not my friend.

When I first read this passage, I realized that I had sought a friend of my mind all those years: someone who didn't see me as a problem or a monster, someone who didn't erase me, someone who considered me central and important. Morrison was the first friend of my mind that I ever felt sure of. And I've sought to reproduce, as an artist, the gift *Beloved* gave me. I've sought to create books that, hopefully, for some people and for some communities, will be a friend of their mind. I write in the hope that someone will realize—yes, they are not alone, there is community in literature the same way we have community in our lived experience.

In many ways, *Beloved* provided me with the first fragment of a map of a vast literature to which, until that moment, I had very little access. It's not as if I was some sort of neutral, blank slate when I encountered Morrison. I had a lot of the stupidities and prejudice that this culture tends to foist on people. Like the idea that great literature resides in places where there are not poor people, where there are not folks of color, where there not immigrants. That's the work, that's the great work, of art I love and am interested in: to open up spaces that society would rather not even exist.

It is not insignificant that Morrison's prototypical friend of the mind is a "she." Morrison partakes in the tradition of black women writers, of women of color writers, and I don't think you can say enough about the foundational importance of African diasporic women, of women of color artists, in giving us the tools that we need as a culture to describe and explore and problematize ourselves and our communities. The philosophies, the lives, that women of color have created in reaction to the societies that marginalize and demonize and attempt to destroy them have transformed citizenship, ethics, literature, reason, being. They are absolutely essential, absolutely invaluable—to all of us.

Toni Morrison allowed me to trace back a tradition, because she, too, was a member of a community, had found support and such friendship in other texts. So many women of color writers, so many African diasporic women, have been a friend of the mind to me, have helped me reassemble, have guided me in this journey. Whether we're talking about Toni Morrison, or Cherríe Moraga, or Gloria Anzaldúa, or Gloria Naylor, or Gish Jen, Maxine Hong Kingston, Paule Marshall, Edwidge Danticat, Sandra Cisneros, Arundhati Roy, Audre Lorde—those certainly, in a literary context, are the friends of my mind and with them and their work I've maintained a life-sustaining dialogue.

But to finish with *Beloved*. As Paul D consoles Sethe in the novel's final scene, she is lamenting that she lost her "best thing"—her child, Beloved, whom she killed in an effort to save her from slavers. But after recalling Sixo's words about the Thirty-Mile Woman, Paul D realizes:

He wants to put his story next to hers.

"Sethe," he says, "me and you, we got more yesterday than anybody. We need some kind of tomorrow."

He leans over and takes her hand. With the other he touches her face. "You your best thing, Sethe. You are." His holding fingers are holding hers.

"Me? Me?"

For me, in these troubled times, this is a passage I return to again and again. That final question at the end of *Beloved*—"Me? Me?"—which the novel does not answer but the reader must—clearly has multiple meanings. To me it seemed that the novel was asking "Me? Me?" not just of Sethe but of all us people of African descent—are we willing to engage in the hard work of healing in order for us to have a tomorrow? The first step of healing is to admit that there has been an illness, to assess, and to do an accounting of the wrongs. That *Beloved* addressed this question not only to its characters but to its readers was really, really valuable to me. Until that point I did not understand the kind of work that a novel, that a piece of literature, can ask of a reader. Until that point I did not understand that a reader could be anything other than a passive consumer of a text. Morrison taught me that literature can invite readers to partake not only in worldmaking but in deeper acts, such as *healing*. That a book written by and for a people shattered by history could be a space of healing was nothing I could imagine before *Beloved*.

After I read this novel, I was no longer the person I was. I had made my thirty-mile journey and I had returned changed. And when I think about my aesthetic aspirations—what I want from a work of art, and what I most wish to make as someone who is creative—it is *Beloved* that guides me.

When Chili first came to Miami Beach twelve years ago they were having one of their off-and-on cold winters: thirty-four degrees the day he met Tommy Carlo for lunch at Vesuvio's on South Collins and had his leather jacket ripped off.

—ELMORE LEONARD, *Get Shorty*

WILLIAM GIBSON

The Handshake

WRITING THE FIRST sentence of a novel, for me, is something like filing, from a blank of metal, the key for a lock that doesn't yet exist, in a door that doesn't yet exist, set into a wall . . . An impossible thing, yet I find it must be done, or at least approximately done, else nothing will follow. The white wall (once of paper, now of pixels) will only open to the right key, or at least something approximating it, as I tend to keep filing, endlessly, through the ensuing composition.

If I were to install a key-logger on my computer, then later watch, fast-forward, as that first line gradually, somehow, finds itself, it would remind me of medieval palimpsests, the magic of writing repeatedly *over* writing, though in my case never quite obliterating the original, that first stroke that managed, however impossibly, to break the white wall.

I know that not all writers go about it that way, but some do, and I've never found that I had any choice in the matter. My first adult attempt at prose fiction, composed secretly over several months, was a single sentence, straining for what I imagined was a tone of sere import, I hoped in the manner of J. G. Ballard. I actually did complete it, that opening line, and have never quite been able to forget it. ("Seated each afternoon in the darkened screening room, Bannerman came to regard the targeted numerals of the Academy leader as hypnagogic sigils preceding the dream-state of film." Ahem.) I knew then, somehow, that that was it, my opening line, yet nothing opened. I think it may actually have been the entire story, such as that was, in which case I suppose it might be considered to have been a successful attempt.

I hope it's not that obvious, how long I labor over an opening line, but then I find it impossible to be certain how long Elmore Leonard, starting *Get Shorty*, labored over "When Chili first came to Miami Beach twelve years ago they were having one of their off-and-on cold winters: thirty-four degrees the day he met Tommy Carlo for lunch at Vesuvio's on South Collins and had his leather jacket ripped off." As plainly quotidian as that might at first seem, he's got it all going on there, damn, and if I were able to write the equivalent, it would take me a good long time. He was a genius at removing every functionally expendable bit of a sentence, right down to punctuation marks, and in my experience that's slow work.

As a new writer of fiction, I imagined that my fussing over first lines (and titles, which at first I felt I needed to even attempt a first line) was about the need to simply *have* something, anything: any one acceptable part of an unwritten whole. Today, it never really having gotten any easier, I suspect it's more organic than that. If writing is like the story of the fiddle-maker, who said that he started with a piece of wood and then removed everything that wasn't a fiddle, the writer is simultaneously charged with having to generate, like ectoplasm, the block of wood. The first line, to very clumsily mix metaphors, is somehow the block of wood in fractal form. The first line must convince me that it somehow embodies the entire unwritten text. Which is a tall order, virtually an impossible one, yet somehow, so far, I have eventually managed to do it. Once that first line succeeds in selling me on the worthiness of some totality that in no way, at that point, actually exists, I can continue.

The Peripheral began somewhat differently, actually. I couldn't get the first line for a long time. This might sound crazy, but initially all I had was the image of a young woman walking down a hill somewhere in the rural

United States toward running water. I don't know why. I didn't know who she was, what year it was, or where she thought she was going. I only had a sense of the landscape—rural, and somewhat impoverished.

I had a long opening paragraph. Sometimes, over the course of two years, it would split into two or three paragraphs, or merge again into a longer chunk. As I toyed with it, a couple of different sentences from that first section would, by turns, rotate into first place.

Eventually, I did finally settle on the sentence that finally wound up at the very top of the text—though it mutated in tiny ways almost daily. Not according to any conscious ideas I might have had about it—just according to my weird process of writing and rewriting.

In retrospect, I think I was looking for the voice of the book. I believe that: A book is going to have a voice and I have to find it.

In the case of this book, I found that voice in what became its first sentence:

> They didn't think Flynne's brother had PTSD, but that sometimes the haptics glitched him.

When the reader first encounters this, it's weird, and not entirely translatable. Yet it helps situate us in place. The phrasing of it is not formal English, not even formal American English. It's colloquial American. It places this character you haven't yet met in an American tradition. (The first sentence of *Huckleberry Finn* does something similar, though for its day it did something infinitely more radical than what I'm doing here.)

The Peripheral has two point-of-view characters—and so the book speaks in two different voices. When you compare the novel's first sentence with the opening sentence from the second chapter, which is the top of the other point-of-view character's thread, you're suddenly in a different kind of language.

> Netherton woke to Rainey's sigil, pulsing behind his lids at the rate of a resting heartbeat.

It's British, or at least faux-British and slightly neo-Victorian, in spite of the hallucinatory raciness of everything else that's going on.

Both sentences have something in common: They both contain words that will not be familiar to the first-time reader. Someone reading the book for the first time will not know what "haptics" are, or what a "sigil" is, or what it means to "glitch" someone—these usages are part of the idiosyncratic lexicon of this particular book. To understand these words, then—and better parse the sentences that contain them—you have to keep reading.

I assume, as a reader myself, that something like this either connects or doesn't, in that moment in a bookshop in which I open a book and glance at an opening line. "It was a bright cold day in April, and the clocks were striking thirteen": I would have bought that instantly, though I never had to, as Orwell's *1984* was canon. Jack Womack's *Random Acts of Senseless Violence* caused me to hear the click as well: "Mamma says mine is a night mind." As a writer, of course, I hope readers will hear the click on opening my book, but it's much more important for me to hear it, in fact essential.

From the shelf beside me as I write this, three first lines wherein I heard the click, however variously:

"There is no greater human hazard than a defeated Irishman abroad."
—*Not Quite Dead*, John MacLachlan Gray

"And so let us beginne; and, as the Fabrick takes its Shape in front of you, alwaies keep the Structure intirely in Mind as you inscribe it."
—*Hawksmoor*, Peter Ackroyd

"to wound the autumnal city."   —*Dhalgren*, Samuel R. Delany

Each of these sentences confronts us with a new grammar, words arranged in a way we can't yet understand. Yet this kind of intentional withholding can be thrilling to encounter. As a reader, one of my greatest pleasures is being dropped into something that's complex and carefully built. Since I haven't got a clue what's going on, I immediately start trying to figure out what the hell is going on. It's similar to the pleasure of the whodunit, but it's really more the pleasure of *what the fuck?*

It is now second nature to me to plunge the reader into the middle of an unfamiliar world, with its unfamiliar language, and let them figure things out. But I must have thought about it in the early eighties when I was writing my first short stories, developing the toolkit that I'd later use. I taught myself to do this through trial and error, and by thinking about the stuff I most liked to read. I loved books that employed a kind of withholding, novels that earned the kind of patience they required. That quality seemed to be an important aspect of my own pleasure in the text.

Of course, there are some kinds of ambiguity you want to avoid. In my mid-teens, I was very frustrated by what I saw as the low imaginative resolution of the science fiction I was reading. There were wonderful writers, of course, but I encountered a lot of lazy visualization. I can still remember being outraged by a story which opened with someone looking out the porthole of something, you didn't know what, and seeing a figure in silver boots sprawled by an airplane. Those "silver boots" totally offended me. Are they lamé? Are they articulated sterling? What the hell am I supposed to be seeing? It was never explained, and I took that to mean that the author neither knew nor gave a shit. Some kind of work had not been done.

Productive ambiguity is not the same as lazy writing. But what's the proper balance of mystery and clarity? This tension is a result of a problem central to science fiction: We're applying hundred-year-old techniques of literary naturalism to imagined futures. This, I think, has been a huge part of what I've wanted to do, but it poses certain challenges. As a writer, you want to describe things so that they speak for themselves. But when you're writing about the future, some objects, ideas, and sensations may be unfamiliar to the reader no matter how well you describe them, because they're not real.

My instinct throughout *The Peripheral* was to play strict science fiction golf, which means to me avoiding the clumsy integration of exposition or contextual information, even when dealing with terms and technologies the reader won't recognize (because they don't exist). It's important to avoid what science fiction writers sometimes call the "As you know, Bob," paragraph, in which you do this big info dump. There's pleasure in working it out. Besides, brief, understated descriptions tend to better serve the lens of character. Real people don't think of things in quite so many adverbs, or adjectives. And then I like to think that withholding information also rewards readers who will go back and reread the whole thing. All of those little enigmas play differently the second time through.

Of course, this approach doesn't work for everyone. I've been doing what no writer should ever do, reading the user reviews of my new book on the Amazon site. Sometimes, I'll hit on one that says something like, "What a pain in the ass! There's all this slang, and I'm expected to know what it *means*?" It's not going to work for some people. But, a novel can't be anything very good in my opinion and simultaneously be totally available to everyone.

Playing by the rules of strict sci-fi golf is a risk, though, one that anyone writing thoroughly imagined speculative fiction—Margaret Atwood, say—runs. Sophisticated science fiction requires a sort of cultural superstructure of reading skill. We forget as readers of longform fiction that at one time we didn't know how to do that—we had to acquire the skill through cultural education. It's the same with good sci-fi, which generally requires a sort of superstructure of cultural experience to make it pleasurably accessible. As a reader, I want to encounter rigorously imagined literature—but anyone working this way risks losing a portion of their prospective audience.

I've sometimes suspected myself of writing, however unconsciously, opening lines that very possibly would put off ("warn off" might be the kinder way to put it) readers who might be less likely to enjoy the rest of the book. Indeed, I suspect I've sometimes written entire opening chapters that way, though today I make some conscious effort not to.

In any case, the first sentence is the handshake, on either side of the writer-reader divide. The reader shakes hands with the writer. The writer has already had to shake hands with the unknown. Assuming both have heard the click, we've got it going on.

The most important things are the hardest things to say. They are the things you get ashamed of, because words diminish them. . . . And you may make revelations that cost you dearly only to have people look at you in a funny way, not understanding what you've said at all, or why you thought it was so important that you almost cried while you were saying it. That's the worst, I think. When the secret stays locked within not for want of a teller but for want of an understanding ear.

—STEPHEN KING, "The Body"

KHALED HOSSEINI

Everything I Meant to Say

MY FRESHMAN YEAR in college, I got a job working security. This was a high-tech building in Santa Clara, engineers coming in and out all the time. During the day I'd sit at the front desk to sign guests in and check their bags. Just as often, I worked the graveyard shift—which started at eleven p.m. and lasted until seven in the morning. Then I'd watch over the building alone, everything totally dark. I'd make a round of the building once an hour, but otherwise had to pass time at my desk.

Trying to read during the day was a nightmare. I had a camera trained on me like Big Brother, and if a book snuck onto your lap you'd get a call from a vigilant boss somewhere: "Put that away, son." Grave, by contrast, was a perfect time to do homework or read—but you weren't supposed to. I found this an unbelievably cruel expectation: to stay up all night alone with nothing to do except stare at surveillance screens and an empty parking lot. Luckily, at night, there was no one around to supervise what I did. So I spent my grave shifts studying, reading books, and writing short stories. (Maybe I'll get in trouble now, thirty years too late.)

I don't remember how I picked up *Different Seasons*, but it was a book I read on a grave shift. I was absolutely floored by it; "The Body," a story about kids who go searching for a corpse in the woods, impacted me especially. I find myself drawn to that period where children are about to leave childhood behind. When you're twelve years old, you still have one foot in childhood; the other is poised to enter a completely new stage of life. Your innocent understanding of the world moves toward something messier and more complicated, and once it does you can never go back. Stephen King captures this brilliantly, and with such humanity, for the boys in this story. By the time they return home, each one has changed fundamentally. None of those four boys is ever going to be the same again.

I read the story not knowing that someday I'd write about similar things. I've written a lot about children—in all three of my books, it turns out. I'm fascinated by the way early experiences haunt and revisit you, remain present in your life for decades and decades—they can even shape who you ultimately become. "The Body" captures this idea as well as any work of fiction that I know. It moved me very deeply, and it still does.

Years later, I can see that the story's wonderful opening has layers I didn't fully appreciate as a young man and unpublished writer. Gordie, the story's adult narrator, looks back on his childhood with fear he won't do justice to the tale he wants to tell:

> The most important things are the hardest things to say. They are the things you get ashamed of, because words diminish them—words shrink things that seemed limitless when they were in your head to no more than living size when they're brought out. But it's more than that, isn't it? The most important things lie too close to wherever your secret heart is buried, like landmarks to a treasure your enemies would love to steal away.

When I first read these lines, I was twenty—not a teenager anymore, but certainly a *young* man. At that age, especially, you feel like the world doesn't get you—if only people could look inside you and see all you carry inside! This passage is an expression of how alone we are, really. How fully we live inside our minds, that the person who walks down the street and shakes hands is only an approximation of the self inside. The personas we inhabit publicly are merely approximations of who we are internally—shrunken, distorted versions of ourselves that we present to the real world. This is because the things that are most important to us, that are really vital to us, are perversely the most difficult to express. I felt all this as a young man reading "The Body" for the first time.

But now I realize what I couldn't have known then: This passage is one of the truest statements I've encountered about the nature of authorship. You write because you have an idea in your mind that feels so genuine, so important, so true. And yet, by the time this idea passes through the different filters of your mind, and into your hand, and onto the page or computer screen—it becomes distorted, and it's been diminished. The writing you end up with is an approximation, if you're lucky, of whatever it was you really wanted to say.

When this happens, it's quite a sobering reminder of your limitations as a writer. It can be extremely frustrating. When I'm writing, a thought will occasionally pass unblemished, unperturbed, through my head onto the screen—clearly, like through a glass. It's an intoxicating, euphoric sensation to feel that I've communicated something so real, and so true. But this doesn't happen often. (I can only think that there are some writers who write that way all the time. I think that's the difference between greatness and just being good.)

Even my finished books are approximations of what I intended to do. I try to narrow the gap, as much as I possibly can, between what I wanted to say and what's actually on the page. But there's still a gap, there always is. It's very, very difficult. And it's humbling.

And then, you must consider another layer. You may not be able to express yourself perfectly, but your audience is composed of imperfect *listeners.* Gordie addresses this anxiety, too:

And you may make revelations that cost you dearly only to have people look at you in a funny way, not understanding what you've said at all, or why you thought it was so important that you almost cried while you were saying it. That's the worst, I think. When the secret stays locked within not for want of a teller but for want of an understanding ear.

We fear we'll be misunderstood—and, at times, we surely will be. The most powerful human emotions are terribly difficult to explain in a way that doesn't diminish them, or that doesn't make you look slightly ridiculous in the telling. How easy to safeguard them then, and keep things close, rather than risk looking foolish or being misheard.

But that's what art is for—for both reader and writer to overcome their respective limitations and encounter something true. It seems miraculous, doesn't it? That somebody can articulate something clearly and beautifully that exists inside you, something shrouded in impenetrable fog. Great art reaches through the fog, toward this secret heart—and it shows it to you, holds it before you. It's a revelatory, incredibly moving experience when this happens. You feel understood. You feel heard. That's why we come to art—we feel less alone. We *are* less alone. You see, through art, that others have felt the way you have—and you feel better.

I began writing at a very young age. From the time I could pick up a pen. I loved the idea of trying to speak what's inside of me—of creating things that felt real to me. And I've kept writing my whole life, kept developing and deepening this compulsion I was born with. At the same time, it's an unbelievable honor and pleasure to know that someone has read my book. To receive an incredibly passionate letter explaining how something I wrote touched another person in an authentic way. What a gift to be on the receiving end of that. There's no greater reward, as a writer, than that.

Do not think, dream.

—RICHARD BAUSCH, "Dear Writer"

Do Not Think, Dream

YEARS AGO, I read a book called *Letters to a Fiction Writer*, which asked about twenty established writers to send their best advice out into the world. There were a lot of heavy hitters in there offering truly wise and helpful advice. But the one that's stayed with me over the years, from Richard Bausch, has become a sort of mantra for me:

Do not think, dream.

We're all born with an imagination. Everybody gets one. And I really believe—this is just from years of daily writing—that good fiction comes from the same place as our dreams. I think the desire to step into someone else's dream world is a universal impulse that's shared by us all. That's what fiction is. As a writing teacher, if I say nothing else to my students, it's this.

Here's the distinction. There's a profound difference between making something up and imagining it. You're making something up when you think out a scene, when you're being logical about it. You think, "I need this to happen so some other thing can happen." There's an aspect of controlling the material that I don't think is artful. I think it leads to contrived work, frankly, no matter how beautifully written it might be. You can hear the false note in this kind of writing.

This was my main problem when I was just starting out: I was trying to *say something*. When I began to write, I was deeply self-conscious. I was writing stories hoping they would say something thematic, or address something that I was wrestling with philosophically. I've learned, for me at least, it's a dead road. It's writing from the outside in instead of the inside out.

But during my very early writing, certainly before I'd published, I began to learn characters will come alive if you back the fuck off. It was exciting, and even a little terrifying. If you allow them to do what they're going to do, think and feel what they're going to think and feel, things start to happen on their own. It's a beautiful and exciting alchemy. And all these years later, that's the thrill I write to get: to feel things start to happen on their own.

So I've learned over the years to free-fall into what's happening. What happens then is, you start writing something you don't even really want to write about. Things start to happen under your pencil that you don't want to happen, or don't understand. But that's when the work starts to have a beating heart.

Okay, I know: It's one thing to quote Bausch. But what does it fucking mean, "dream with language"? I think this is what happens. Habits of writing can be learned. We can choose concrete language over overly abstract language. We can learn to use active verbs instead of passive verbs. To bring in at least three of the five senses to activate a scene. All these things we can be taught, or learn on our own from reading. These are all part of your toolbox—but that toolbox will always remain locked if the writer *is not genuinely curious about what he or she is writing about*. To me, that is the essential ingredient. Late in his life, Faulkner was asked what quality a writer most needs—and he said not talent, but curiosity. I know the quote by heart: "Insight, curiosity, to wonder, to mull and to muse why it is that man does what he does. And if you have that, talent makes no difference, whether you've got it or not."

So you can dream by being curious—by being curious enough to report back what's in front of your narrative eye. I love that line from E. L. Doctorow, who said in essence: "Writing a novel is like driving at night. You can only see as far as your headlights"—but you keep going until you get there. I've learned over the years to just report back anything that I see in front of the headlights: Are they yellow stripes or white? What's on the side of the road? Is there vegetation? What kind? What's the weather? What are the sounds? If I capture the experience all along the way, the structure starts to reveal itself. My guiding force and principle for shaping the story is to just follow the headlights. That's how the architecture is revealed.

You must also be curious not just about perceptions, and the physical word, but about the character. "Why it is that man does what he does," as Faulkner said. Or another great line from Flannery O'Connor: "The writer must write not *about* character, but with character." Or, Eudora Welty, who says the artistic act she holds most high is entering the private skin of another. Writing *with* character. It's every eight or nine or ten days with me when most of the entire writing session feels I'm just moving with the character, a strange observer in their chest some way as they go about their business. I think it's why a lot of writers write, is for that feeling. It's certainly why I write.

I write longhand pencil, and every other word's crossed out. The words I strike are not usually because they're clichéd, or not good words, but because they don't reflect the character's essential truth. Through a series of micro choices made as I'm writing a sentence, I'm trying to find the true word, the word that reflects the character's truth. Is that the smell she's smelling in that bar? Is that the light she's seeing in her car, with the snow falling? Is that really what she hears, and thinks and feels?

Now, I have days when this doesn't happen. I would say most days. I would say I feel I've had a good writing session every nine or ten days. That's not to say I don't have any contact on those other eight or nine days—it's like dancing with somebody in the dark, you catch glimmers of her face in the shadow light. But other days, the moon's right on her—and those are the days I write for.

I'm one of these writers who rewrites pretty constantly all the time. If there's any moment that feels even slightly false I cannot continue. Even if a character says one thing I don't quite believe, or has an association I don't quite buy, I cannot continue. I've learned the hard way that this novel is a twelve-story building. If there's a faulty brick on the fourth floor, that means that the eight stories I've put on top have to go. So I constantly am a vicious, merciless rewriter when it comes to truth.

Now, dreaming your way through a story is very useful at first—for the first draft, maybe the first two drafts. But once the revision process begins, you've got to change your approach. Bausch would be the first to say that once you dream it through, try to look at the result the way a doctor looks at an X-ray. You've got to be terribly smart about it. In the secondary period, you get more rational and logical about what you've dreamed—while still cooperating with the deeper truths of what you've made.

So once I have a beginning, middle, and end, I walk away from it for at least six months and don't look at it. At *least* six months. To revise means "to see again"—well, how can you see again when you just looked at it ten days ago? No. Have two seasons go between you. And then when you pick it up and read it, you actually forget some of what happens in the story. You forget how hard it was to write those twelve pages. And you become tougher on it. You see closer to what the reader is going to see.

What I look for at this point is dramatic tension, forward movement, and, frankly, beauty. I try to make it as truly itself as possible. And that's when the major plotting comes in—plot, not as a noun but as a verb— the ordering of events and material. I get really merciless. I don't care if I spent a year writing pages 1 through 96. If I feel some real energy on page 93, and I think that should be page 1? Those first ninety-two pages are fucking *gone*. A merciless reviser is in a much better position to write a really good book than one who hasn't got the stomach for it.

That may be the distinction between what makes a really good book and a great book.

It's very difficult to achieve this dream state, and it requires a lot of courage. And I don't think it's going to happen unless you can cultivate two qualities in yourself, which William Stafford, the poet, taught me when he said, "The poet must put himself in a state of receptivity before writing." Stafford said you know you're being receptive when a) you're willing to accept anything that comes, no matter what it is, and b) you're willing to fail. But Americans are very impatient with failure. I think one of the many reasons people don't end up living their authentic lives is because they're afraid of failing—they don't take chances. And I understand it. This is very risky, terrifying territory writing this way. But it's the only way I can do it. Frankly, I just feel so alive when I write that way.

Here's how it happens for me. The first thing I do is go to my office, which is a nearly soundproof cave in my basement. (But I also have to write in hotels and on planes and shit all the time, so.) The big ritual is that I read a few poems. I don't write poetry, but I read poetry daily. I must have 500 volumes of poetry. And I read it just to, you know, sprinkle flower petals on the bed and put a little Luther Vandross on. To get me in the mood. And it brings me down into a pretty good meditative state.

I write longhand pencil every day in composition notebooks, even on my birthday (today's my birthday, and I think I had a good session). I read some poems, then I put on some headphones and play some music. While I'm listening to music I'm just typing the previous day's handwritten work into the computer. Then I turn off the music, rewrite some sentences—I don't go nuts, just making sure I believe everything that happened. I know that later I'll be rewriting constantly, and I don't want to go to that rational, critical, logical part of my brain too much. That can get in the way of the dream state.

Then I go back, get rid of the machine, and I sharpen my Blackwing 602 Palomino pencil, and I just go at it. It's a ritual. It's O'Connor: "There's a certain grain of stupidity that the writer of fiction can hardly do without, and this is the quality of having to stare." And she goes on to say that writing is waiting. And I think what she means is, you're not waiting for inspiration. You're staring or waiting for the image or the moment or the smell or the sound to emerge—and when you start to write it, just trust me that things happen.

I really wrestle with religious faith, but I don't wrestle with this. I used to think I had no religious faith of any kind. I've been a father of three for years, and I never prayed until I became a father for the first time at the age of thirty-three. I don't believe in God, but I believe in something: Something's out there. And the main reason I believe that something's out there—something mysterious and invisible but real—largely has come from my daily practice of writing. There's a great line from an ancient anonymous Chinese poet: We poets knock upon the silence for an answering music. The way I write, the way I encourage people I work with to try to write, is exactly this: Trust your imagination. Free-fall into it. See where it brings you to. It's scary, it's unorganized, and you're going to have to prepare yourself for some major fucking rewriting—and maybe cut two years of work.

I know, putting up with this kind of uncertainty is very difficult. We bring ourselves into these rooms. We bring all of our hopes, all of our longings, all of our shadows. What writing asks of us is the opposite of what being in the American culture asks of us. You're supposed to have a five-year plan. Young people now are so cautious. Oh, we can't get married until we have a house. Oh, we can't have a baby until we have twenty grand in the bank. These crazy, careful people! You know, look: Life is short if you live a hundred years. Better to die naked and reckless and with passion—and not be afraid to fuck up and fail.

Sometimes the fear is, I won't publish the novel by the time I'm thirty. Or my mother's sick—she'll never see me publish a book. Or all my friends have published, when am I going to publish? All of these demons we bring to the desk. Often, subconsciously buried. And I think it's really important to be clear on what's at stake for you.

I think one of the downsides of MFA programs is they make people really career-conscious. *Fuck career.* Let me tell you something: I'm so grateful to have had a publishing career so far. It's how I make most of my living. It's been an incredible blessing. It's helped me take better care of my family than I could have ever thought possible. *But I do not ever think about career when I'm in my writing cave.* I do not. I try not to think; I dream. It's my mantra. I just get in there and try to be these people. It's not so I can write a book and get paid and have another book tour—though those are good problems to have. It's because I feel an almost sacred obligation to these spirits who came before: to sit with them and write their tale.

There is another woman in me, I'm afraid of her—she fell in love with that man, and I wanted to hate you and couldn't forget the other one who was there before. The one who is not me. Now I'm real, I'm whole.

—LEO TOLSTOY, *Anna Karenina*

MARY GAITSKILL

I Don't Know
You Anymore

I READ *ANNA KARENINA* for the first time about two years ago. It's something I'd always meant to read, but for some reason I didn't expect to like it as much as I did. When I finally settled down to read it, I loved it. What strikes me about the book is how precisely rendered the characters are, how recognizable they are as people. It was written so many years ago, and yet the characters are descriptions of people I know and see.

I found one section in particular so beautiful and intelligent that I actually stood up as I was reading. I had to put the book down, I was so surprised by it—and it took the novel to a whole other level for me.

Anna's told her husband, Karenin, that she's in love with another man and has been sleeping with him. You're set up to see Karenin as an overly dignified but somewhat pitiable figure: He's a proud, stiff person. He's older than Anna is, and he's balding, and he has this embarrassing mannerism of a squeaky voice. He's hardened himself against Anna. He's utterly disgusted with her for having gotten pregnant by her lover, Vronsky. But you have the impression at first that his pride is hurt more than anything else—which makes him unsympathetic.

Then he receives a telegram from Anna that says: *Please come, I'm dying, I need you to forgive me.*

At first, he thinks it's a deception. He wants to refuse to go. But then he realizes that it would be too cruel, and that everyone would condemn him—he *has* to go. So he does.

As he walks into the house where Anna's dying, in the highest point of her fever, he thinks to himself:

> He drew a resolution in the far corner of his brain and consulted it. It read: "If it is a deception, then calm contempt, and depart. If true, observe propriety."

He comes off as very rigid, even in this moment. We think nothing could shake this man's stolidity. And when he finds out Anna's still alive, he suddenly senses how much he was hoping for her to be dead—though this realization shocks him.

Then he hears her babbling, in the height of her fever. And her words are unexpected: She's saying how kind he is. That, of course, she knows he will forgive her. When Anna finally sees him, she looks at him with a kind of love he's never seen before. She says:

> There is another woman in me, I'm afraid of her—she fell in love with that man, and I wanted to hate you and couldn't forget the other one who was there before. The one who is not me. Now I'm real, I'm whole.

Anna's speaking about the decisions she's made in the third person—as if the person who betrayed Karenin was a stranger. And she does seem to be transformed here, as though she's become a different person. I was so surprised by that. I think of it as a very modern insight, Tolstoy's idea that there may be two, or more, different people inside of us.

And it's not just Anna. As his wife tells him she loves him, begging his forgiveness, Karenin transforms, too. The man we'd thought could never be anything but stiff and dull turns out to have this entirely different side to him.

Throughout the book, he's always hated the way he's felt disturbed by other people's tears or sadness. But as he struggles with this feeling while Anna's talking, Karenin finally realizes that the compassion he feels for other people is not weakness: For the first time, he perceives this reaction as joyful, and becomes completely overwhelmed with love and forgiveness. He actually kneels down and begins to cry in her arms; Anna holds him and embraces his balding head. The quality he hated is completely who he is—and this realization gives him incredible peace. He even decides he wants to shelter the little girl that Anna's had with Vronsky (who sits nearby, so completely shamed by what he's witnessing that he covers his face with his hands).

You believe this complete turnaround. You believe it's who these people really are. I find it strange that the moment these characters seem most like themselves is the moment when they're behaving in ways we've never before seen. I don't fully understand how this could be, but it's wonderful that it works.

But then the moment passes. Anna never talks about the "other woman" inside of her again. At first, I was disappointed. But then I thought: *No, that's actually much more realistic*. What Tolstoy does is actually much better, because it's more truthful. We feel a greater sense of loss, knowing it will never happen again.

I very much saw that as the core of the book. Everyone says *Anna Karenina* is about individual desire going against society, but I think the opposite perspective is stronger: the way social forces actively go against the soft feelings of the individual.

Karenin, for instance, talks himself down from his most generous moment, knowing that the feeling can't endure the judgment that would be aimed his way:

> The more time that passed, the more clearly he saw that, natural as this situation was for him now, he would not be allowed to remain in it. He felt that, besides the good spiritual force that guided his soul, there was another force, crude and equally powerful, if not more so, that guided his life, and that this force would not give him the humble peace he desired.

As powerful as these emotions are, basic social expectations are "crude and equally powerful." He knows everyone will utterly look down on him if he does what he wants to do. Actually, I feel that he would do it anyway if Anna stayed with him—but she doesn't stay with him. When she comes out of the fever she no longer remembers what she felt, and she looks at him with fear. She feels guilty, and she simply can't be the way she had been. Perhaps she doesn't even remember—as if the other woman has taken over again. And that's what destroys him.

But which is the real Anna, and which is the real Karenin: the people they are at the tender bedside moment, or the people they become afterward, when the fever subsides? I don't think you're given a clear answer—that's part of what I like about it. The person Anna reveals when she really believes she's going to die may be in fact the truer part of herself. As in real life, you can't know.

I believe that the truest parts of people can be buried, and for many different reasons. It's mysterious and strange, and though I don't think about it consciously while I'm writing, I do believe this about people—so it probably does show up in my work.

People sometimes turn out to be almost the opposite of how they present. It isn't because they're trying to fool you, or because they're hypocrites. It's because they badly want to be that thing, and so they'll try to be it. It's not even like they're deliberately pulling the wool over anyone's eyes. That's their ideal, and that's what they try for. But it's not who they are.

Fictional characters are different. I wouldn't go so far as to quote Nabokov and say they're galley slaves, but they are your creations—so they'll do whatever you want them to do and be whatever you want them to be. Still, you don't always know exactly what that is when you first conceive of them. And sometimes they do change. I wouldn't say they surprise you, but your idea of them certainly changes as you go along.

In the book I just wrote, one of the characters behaves in a way that could seem out of character and I suppose some people could say it's unbelievable. But I think that people in real life do unbelievable things all the time, that, in fiction, the things that are realistic or literally true don't always *feel* true. It happens in my writing classes over and over again: The thing that everyone, including me, picks out as unbelievable sometimes is exactly the thing the writer will say, "But it really happened!" And it probably did. But it means they haven't done enough to make that incident enter the world of the story, which becomes a reality with its own logic. When something genuinely surprising happens in a work of fiction, you have to be very in the story, and very in the moment, to make the reader accept it.

I don't know if I can say exactly what I seek in books, but one of them would be to expand my understanding of the world. And that can happen through characters. Karenin, the husband, is a character that I probably would never get to know in real life. I could know a person like him, and we wouldn't have anything to say to each other; each would find the other uninteresting and even repellent. But through a book like *Anna Karenina*, we can be enticed to go beyond the uninteresting, day-to-day appearance—and find the true person beneath the surface.

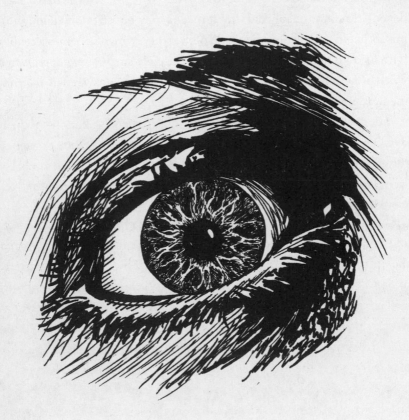

I felt infinite wonder, infinite pity.

—JORGE LUIS BORGES,

"The Aleph"

MICHAEL CHABON

To Infinity and Beyond

"THE ALEPH" IS about a weird house, and a weird family with a secret, and the innocent but involved narrator who is inexorably drawn toward the horrible thing hidden in the basement. It follows the classic pattern of one of H. P. Lovecraft's horror stories, which are themselves modeled after certain stories by Edgar Allan Poe—though this is more of a wonder story than a horror story. "The Aleph" is like what a Lovecraft story would be if Lovecraft were a truly great writer, one of the greatest of all time. I'm a lifelong lover of H. P. Lovecraft, but he's no Borges.

In Lovecraft, the universe is a vast malign entity separated from our humdrum existence—what we'd call "reality"—by the thinnest of membranes. Very persuasively, with all the obsessive fervor of a great writer, he conveys that cosmic, carnivorous destruction is always out there looking for a way in, always feeling for the spots where that membrane is thinnest. But he doesn't take that next step—making you believe that this experience is being undergone by a fully developed, conscious individual human being with a long past of heartache and sorrow and romantic entanglement. In "The Aleph," Borges manages to do what Lovecraft can't: He fully integrates an encounter with the infinite into the consciousness of what feels like a living, breathing human being with stale breath and lint in his pockets.

As "The Aleph" begins, we learn the narrator is in love with a woman who has just died. We witness his heartbreak in the incredible first sentence, one that would definitely be in contention if I had to choose a favorite opening line:

> On the burning February morning Beatriz Viterbo died, after braving an agony that never for a single moment gave way to self-pity or fear, I noticed that the sidewalk billboards around Constitution Plaza were advertising some new brand or other of American cigarettes.

When I first read that sentence, it sounded amazing to me. I loved its language and its pacing, though I had never actually experienced the phenomenon it's trying to capture: the sense, after somebody you love has died, of how things plod on in such a banal way. In this one sentence, Borges captures the complete indifference of the universe to the people you love. It's definitely one that, over the years, I've tried to model various of my own first sentences after.

The narrator begins paying regular calls on Beatriz Viterbo's family, every year on the anniversary of her death. As a consequence, he develops a complicated and not entirely amicable relationship with her cousin, a man named Carlos Argentino Daneri, who lives in the family home. The narrator is a literary man, and Daneri also has literary aspirations. Eventually Daneri lets on that he's working on this epic poem—one that is going to, according to him, describe everything in the world, almost like a catalog of the universe. One day, Daneri invites the narrator over to see something, a secret he's been concealing in the house for his whole life. A "discovery," he calls it.

He brings the narrator down into the cellar of his house, and gives him a cloth—a kind of folded sack to kneel on, to protect his knees— and tells him to look up at a certain spot, a kind of window he can look into if his head is at just the right level. There's a deliberate invocation of Poe's "The Cask of Amontillado" in that moment when the narrator briefly wonders if Carlos has lost his mind, and has brought him down into the basement to kill him.

But when he opens his eyes, suddenly, he sees the Aleph.

An Aleph (which is the first letter of the Hebrew alphabet) turns out to be a point from which you can see every point in the universe, from every possible point of view. Borges uses the word "universe," but what's revealed here is not a Carl Sagan thing, with billions of stars—it's a more local version of the universe, what we would probably call "the world." Yet it's still infinite, nonetheless. The narrator admits he lacks the words to describe what he saw:

> In that single gigantic instant I saw millions of acts both delightful and awful; not one of them occupied the same point in space, without over-lapping or transparency. What my eyes beheld was simultaneous, but what I shall now write down will be successive, because language is successive. Nonetheless, I'll try to recollect what I can.

I love the way he sets this up. Because this is impossible, right? There's no way to convey the experience of seeing the entire world from every possible point of view, all at the same time, without any of those views overlapping. You can't do it in the space of a paragraph, or the space of a story, or of a novel, or of an entire book, or an entire library of books. So the way he handles it is by acknowledging the impossibility at the beginning—which is a really useful strategy for a writer, something I definitely learned from studying the story. Before you've even seen anything, Borges discreetly lowers your expectations.

Then, having lowered your expectations, he presents you with this long, miraculous paragraph, one of the most stunning passages I've ever read. It starts this way:

> I saw the teeming sea; I saw daybreak and nightfall; I saw the multitudes of America; I saw a silvery cobweb in the center of a black pyramid; I saw

a splintered labyrinth (it was London); I saw, close up, unending eyes
watching themselves in me as in a mirror; I saw all the mirrors on earth
and none of them reflected me.

It's just a list, this paragraph; the listiness of it is far from being con-
cealed. Borges goes right ahead repeating those two words, "I saw"—*I
saw this, I saw that*, on and on. But somehow that repetition gives the
passage this incredible incantatory power, managing to convey a kind
of infinitude. It casts this magical spell, and it convinces you.

After a long catalog—including the insects and animals and gardens
and snows of the world, a translation of Pliny, a Scottish woman with
cancer in her breast—the paragraph ends this way:

> I saw the rotted dust and bones that had once deliciously been Beatriz
> Viterbo; I saw the circulation of my own dark blood; I saw the coupling of
> love and the modification of death; I saw the Aleph from every point and
> angle, and in the Aleph I saw the earth and in the earth the Aleph and in
> the Aleph the earth; I saw my own face and my own bowels; I saw your
> face; and I felt dizzy and wept, for my eyes had seen that secret and conjec-
> tured object whose name is common to all men but which no man has
> looked upon—the unimaginable universe.
> I felt infinite wonder, infinite pity.

I love the last, dazzling item on the list: I saw *your* face. Borges wrote
the story in 1939 or 1940, and the line would have had power then. You,
the reader, become an object in the universe depicted here. But reading
in 2016, it's as if he's reaching out to you across time. You feel so impli-
cated. They have such power, those four simple words coming right at
the end, the culmination of everything else that's been said.

Of course, Borges doesn't reveal *everything* here, a complete universe
in all its chaos and complexity. How could he? Instead, the passage is an
incredible mixture of cosmic things, things the narrator has never seen
and places he has never been, layered very poignantly and strategically

with quite personal things. Details that reinforce the romantic, emotional predicament of a man who was hopelessly, wordlessly in love with a woman who did not love him in return. That unrequited love he's been carrying with him for all these years emerges through the details. That's one of the fundamental things you have to do as a fiction writer: learn to produce the right details from a sea of choices—not just the ones that are plausible, but the things that convey a sense of who a character is. As a writer, you, too, have essentially infinite details to choose from, and in a way this passage both postulates and demonstrates the technique by which you have to choose.

For me, almost everything in literature almost always comes down to the question of point of view. Whose story is this, and who's telling the story of that person? Ultimately, it just boils down to word choice, the words you choose to persuade the reader that this is the point of view of a particular human being. In my own work, it comes down to finding the right voice for the story that I'm trying to tell. Trying to hit on that right narrator, on that right voice, on that correct point of view—whether it's a limited point of view, or an omniscient point of view, or a first-person or third-person one. Once I have a sense of that, then it's about what kind of tone to adopt, and the narrator's relationship to the material. If it is a first-person narrator, is it retrospective, looking back with the gathered wisdom of all the time that has passed since the events that are under discussion occurred? Or is it someone who's in the thick of it, narrating?

Sometimes those questions all get settled instantly. In my second novel, *Wonder Boys*, the first sentence came to me as I was writing it, just as it was eventually published. It's a first-person sentence: "The first real writer I ever knew was a man who did all of his work under the name of August Van Zorn." That gave me a series of questions to answer: Who's August Van Zorn and who's this narrator, and why is Van Zorn the first writer he ever knew? The seed of the novel—who would tell the story and what it would be about—was in that first sentence, and it just arrived. I just had to tease it all out, and that was how I wrote the book. That book actually did write itself fairly quickly.

Much more often, I struggle for a while to find the right point of view, the right place to stand and peer into the Aleph of the novel. Your eye lights on things that seem relevant somehow, and you grab hold of them, hoping that the details assemble themselves into what feels like a coherent narrator. Once you've found the voice, then you have to keep at it through the whole piece. That seamless uniformity of tone is probably the most satisfying experience you can have in reading, and it all comes down to those word-by-word choices.

In the Borges story, the narrator's reaction to the Aleph—"I felt infinite wonder, infinite pity"—is not how I feel on a daily basis when I'm writing. But it serves as a reminder of what I *ought* to be feeling while I work, as I'm describing the behavior of human beings and of the world. I ought to be full of infinite wonder and infinite pity when I sit down at my desk, look into an Aleph, and see things, report them, and try to set them down. Wonder, because it's the appropriate response to that which is new. You have a responsibility, when you're looking into the personal Aleph of your work, to always try to see things afresh. You are seeing through the eyes of fictional characters who are not you, and they will see things in ways you have never seen them before.

Infinite pity, I think, is the proper attitude to have toward your characters. Not pity in the way we mostly tend to understand it—which is the condescension of a superior looking down at an inferior and feeling sorry for them. That's not the kind of pity Borges was talking about, and that's not what's required in this process. It's a much more self-implicating pity, where you see and understand the tragic and routine flaws people have, the ways in which your characters fall short of the marks they set for themselves—just as you fall short of the marks you set for yourself.

There are some fantastic writers out there who are relatively pitiless, whose work demolishes not only the foibles of its characters but the foibles of all of humanity in a merciless, remorseless way. Some of those writers are important and wonderful. But I think the greatest writers are like, say, Tolstoy, who's celebrated for that quality of extending, if not forgiveness, then profound understanding and sympathy to even his most weak, vacillating, or blinkered characters. Not only saying, *Aren't we all this way?* But fundamentally saying, *This is how I am. And since I am this way, too, I can't judge. I can only present with sympathy the way all of us are.* This is not something that I manage to accomplish every time I look into the Aleph. But I think it is a useful, valuable codification of what to try for.

He was looking at me and neither his eyes nor the gun moved. He was as calm as an adobe wall in the moonlight.

—Raymond Chandler, *The Long Goodbye*

WALTER MOSLEY

How I Awoke

Forty-four years ago, I came across a passage that changed my life. I was a teenager then, reading just about anything that struck my fancy. In those days I was pretty much an unconscious reader taking in one book after another looking for good stories. When I was finished with one novel it receded into the background and made way for the next. I had no notion of becoming a writer. Writers were, for me, long dead practitioners of a lost art.

And so it went. I read, let's say, *Treasure Island* by Stevenson, then *Demian* by Hesse, and on to *The Long Goodbye*. One page after the other went by and I was as happy (and as unaware) as a clam. And then two sentences, toward the end of the novel, shook me from my waking slumber. It was like a one-two combination punch. The jab was a man, a dangerous man, looking at the protagonist without the slightest concern. He had a gun but didn't bother lifting it. He was sitting down but saw no reason to stand. And then came the straight right cross: The first-person narrator told me that this dangerous man was as calm as an adobe wall in the moonlight.

I was overcome by an image that I had seen many times but that I had never stopped to mark in my mind. It took Raymond Chandler to show me something that I already knew but had never been aware of. Adobe walls in the lunar light of the southern California desert had the most passive demeanor—they were the ideal of peacefulness.

Then the writer contrasts this nearly absolute tranquility to an armed and dangerous man . . . For the first time I understood the power of language to reach beyond the real into the metaphysical and into metaphor.

Those twenty-four words alerted me to the potential power of writing. It was a step beyond the limitations of the physical world into a realm where a thing and its opposite could meet and magically become something else.

Tinker, tailor
Soldier, sailor
Rich man, Poor man
Beggar man, thief.
—ENGLISH FORTUNE-TELLING RHYME

JIM CRACE

Stealing Plums and Counting Stones

I WAS BROUGHT up in a flat in what was virtually the last building in London. North of us was countryside all the way to the coast, and south of us was nonstop city for twenty miles.

My father had an allotment there, a small garden that we rented to grow our own vegetables. And next to that was a farm. My father used to send me and my brother across to a row of damson trees on the farmland. The trees hung thick with damsons that were hanging there not getting picked.

So we would go scrumping—do you know the term "to scrump"? It's an English word that basically means to steal apples, but also has come to mean to steal any type of fruit. My father would send us across to scrump the damsons. Of course, in a way, it wasn't truly theft: The fruit would have rotted if we didn't take it. But really, it *was* theft. We were trespassing on a farmer's land, and we were stealing from him.

Even though my brother and I loved scrumping—we loved the act of climbing trees and grabbing fruit—there was always fear we would be caught. We feared we'd be imprisoned, sent to Australia. You know how you are when you're a kid? We were terrified and excited by it at the same time.

The story didn't end there, because we'd take the damsons back home. My mom would bottle them—and all through the winter we'd have damson pie. In our generation in England, you'd have damson pie for Sunday lunch. You'd get your portion of pie, and as you'd get through it, the pips—the stones in the center of the fruit—would end up in your mouth. You'd take them out and place them on the tablecloth in front of you, and they'd remain on the table throughout the meal. Then at the end, you could recite a little rhyme:

Tinker, tailor
Soldier, sailor
Rich man, Poor man
Beggar man, thief.

We used this rhyme around the table to tell our fortunes. Eight men! You'd count off each pip you had, stopping when you ran out, looping around to the beginning if you had more than eight stones. Every single one of the choices would invite you to have a little imaginative spree. If you had five of these stones, you could for a few minutes think about being a rich man, and how close you'd come to being a poor man.

And there's another level here—a sexist level—because it was different for girls and for boys. If you were a boy, you would chomp a bit, and it would tell you who you would become later in life. But if you were a girl, when you reeled off this little rhyme, it would only tell you who you were going to *marry*. When we were kids we wouldn't have seen the feminist aspect of it, the fact that women had different outcomes from men, that women were only defined by marriage, while men were defined by what they did.

This influential little verse had enormous power for me, in part, because of my fear of being accused of stealing. Imagine: My brother and I would thrill ourselves by stealing the damsons when my father ordered us to do it. We'd eat and enjoy them, and what was left over would come out again six months later in preserving bottles, baked in pies. And as we ate we'd end the rhyme with that accusatory snare-beat:

thief. For me, the fear of being called a thief was resurrected again in that moment. The plums came back in a different form, and with them the ghost of the accusation.

There were happy memories associated with it, too. My father had a North London accent—he said *thief* like *feef.* My brother and I used to sneak pips into his pile to give him the right amount so that he'd fall on "thief." And we'd laugh ourselves dry—because not only did he become a thief, but he'd mispronounce the word.

So I loved this, but I didn't know why it had invaded my imagination so thoroughly until I started writing. I began to see the power of the twinning of narrative and rhythm, which is something my books go into very much. It taught me to think about the difference between what poetry does—old-fashioned thumping, rhyming poetry—and the effects that really beautiful, percussive, musical, melodic prose can achieve with rhythm.

In this simple little rhyme, you're seeing an unraveling of the tightest form of poetry into free verse. The rhyme form is immensely interesting; it sets a tight, highly versified and melodic opening against a free-verse and percussive closing.

It goes like this. You're starting off in that first line: "Tinker, tailor," not only with alliteration, but with matching pairs of syllables: Tinker. Tailor. Soldier. Sailor. And, you've got a perfect rhyme: "tailor" and "sailor." Those four words there could not be stitched more tightly together than they are in the form that I've just given them to you.

Then you come to the third line. Again, we observe pairs of syllables— but there's a subtle change, and a weird change. Tinker, tailor; soldier, sailor; *rich man, poor man.* You've got repetition—but exactly matching words don't rhyme with each other. "Pear" doesn't rhyme with "pear"; "bear" rhymes with "pear." "Man" and "man" don't rhyme—they're simply repetitions. There's a kind of loss of verve about repeating a word. So the verse is subtly, subtly starting to fall apart.

Then you've got a real falling apart on the next line—because with "Tinker, tailor," "Soldier, sailor," "Rich man, Poor man," you've got pairs of syllables. And then you've got this tricky three-syllable phrase: "Beggar man." It's three syllables, which breaks the pattern—and yet you've got the repetition of the word "man" that links them together. But it's loosening up its form. And then finally, the percussive note, the little drumbeat at the end—that slap on the skin of the drums—is the word "thief."

"Thief," out of all the words in this small piece, stands alone. It's only one syllable. It doesn't complete the rhyme. It's the only one that implies a kind of moral failing. On all three levels, it subverts the established pattern. And so the "thief" moment is the moment of prose—the moment I go after in my writing. I never achieve the regularity of "Tinker, tailor/ Soldier, sailor." I'm trying to achieve melodic and rhythmic beauty in prose that is expressed here in this nice little so-called poem.

This poem registered profoundly in my imagination, even though I didn't understand it until later. But it created a literary consciousness in me. We should never underestimate what it is that will turn a young person into someone who wants to love literature. Or the young person who wants to make music, or the young person who is attracted to lyric. How are these people formed? They're not formed by being sent to do MFAs in creative writing. That's too late. They're formed by early encounters. They're formed by something that their mother said that made them laugh because it was so well-shaped. And "Tinker, tailor" is something that seems so simple, that seems so one-dimensional—this little rhyme. But if you start to pick it apart—well, I'm having no trouble talking with you about it for twenty minutes. And those things enter into you. Straight from the plum tree, into the plum pie, and onto the family table counting the stones: That's where my writing voice was formed.

I hate to think how this whole story might not have been possible today—that I caught just the tail end of a world that's all but disappeared. We are in a society where everything is getting more "user-friendly," to use that horrible phrase. Food is being packaged so thoroughly. Fewer and fewer people are scrumping. There are fewer damson trees to raid—and if there were more, they'd be fenced off. Fewer people are buying fresh fruit—they're buying it tinned, they're buying produce which doesn't have pits or stones. Parents aren't sitting at the family table chatting around—they're in front of the TV set. Now I sound like an old fart, but you see what I'm saying: The life of that little rhyme, the content of that little rhyme, is to some extent threatened. And I'm not wagging my finger at change; I favor change. But this is one of the things we're going to lose. The great, rich oral tradition, and the narratives embedded in the land—these spoil when we abandon them, like summer fruit left hanging on the tree.

In some ways, my encounter with the stones—both when I was scrumping them and then again when I was eating them—somehow helped forge my passion for the natural world. Natural history and the landscape are my characters, in a way more important than the human characters. And it was this nursery rhyme that helped me realize that the natural world has powerful and deeply embedded narratives. Trees across the road flowering with perishable fruit. The thrill of a young boy going out scrumping, and the terror of being caught. The fact of a family gathering at a family table to eat their food together, some of it grown and some of it borrowed. All of this is made sense of by a little snatch of beautiful language, one I've carried all my life. To encounter it is to reencounter the dining table, to relive my love for my parents, which has not abated one bit. This little rhyme is one of my most powerful reminders of my family's love. It shows exactly how big things of childhood and transgression can be powerfully expressed, and recalled whole again, by the form of beautiful prose.

"It's not the same, Papi," I'd tried, but he shook his head.

"Pero of course it is, mijita. All your life is a work of art. A painting is not a painting but the way you live each day. A song is not a song but the words you share with the people you love. A book is not a book but the choices you make every day trying to be a decent person."

—PATRICIA ENGEL, *It's Not Love, It's Just Paris*

EDWIDGE DANTICAT

All Immigrants
Are Artists

As I thought about my choice for this book, I felt nervous to choose something that isn't a classic. But Patricia Engel's *It's Not Love, It's Just Paris* struck such a chord with me that I feel I have to talk about it. I got the book in galleys earlier this summer, just as I was about to travel to Haiti. I took it with me while I was there, and was totally absorbed. So much of the book is familiar to me. It's set in Paris, where I spent my junior year abroad, and it's about being a kind of double-foreigner: The narrator is a foreigner in Paris, but she's also a foreigner in the United States, her home.

I came upon one paragraph that really jumped out at me, one that I read over and over and over:

I thought of my father. Once, before my graduation, I'd mentioned the possibility of changing direction and not studying diplomacy as I'd been planning. Papi thought I meant I'd join him and Santi at the family business, but when I said I was considering something more creative, he shook his head as if I'd been terribly mistaken and said there was no need for that; I was already an artist by blood; all immigrants are artists because they create a life, a future, from nothing but a dream. The

immigrant's life is art in its purest form. That's why God has special
sympathy for immigrants, because Diosito was the first artist, and Jesus,
un pobre desplazado.

"It's not the same, Papi," I'd tried, but he shook his head.

"Pero of course it is, mijita. All your life is a work of art. A painting
is not a painting but the way you live each day. A song is not a song but
the words you share with the people you love. A book is not a book
but the choices you make every day trying to be a decent person."

The narrator encounters resistance when she tells her father she's considering a creative path. Often, in an immigrant family, it's a very big
departure for a child to say: I want to be an artist, not a doctor, not a
lawyer, or an engineer. The father, here, tells his daughter what so
many immigrant parents tell their children: *Art is not the safest route in
life. We didn't sacrifice all this for you to take up a precarious profession.*

He tries to comfort her, at the same time, by insisting that being an
immigrant makes her an artist *already.* And this is a fascinating notion:
that re-creating yourself this way, re-creating your entire life, is a form
of reinvention on par with the greatest works of literature. This brings
art into the realm of what ordinary people do in order to survive. It
takes away the notion that art is too lofty for the masses, and puts it in
the day-to-day. I've never seen anyone connect being an artist and an
immigrant so explicitly, and for me it was a revelation.

My parents spent their entire lives in Haiti before they left. They
didn't know much about the United States except that, at that time,
there were opportunities there. They basically packed two suitcases
and came. That experience of touching down in a totally foreign place
is like having a blank canvas: You begin with nothing, but stroke by
stroke you build a life. This process requires everything great art
requires—risk-taking, hope, a great deal of imagination, all the qualities that are the building blocks of art. You must be able to dream something nearly impossible and toil to bring it into existence.

As in art, there are always surprises. For my parents, one thing was snow. Cold. They'd never had to worry about being cold before! It took creativity to know how to cope with it. My mother, because of a rule in her religion, wasn't allowed to wear pants. Other women told her that pants would help quite a bit with the cold, but she knew she had to find another way. In the end, she learned to sew these legwarmer-like things for herself, which she wore under her dresses to stay warm.

Alice Walker has a wonderful essay called "In Search of Our Mothers' Gardens," where she talks about women who were slaves and dying, perhaps, to paint or write. Because they couldn't, they channeled their creativity into domestic forms of art—into their quilts, say, or gardens. I see this impulse in my mother. She could have been an extraordinary designer in another place, in another situation—she was an excellent seamstress. When we'd walk through a clothing store together, I'd pick out a dress—she'd always touch the fabric and say, "This is such cheap quality." And she'd tell me, "I'm going to make you this dress—but better." So we'd go to the cloth shop, buy some fabric, and she'd make me a beautiful replica of the dress.

When I was little, I bought her reasoning: It was the quality of the cloth, she wanted better for me. And it might have been. But when I got older, I realized it was just cheaper for her to make my clothes. My mother made most of the clothes I wore through high school. Until I had my own money, we didn't buy dresses. Sometimes it was weird—I wore more dresses than other things. But these are ways people find to survive. If you can't afford clothes, but you can make them—make them. You have to work with what you have, especially if you don't have a lot of money. You use creativity, and you use imagination.

And that's another thing this passage hints on: that first-generation immigrants often model artistic behavior for their children. They don't necessarily realize it, like the father who says the immigrant life is art in its greatest form. But I realize now I saw artistic qualities in my parents' choices—in their creativity, their steadfastness, the very fact that we were in this country from another place. They're like the artist mentors people have in any discipline—by studying, by observing, by reading, you've had this model in the form of someone's life. My mother could not have found time for creative pursuits with four children and a factory job. But she modeled the discipline and resourcefulness and self-sacrifice that are constant inspirations in my own life's work. The things she did, the choices she made, made the artist's life possible for me. I didn't know it, but she taught me that being an artist makes sense.

While it's natural for the children of immigrants to want to be artists, it is natural for the parents to feel threatened by artistic vocations. As a parent myself, I completely understand that impulse. When you've given so much, when you've sacrificed everything to make this huge transition, you want to see your child have an easier life as a result. You want to spare them the anguish of worrying always about survival, especially after all the sacrifices you've made. The first generation feels they created a path, they sacrificed, they made the way—and now their children should have stability and peace of mind. This, of course, is not the emphasis of being an artist.

And so, for children of immigrants, the creative path is fraught with added risk: There's so much more at stake if you fail. There's a feeling that—as the character in the passage feels—if you fail, you're not only failing yourself, but your family, your parents who have gone through so much to give you this opportunity. It's not just your own failure at stake—artistic failure can mean the failure of your family's entire enterprise.

My father died of pulmonary fibrosis in 2005, after a very long illness. On his deathbed, he wrestled very much with the idea that his life ultimately meant nothing. He'd ask me questions like, "What have I contributed to the world?" And the conclusion he came to was: *Well, you guys—my children. You are my contribution.* I think the fact that my brothers and I had some success in life helped him come more readily to this conclusion. My father always wanted me to be a doctor. As he was dying, if I had become neither doctor nor writer, I fear he might have felt like his life meant nothing. That weight was on my back, this feeling that success—however it's defined—was somehow crucial.

The worst feeling that immigrant parents can have is, "Maybe we shouldn't have come here. Maybe we should have stayed." Often, their feeling about their decision to leave home is bound up in the fates and careers of their children. If they *do* succeed, though, this wonderful thing can happen: when they speak to the culture about the journey a particular family went through, and it validates the parents' decision publicly. I found that, as my father was dying, this counted for him somehow—the fact that other people, through things I had written, knew how much he sacrificed to raise me and my brothers. This success ultimately convinced him that he made the right choice. It validates the decision he made all those many years ago.

This passage made me feel something different: a new and sudden connection with the generation before. After having read this, I can no longer say I'm the only artist in my family. This passage broadened my artistic community beyond my fellow writers. It makes my community larger in terms of who I think of being artists, and how I think of others. It makes me honor, through the prism of art, the way other immigrants have lived their lives, all the difficult choices they have made. I'm part of a broader community—beyond just artists and just immigrants—one that links them both. It makes me look at my work differently, and I see my parents in a different way.

I will arise and go now, for always night and day
I hear lake water lapping with low sounds by the shore;
While I stand on the roadway, or on the pavements grey,
I hear it in the deep heart's core.

—W. B. Yeats, "The Lake Isle of Innisfree"

BILLY COLLINS

Into the Deep
Heart's Core

I FIRST CAME across "The Lake Isle of Innisfree" in college, with other anthologized poems by Yeats. At that time, I found some of his work difficult—especially poems like "Sailing to Byzantium" and "Easter, 1916" that required historical context. But "The Lake Isle of Innisfree," this little twelve-liner, had immediate appeal.

The sentiment is very clear: The speaker has committed to go off to an island, and imagines himself there. The language is gorgeous—it has a beautiful, rhythmic, almost hypnotic spell. It also has a very tightly organized structure, despite its lyric quality. Each four-line stanza makes its own argument, starting with the first grouping of four lines:

> I will arise and go now, and go to Innisfree,
> And a small cabin build there, of clay and wattles made:
> Nine bean rows will I have there, a hive for the honey-bee,
> And live alone in the bee-loud glade.

First, he puts you on the island in this idealized retreat, where he's going. He talks about the physical place, and his physical needs. He needs shelter—so he'll build a cabin. And he'll need food: He describes the beans he'll raise and the bees he'll keep for honey. (I don't know what kind of dish you can make from beans and honey, but—okay.)

In the second stanza, the poem escalates. He pivots away from his material needs and addresses his spiritual needs:

> And I shall have some peace there, for peace comes dropping slow,
> Dropping from the veils of the morning to where the cricket sings;
> There midnight's all a glimmer, and noon a purple glow,
> And evening full of the linnet's wings.

In addition to honey and beans, then, he'll have peace. And we see how this feeling manifests, as he takes us through the day from the "veils of the morning" until very late at night. He runs around the clock, showing how peace spreads in this diurnal way.

In the final stanza, he recommits, reiterating his intent to leave:

> I will arise and go now, for always night and day
> I hear lake water lapping with low sounds by the shore;
> While I stand on the roadway, or on the pavements grey,
> I hear it in the deep heart's core.

He continually hears this "lake water lapping with low sounds by the shore," but then there's the shock: He hears this island sound in the *city*. He hears it "on the roadway," and "on the pavements grey." It's all wishful thinking. He says "I will arise," but he never *does* arise. He hears the sounds of the water lapping at the shore, but he hears it in the city. He hears it in London. And we begin to understand that Innisfree is an internal place, a fictive place, a refuge that calls to him from the inside, not a place that he can physically go and visit. The poem ends with a strong sense of this internal motion, going in and down, in the final line: "I hear it in the deep heart's core."

It's a powerful, unexpected statement of a simple sentiment: I want to go somewhere better than where I am.

Shortly after coming across the poem, I heard a recording of Yeats reading it. I loved to hear his performance of the poem. It's as though he *sings* it, elongating the words and phrases with his musical voice. It gives you the shivers.

In this recording, as he introduces his recitation of the poem, Yeats gets rather testy. It took him a lot of bother and time to put the rhythm and the sound into the poem, he says, and he's not going to take it out in the reading. It's a justification of his incantatory, singing style of reading aloud.

One of the disadvantages of poetry over popular music is that if you write a pop song, it naturally gets into people's heads as they listen in the car. You don't have to memorize a Paul Simon song; it's just in your head, and you can sing along. With a poem, you have to will yourself to memorize it. That's what happened to me with "The Lake Isle of Innisfree." I knew the poem well—through many rereadings and through teaching it in my classes—but at some point, I remember thinking, "I'm just going to get this poem down." This process—going from deep familiarity to complete mastery—is a challenge and a great pleasure. In repeating different lines, your reading becomes more focused than it's ever been before. You become more sensitive to every consonant and vowel.

Years ago, I wrote an article called "Poetry, Pleasure, and the Hedonist Reader" in which I enumerated five or six of the principle pleasures of poetry. One of the final pleasures, for instance, is the pleasure of meaning—the moment when a poem's emotional effect begins to crystallize into significance you can articulate. But the very final pleasure is what I called "the pleasure of companionship"—and this was a way of talking about memorization. When you internalize a poem, it becomes something inside of you. You're able to walk around with it. It becomes a companion. And so you become much less objective in your judgment of it. If anyone criticizes the poem, they're criticizing something you take with you, all the time.

Some years ago, I had an MRI—and a very insensitive blockhead of a neurologist. The technology hadn't been in wide use for very long, and I'd never had an MRI before. I assumed it was like an X-ray or a CT scan. The neurologist didn't prepare me at all. He didn't tell me it was like being buried alive in a very high-tech coffin. He didn't say, take half a Valium. He didn't say, don't drink coffee.

So when I got there I was shocked to hear the technician ask: "Would you like music or no music?" I didn't know what he was talking about. Then he pointed to this high-tech, plastic coffin. "You'll be in there half an hour," he said. So, I asked for no music—afraid I might get caught with Neil Diamond classics or something.

I'm not a claustrophobe, but you don't need to be to feel claustrophobic inside an MRI. It's like being buried alive. I lay there with my eyes closed, and pulled "The Lake Isle of Innisfree" up in my memory. I pulled the whole poem up before me in my mind. Slowly, I started reciting it. And then more slowly. After saying it straight through a number of times, I used the poem as a kind of diagram to focus on. I said just the rhyme words: Innisfree / made, honey-bee / glade, slow / sings, glow / wings, like that. Then I tried to say every other line. By the time the MRI was over, I was in the process of saying it backward. And the poem—like a good companion—had saved me from really freaking out.

"The Lake Isle of Innisfree" is very soothing in that way. After all, it's wishing for this rural and insular paradise from within the bowels of the city. It's about hearing the call of a safe, peaceful place, especially while under duress. Yeats hears that call while he stands "on the pavements grey," he says—but it could be "I hear it while I'm lying in the MRI." Or "I hear it while I'm in jail for the night," or "I hear it while I'm stuck on an elevator," or "I hear it while I'm waiting for the bus." You don't need to be in an extreme situation, or you can be. Once you've installed the poem in your memory, it's there to comfort you—or at least distract you—wherever you are.

I think that's one reason I've always made my literature students choose a poem to memorize, even if it's just something short—a little poem by, say, Emily Dickinson. They're very resistant to it at first. There's a collective groan when I tell them what they're going to have to do. I think it's because memorization is hard. You can't fake it the way you might in responding to an essay question. Either you have it by heart, or you don't.

And yet once they *do* get a poem memorized, they can't wait to come into my office to say it. I love watching that movement from thinking of memorization as a kind of drudgery, to seeing it as internalizing, claiming, owning a poem. It's no longer just something in a textbook—it's something that you've placed within yourself. And if you learn something written by a living poet, you might have an edge on the writer himself. Not all formal poets memorize their poems—so you may own it in a way he or she doesn't. It becomes an exciting thing.

Poetry tends to be easier to memorize than prose, because it's designed to be memorized. A formal poem like the one we're talking about—with a steady beat, and with lines that divide neatly into two—almost asks to be remembered. And because the poem is so perfectly organized into twelve lines, three four-line stanzas, an ABAB rhyme scheme in this common rhythm, it becomes a kind of grid that you can move around in. Unlike prose, which is complete, linear, headlong movement forward—a poem is a design that displaces silence on the page. You can look at it as a thing to wander in. You can say every other line. You can play with the design by getting inside its structure. When you're in duress, as I was in the MRI, you can put the poem to all kinds of diagrammatic uses.

Formal poems remind us that the origins of poetry lie in its mnemonic features, in rhythm, end rhyme, assonance, alliteration. All these devices were presumably ways of storing information, tricks pre-literate cultures developed to help commit things to memory before they could write things down. Poetry made it easier to recall basic survival information, like how to hunt or what to plant. But it also helped store vaguer or less material things, answers to questions about where your people came from, or what your tribe did hundreds of years ago. It helped store things about individual and collective identity, really. And the shamans or griots or bards—the society's poets—would be the people best at retaining that information, and most enchanted with the process of learning it and reciting it.

Once we did develop written language, practically speaking, poetry had outlived its practical function. And so, poetry has taken on other uses: as a form of enlightenment, a way of recording your internal life. But basically it still retains the powerful features that we put to use before we had writing.

I'm aware of these things as I go about my own work. The things that make a poem memorizable are important to me: the cadence of the lines, the cadence of the sentences, the flow of the syntax. These things consume a lot of my creative effort, even though my poems aren't formal, and they don't run to a metronomic beat, and they don't usually feature end rhyme. Free verse is obviously harder to memorize than formal poetry, but it's easier to memorize than prose because it does come in lines that are units—units of thought, units of syntax. I try very much to make the poem roll, and syntactically hold together, in the same way that Frost or Yeats would try, only without the exact metrics, and without end rhyme. I'm very conscious of the rhythm of it. And I think that poems of mine are somewhat memorizable for that reason.

Writing free verse, it's hard to know exactly when a line has the feel or rhythm that you want. It's hard to describe, though you know it when you feel it. For me, it's often about gracefulness. I want graceful lines and graceful sentences. I try to write very simply. The vocabulary is simple, the sentences tend to be quite conventional—subject, verb, object. I try to be very unchallenging in syntax. I want the trip to be one of imagination and not completely of the language. But I'm also thinking about the reader, whom I'm trying to guide through an imaginative experience. I want the excitement of the poem—if I can generate some—not to lie in a fancy use of language, or an eccentric use of language. I want the poem to be an *imaginative* thrill. To take the reader to an odd place, or a challenging place, or a disorienting place, but to do that with fairly simple language. I don't want the language itself to be the trip. I want the imaginative spaces that we're moving through to be the trip.

I know that goes against some of the poetry you might encounter, where the language is the thing. Well, of course, poetry is all made of words and that's what we're working with here. But I don't just want the reader's staring at language to be the experience. I want to take the reader from Kansas to Oz: from a simple, familiar place, to a slightly unusual place.

Poetry's kind of a mixture of the clear and the mysterious. It's very important to know when to be which: what to be clear about and what to leave mysterious. A lot of poetry I find unreadable is trying to be mysterious all the time. The reader needs to feel oriented in the beginning of the poem, or else he or she can't be disoriented later. Often, the first lines of a poem—many times, I find them completely disorienting. I'd like to go to that place, but I like to be taken there rather than being shoved into it. It's like being pushed off the title into the path of an approaching train.

I think part of the reason for this is that the audience for poetry has decreased in recent years. There's really only one audience for poetry these days: poets themselves. In the last thirty years, this has been good news and bad news. The good news is there's all this poetry activity: open mikes and workshops and readings and prizes. The bad news is that these events are populated largely by card-carrying fellow poets. Poetry's not getting out to nonpractitioners as much as it used to. And the anxiety these days is not the anxiety of influence, but the anxiety of clarity. I think a lot of poets feel anxiety about being clear.

And yet I think poetry is as important today as it's ever been, despite its diminished public stature. Its uses become obvious when you read it. Poetry privileges subjectivity. It foregrounds the interior life of the writer, who is trying to draw in a reader. And it gets readers into contact with their own subjective life. This is valuable, especially now. If you look around at the society we live in, we're being pulled constantly into public life. It's not just Facebook, which is sort of the willing forfeiture of one's own privacy. The sanctuaries of privacy are so scarce these days. Every banality, from "I'm going out for pizza," to "JoAnn is passed out on the sofa," is broadcast to the wide world. I think I read recently that we're not suffering from an overflow of information—we're suffering from an overflow of insignificance. Well, poetry becomes an oasis or sanctuary from the forces constantly drawing us into social and public life.

Poetry exerts a different kind of pull on us. It's a pull toward meaning and subjectivity. It's the sound of lake water lapping by the shore. In "Dover Beach," when Matthew Arnold describes hearing the waves coming up from the English Channel, he says Sophocles heard this long ago in the Aegean. And it's one of those sounds that everyone has heard—Joan of Arc heard this, Cicero. Poetry presents us with these sensations: the things that cut through history, into the deep heart's core.

For
darkness restores what light cannot repair.
—Joseph Brodsky, "On Love"

KATHRYN HARRISON

Please Stop Thinking

I DON'T KNOW when I first encountered Joseph Brodsky's poem "On Love," but I know what reawakened my interest in it. I was in Boston looking at the collection of Rothkos at Harvard, and a line from the poem popped into my head—as if the Rothkos had summoned it.

It's a poem about a man who has dreamed about his dead partner. The possibilities that were destroyed by losing her are restored in the dream: the idea of their making love, and having children, and being in each other's company. It ends by underscoring the commitment that extends beyond mortal life—in a realm that is not conscious, not present here, not material, not cerebral. You might call it the realm of the mystical, or the ineffable. Whatever you want to call it, it's a realm I believe in.

Throughout the poem, Brodsky sets up a contrast between light and darkness. With the lights out, memories of the dream-woman consume the narrator—so much so that she seems to become real. When he flicks the light on, though, she vanishes:

> And with the bulb turned on
> I knew that I was leaving you alone
> there, in the darkness, in the dream, where calmly
> you waited till I might return.

Many human transactions take place in this realm of darkness. On unconscious planes, through dreams—even, on some level, in people's ability to communicate without words. By darkness, I don't mean black, as in lacking light. I mean *dark*: the aspect of life that is not accessible through our conscious processes of analysis.

The poem's essence is in this line:

> For
> darkness restores what light cannot repair.

I think Brodsky means that light can "repair" things in the *material* world, but that there are limitations of that kind of fixing. Medicine, for instance, can heal in the light. But if the spirit isn't well, there is no life. And there is no way to restore what's lost, sometimes, other than through dreams and imagination.

I don't think I'm saying something sad when I say that. There's huge redemption in the fact that there is a world that is dark, or opaque, to conscious life. The realm of darkness that heals and restores, and allows memory to bind up, provides the present with a kind of solace that is almost holy. The line is about the holy and generative properties that exist within us. And so, I think the line is about God. A realm that God inhabits.

We could probably say that about a Rothko, too.

The line also defines writing, at least writing the way I experience it. For me, writing is a process that demands cerebral effort, but it's also one informed by the unconscious. My work is directed by the needs of my unconscious. And through that dark, opaque process, I can restore what might otherwise be lost. In a novel, I can restore lost voices—usually a woman's—and give words back to the silenced. Or in memoir—*The Kiss* restored my voice, broke a silence imposed on me.

I have to write. It's not an option. When I write, I am literally building myself a place in which to live. Once I'm firmly established within the narrative I pop awake in the morning and it's the first thing I think about. Not in an analytical way, as in "Oh, I haven't really reached the crisis point and it's already page 200—I'd better work on that." It's very much just running toward and into the place I most want to be.

When I can't go to that place, I feel anxious and unhappy. I love writing, and I'm miserable without it—and as time goes by, the people around me are miserable also.

It's funny, I teach writing, and before I taught I never would have guessed the thing I say most often is: "Please stop thinking." But people really write better without thinking, by which I mean without self-consciousness.

I'm not calculating about what I write, which means I have very little control over it. It's not that I decide what to write and carry it out. It's more that I grope my way toward something—not even knowing what it is until I've arrived. I've gotten better over the years at accepting this.

Of course, the intellect wants to kick in—and, in the later drafts, it should. But in the early stages of a book, I deal with potential self-consciousness by literally hushing the critical voices in my head. The voices that tell you: "Oh, those aren't the words you want," or "You shouldn't be working on this part now," or "Why not use the present tense?"—on and on. Anyone who's ever written anything is familiar with that chorus.

Writing a first draft, you can become paralyzed by these thoughts. So I literally tell the voices to quiet down. I praise them for their perspicacity, and I tell them how much I need them—that I will want them later. But I cannot listen to them right now, because I am confused by them.

And I don't sit there waiting for that perfect, beautiful sentence, because I know I'm going to sit there forever. So, as I tell students—start out by tripping, why don't you? Then get up and fall over again. Just as long as you *go.*

When I'm writing the way I want, the way I love, which is without thinking about what I'm writing, a strange thing happens: I feel simultaneously the most myself I could possibly be, and at the same time totally relieved of self. I become, I guess, a version of myself that isn't filtered through the detritus and clutter of experience. We can't control so much of what happens to us in life. Even our own actions unfold in time in ways we can't possibly imagine. But there is someone inside who remains untouched by all of that. That person may not really exist in the light, but she is there, waiting, in the dark.

Once a book is out of my hands, I have no illusion that I have much control over its future in the world. It's like giving a radio to a reader: They turn the knob, it plays, and they think, "Oh great!" Or it doesn't play, and then they throw it out. Giving a book to critics is different, and worse—more like watching your radio being taken apart, not even hearing it play.

I don't really like publication. Don't get me wrong, I'm grateful to be making a living doing what I love. But though I love to write, I don't much like *being* a writer. I don't really have much sense of who Kathryn Harrison, the writer, is. She has little to do with me, actually.

Sometimes, I have to run out and pretend to be that person for a while, which requires a lot of energy. I'm very much an introvert. But I am also a willing and cooperative person in terms of serving the thing that I care about, which is writing. So if that means that I show up and give readings and interviews, even if it takes a lot of energy just for me to work myself up to appearing in public, that is something I'm happy to do. I'll present myself to the world as a writer if it helps me continue writing.

I always think of that beautiful Kafka quote: "A book must be an axe for the frozen sea within us." I want art to be that axe. I want art to tear through the veil between the dark and the light. Art has to exist that way, because art is material even though what it expresses is ineffable. A book might be inspired by darkness, but it is a material, concrete thing made from words—real things that, put together, mean approximately the same thing to me as they do to you. That's what I do, what a painter does, what it means to engage in any creative act: balance there, on that line between the dark and the light.

I lean back, as the evening darkens and comes on.
A chicken hawk floats over, looking for home.
I have wasted my life.

—JAMES WRIGHT,
"Lying in a Hammock at William Duffy's
Farm in Pine Island, Minnesota"

DAVID MITCHELL

Neglect Everything Else

BEFORE I WAS published, when I was about twenty-nine years old—I'm forty-five now—I was looking through the poetry section in a bookshop. I found this very slim volume of poems by a man I'd never heard of before, James Wright, called *The Branch Will Not Break*. I flicked through it, and found a poem that is still one of the most beautiful things I've ever read: a short piece called "Lying in a Hammock at William Duffy's Farm in Pine Island, Minnesota." I bought the book, and for much of my life I've had a copy of the poem just above my desk, or wherever I've worked. Whatever else is going on in the day, my eyes can go and find this textual hammock.

For most of the poem, the narrator describes the scenery that surrounds him during a summer lounge:

> Over my head, I see the bronze butterfly,
> Asleep on the black trunk,
> Blowing like a leaf in green shadow.

I love the poem's leisurely rhythms (and it should be leisurely, he's lying in a hammock). I love the colors—"bronze," "black," "green"—its tones and hues are exquisite. I love the unflashiness of the language—as in "I lean back, as the evening darkens and comes on." "Comes on" just isn't a literary turn of phrase, but it's the language that we use. And I love the way all Wright's prepositions locate us so concretely in space: We've got "over" and "down" and "into" in addition to "to my right." Each line has kind of a key word—"empty," or "cowbells." It's almost a kind of cryptogram. Every single word is earning its place—it's unfussy, brilliant, deceptively simple.

Wright ends the poem on a surprising turn:

A chicken hawk floats over, looking for home.
I have wasted my life.

What to make of this famous last line? I hear him exhale it with a wry laugh: I've wasted my life! He's kind of smiling. *I've done it again, all this wasted time,* he thinks—*but at least I know it.* Though he hasn't really wasted all of his life—he knows that, too. You have to enter the hammock, put the world on hold, to really see things clearly the way the poem does. He's been to this hammock before, and he's had moments like this before, and it's mostly positive. It's self-deflating, but not depressing. It's sad, and longing, and nostalgic, and wry—the ironic half-bark of a laugh.

For me, the poem's chief value is as a reminder to stay inside the moment. It asks us not to let our minds rerun things that have already happened, not to trouble our head fruitlessly about things that haven't happened yet. Inhabit the now, the poem urges—just see the beauty around you that you don't normally see.

We have a hard time remaining in the present: Our monkey minds are continually jumping through the jungles of the past and the forests of the future. But Wright's poem says: *Stop!* Just stop. Calm down, be quiet, and look around. It's an homage to, and an exhortation of, the act of seeing.

I forget this all the time, all the time. If I remember to do what the poem asks for 0.1 percent of the day—slow down, look closely—then that's a great day. An enlightened day. Usually, though, it's nowhere near even that.

The world is very good at distracting us. Much of the ingenuity of our remarkable species goes toward finding new ways to distract ourselves from things that really matter. The Internet—it's lethal, isn't it? Maintaining focus is critical, I think, in the presence of endless distraction. You've only got time to be a halfway decent parent, plus one other thing.

For me, that one other thing is: I've got to be writing. I have a few ways to make sure I can carve out time.

Part one: Neglect everything else.

Part two: Get disciplined. Learn to rush to your laptop and open it up. Open the file without asking yourself if you're in the mood, without thinking about anything else. Just open the file—and then you're safe. Once the words are on the screen, that becomes your distraction.

Of course, it's not distraction—it's work, and it's wonderful when it goes well. I'm sure other, more disciplined people can do it without needing to rush, but I have to. The moment you think, *okay, it's work time*, and face down the words, you rush past all the other things asking for your attention.

Part three: Keep the Apple homepage, because it's rather boring. If your homepage is the website of your favorite newspaper, you've had it.

Just remember, this is how you earn a living. Really hardworking people at the publisher are relying on your next book for their bonuses, to feed their kids, pay their mortgage. You owe it to them not to let years fritter away fruitlessly. First and foremost, of course, you owe it to yourself, and you owe it to your book—but if that isn't getting the job done, remember that it's other people's livelihoods on the line as well, not just yours.

These are just some of the sticks I use to beat myself into opening up the file. Once I do, I'm safe. I'm home free.

I do think there's some relationship between maintaining focus, looking closely, and the act of writing itself. The more you practice really looking, the more convincingly you can build a set for a scene. You become used to looking at the relationships between objects and people and light and time and mood and air. That's what you're doing when you're having a James Wright's hammock moment, and it's also what you need to do to bring a scene into being. I think all writers do this. I don't think I'm remarkably gifted at it or anything, but if there is an overlap between the skill of perception and the skill of populating a scene with objects and people, then this would be the connection.

Much of my work involves writing about scenes set far in the future or deep in the past. How to immerse oneself in the moment-to-moment nature of a time and place you've never personally experienced—and perhaps cannot?

Well, I would put a question to you. What's the difference between you and your great-great-great-grandfather? What makes you different?

I think the answer is this: what you take for granted.

What you take for granted about your life, about your rights, about people around you. About ethnicity, gender, sexuality, work, God. Your relationship with the state. The state's obligations and duties to you: health care, education, recreation. What you take for granted about all these things is I think what marks one culture from another, and one generation from another.

So when you're writing about the future, you simply try to work out what people in that future point will be taking for granted. In *The Bone Clocks*, there are two future sections. The 2025 one is only about eleven years away—there's just a few gizmos about the place and we're basically there already. In the 2040s, however, more dramatic changes have taken place. There's no more oil—or very little oil—left. So you think about what people at that point will be taking for granted about travel, about the ability to hop on an airplane and be hundreds of miles away in an hour or two. Or to have a conversation like this one, to speak across a continent—which, in the context of human history, is a profoundly bizarre thing to be doing. An *impossible* thing to be doing, an unthinkable thing to be doing! We can take a device out of our pockets and speak to somebody in Auckland on it. And the miracle is that we don't see it as a miracle. We've only had this skill—to take out a smartphone and call anywhere on earth—for ten years, maybe twenty. But, already, we take it for granted. It is part of what it means to live in our time.

When there is no more oil to power the system of power stations, which power the electric grid, which we power our devices on—we will no longer take it for granted that we can do it. It will be something that our grandchildren will marvel at—my grandfather lived in a world when you could phone someone in Auckland, my god! So that's how you project yourself, narratively, into another time. You work out what people will be taking for granted and whatnot.

Having a spectrum of worlds where different things are being taken for granted, because they are in different times or different cultures, allows me to examine similarity and difference. It allows me to examine change. And isn't change interesting? What is it, after all? It's invisible, like the wind, but you can see its effects when a tornado blows through. The way my books are—spectra across time, across cultures—perhaps allows me to render visible things that are normally invisible, or nontangible. And focus on things that defy focus, perhaps.

It allows me to examine what stays the same, too. For instance, I think we all believe that things are changing faster than they've ever changed before. But if you'd been in England during the Reformation, people would say—I can't believe the way that change is accelerating. Or if you'd been alive during an industrial revolution, or during the Civil War, or as German and Russian and British and American bombs fell during the twentieth century—you'd feel change taking place at a rapidly accelerated pace. The digitization of our existence, what feels like a new reality, is probably just our generation's version. The clothes in which change garbs itself for our generation. In a sense, we're not that special.

Arguably, change and permanence are two of the default themes of all novels—along with memory and identity. It would be hard to keep change out of a novel if you tried. In *The Bone Clocks* it's a salient, foreground theme, but you see it everywhere if you look. In James Wright's poem, too—where you see eternity and reincarnation in the line "The droppings of last year's horses / Blaze up into golden stones." The poem's pastoral scene is timeless, universal: It could very nearly have been written at any point in 5,000 years. Aside from the title, nothing locates Wright's poem in history—not since the invention of agriculture, at least. And the words chosen—"butterfly," "ravine"—are just so elemental and primal. The experience of reading the poem is primal, too, the way it's sonic—we've got the cowbells clunking in the distance—and visual. We've got extreme visual nearness, close enough to see the butterfly; we've got extreme distance in the glimpsing of the chicken hawk, just a speck on the sky.

In this way, Wright captures the most timeless, unchanging human experience: the simple, profound act of perceiving the world. Here, he does it so fully, so beautifully, it's as if the bond between his mind and the world around his head have become one—it's a skull melter. His skull has melted, he's perceiving that purely.

It is an exquisite little gem, and I'll keep it over my desk for the rest of my life.

Daughter drag. Sister drag. Mother drag. Wife drag. Court drag. Rich drag. Poor drag. British drag. Jamaican drag. Each required a different wardrobe. But when considering these various attitudes she struggled to think what would be the most authentic, or perhaps the least inauthentic. —ZADIE SMITH, *NW*

ROXANE GAY

Dreaming in Drag

HOW DO WE inhabit multiple identities? This question has long con-
sumed me and my writing. Perhaps it still does, though I have learned
to ask more rigorous questions. The first essays I published, nearly fifteen years ago, were ones where I tried to write through my conflicted
feelings about identity. As the child of Haitian immigrants who was
raised in the suburbs, mostly in the Midwest, I often wondered where I
belonged—never Haitian enough or American enough or black enough
to feel like the world had a place for me.

I grappled with being black in America and being Haitian in black
America and being black American in Haiti and being middle class
when that was rarely considered a possibility for someone who looked
like me. I was also trying to make sense of desire and sexuality and
wanting so much for myself that felt forbidden. I was trying to figure
out who I was and what might be possible for me. I was trying to write
toward a space where I could reveal my most authentic self to the people who knew me but did not.

My fiction has also taken on a lot of these issues. A black woman in
Michigan's Upper Peninsula tries to close herself off from grief but meets
someone who makes her want to open those parts of herself she is

protecting and make a home in a strange land. In a near future where the South has re-seceded from the United States, a father must decide between his wife and son and his own family whose roots run deep into Southern soil. In my novel *An Untamed State*, a Haitian American woman is kidnapped and has to overcome the betrayal of father and country as she tries to return to the woman she once was.

Where do we belong, I am always asking. How beholden are we to the places and people to whom we belong?

Writing requires courage, audacity. I'm not suggesting that there is something heroic about writing, but I do believe that to commit words and ideas to the page demands something of the writer. Whether fiction or nonfiction, most writers are baring some part of themselves. They are making themselves vulnerable because the writing demands it. Whenever I come across a writer who takes bold chances and exposes their vulnerability at the same time, I am in awe. Zadie Smith is one such writer. Since its release, I have marveled over her novel *NW*, polyphonic, messy, sly, and tender in the most unexpected places.

The energy throughout the novel holds me in its thrall. *NW* is a novel about place and identity and the ways people compromise themselves and the people in their lives. Smith blends narrative styles and narrative voices to tell a story about two friends growing up in a working-class neighborhood. There is a section, telling the story of Natalie Blake née Keisha Blake, offered entirely in list form. As Keisha grows up, becomes a lawyer, wife, and mother, and changes her name to Natalie, we see her grapple with identity and finding a place to belong in the life she has created for herself.

In one section, Smith depicts Keisha/Natalie's struggle with her identities using the metaphor of drag. She tries to make sense of which of her selves is the truest.

170. *In drag*

Daughter drag. Sister drag. Mother drag. Wife drag. Court drag. Rich drag. Poor drag. British drag. Jamaican drag. Each required a different wardrobe. But when considering these various attitudes she struggled to think what would be the most authentic, or perhaps the least inauthentic.

By the end of the novel, Natalie Blake who is Keisha Blake who is Natalie Blake is still searching for the least inauthentic drag to wear. With her friend Leah, she calls the police to report a crime.

"I got something to tell you," said Keisha Blake, disguising her voice with her voice.

This moment is what we are left with, such fitting and gorgeous ambiguity. It is an audacious, elegant choice Smith makes, to offer closure without offering closure, to offer answers to the question of who a woman inhabiting multiple identities is without offering answers. This is what I do when I write, or at least this is what I try to do, what I hope to do— disguising my voice with my voice as I tell some version of the truth.

At least, choose an unimportant day. Choose the least important day in your life. It will be important enough. —THORNTON WILDER, *Our Town*

TOM PERROTTA

Ordinary People

WHEN I WAS a kid, I got a lot of my information from *Reader's Digest*—and I first saw *Our Town* referred to in a copy my parents had lying around. The magazine didn't excerpt the play directly, but used a few details to craft an uplifting little life lesson. It explained how, in the play, a dead woman re-lives her twelfth birthday and discovers how much in life she took for granted. The goal was to remind people that every day is precious; *appre-ciate the time you have*, it said, *and love the people in front of you.*

Though the takeaway was banal—*carpe diem!*—something about it still made a big impression on me. There was a compelling, *Twilight Zone*–like quality to the idea of someone coming back from the dead, looking on in anguish and regret at her own life. I remember thinking *Our Town* was something I should try to read.

But I never came across it in high school. I took the advanced English seminars, and *Our Town* was relegated to the basic courses. In college, I never had Wilder on an English syllabus. I'm sure if I took American Play-writing I would have come across it, but I didn't. I was in my late twenties when I first saw the play performed—the Spalding Gray version put on in New York in the late '80s—and I loved it. When I went to see a new pro-duction about a year ago in Boston, I made sure to bring my kids.

And something caught me totally off guard—I just lost it. During the third act, I started to weep. I think I scared my kids, but I simply couldn't help it.

Our Town can take you by surprise that way. If you know the play, you know how it builds from an innocuous premise toward a cosmic, emotionally punishing finale. It works the kind of magic that certain works of art achieve in that it forces you to do the very thing it says is impossible. The play laments the fact that we can't see our lives from the perspective of the dead—and that's exactly what it makes us do.

Our Town is a play in three acts. There's an ordinary day, then three years later a wedding, and then nine years later there's a death. So an ordinary day, a celebration, and a death—using just those three elements, he provides a crushing sense of how quickly and irrevocably time slips by. It's an amazing work from an artistic standpoint. The play strips away almost everything. The stage directions suggest a barebones set, and there are no props—characters mime their actions. The characters are mostly boiled down to stock types, and there's really no plot. It all boils down to this essential fact: These people live, and then they die. The play generates an enormous amount of emotion from just that basic fact of existence.

But there's no way to make the cosmic moves that Wilder pulls off unless we first believe in the mundane reality of the characters. That's why the first two acts mostly serve to build the world and make the characters feel real. Act One depicts daily life in Grover's Corners using a series of vignettes: children getting ready for school, local housewives complaining about their husbands, the milkman delivering milk, the country doctor returning from his rounds. The kids banter, the adults discuss and gossip, and though most of what we see is wholesome, innocent—*Our Town* prefigures *Happy Days* in this sense—all the little moments ring so true.

Act Two deals with love and courtship—with a focus on the deepening relationship of two characters, George and Emily. Again, Wilder builds upon the small moments. We get this touching flashback when

Emily accuses George of growing too conceited—as George resolves to be better, and Emily apologizes for calling him out, we begin to realize this mundane teenage confession is really a marriage proposal. There are so many small gestures surrounding the wedding that convince completely: the parents' awkward dispensing of advice, the cold feet felt by both bride and groom. It's fairly conventional stuff, but that's the sleight of hand—the play only works if the small moments feel completely real.

It's by building this believable, mundane world that Wilder can pull off a radical move in Act Three. Suddenly, we're in the cemetery. It's nine years later, and many of the characters we've come to know are dead. The cemetery functions like a town all on its own—the inhabitants gather and converse with one another, beyond the grave. Though they're able to watch what the living do, they feel it's too painful to do so; slowly, they learn to turn away from that world.

It's a terrible, frightening thing to imagine your life from the perspective of the dead, but that's what Wilder asks of us. And then we're dealt this emotional blow: Emily, who we've seen grow up, fall in love, and get married, enters the cemetery—a fact the other dead greet with indifference. She died giving birth to her second child. Suddenly, the play's innocence—its light and laughter—becomes cast in a completely different light.

What we don't expect is how painful it will be for the dead to watch the living. And Emily, a new arrival who still clings to the life she had, learns the hard way. "How can I *ever* forget that life?" she says. "It's all I know. It's all I had."

The other dead people, who have been in the cemetery longer, know it's best to forget. But Emily insists on going back to relive a day from her past, even though all the ranks of dead citizens warn against it. Of course, she wants to choose a happy day—maybe the day she fell in love with George. But Mrs. Gibbs, Emily's mother-in-law (killed by pneumonia), warns her that she shouldn't choose something so special—it will be too intense.

At least, choose an unimportant day. Choose the least important day in your life. It will be important enough.

When Emily reluctantly goes back to watch her twelfth birthday—a day she thinks will be commonplace enough—she's shocked to find every moment suffused with great significance and a terrible sense of loss. The simple scene—her mother giving her presents, relatives paying their respects—is the kind of thing we watched, blithely, in the play's first two acts; glimpsed from inside the cemetery, though, that everydayness has a kind of terrible power. Emily wants to savor every moment, because all of it's gone for good. She becomes completely overwhelmed:

> I can't bear it. They're so young and beautiful. Why did they ever have to get old? Mama, I'm here! I'm grown up! I love you all, everything! I can't look at everything hard enough.

"I can't look at everything hard enough": The tragedy is that, while we're alive, we don't view our days in the knowledge that all things must pass. We don't—we *can't*—value our lives, our loved ones, with the urgent knowledge that they'll one day be gone forever. Emily notices with despair that she and her mother barely look at one another, and she laments our self-possession, our distractedness, the million things that keep us from each other. "Oh, Mama," she cries, "just look at me one minute as though you really saw me. . . . *Let's look at one another.*" But mother and daughter remain self-absorbed, each in a private sea of her own thoughts, and that moment of recognition, of connection, never comes. Eventually, Emily has to turn away.

Some people think of *Our Town* as being sentimental. Obviously, there's a wish-fulfillment aspect here: the character who returns to the past, in a sense conquering death for a moment. But what's unsentimental is that it's too much, the way the experience is heartbreaking for the character. There's a real emotional courage in the fact that there's *not* a catharsis: only an unflinching acknowledgment of the gulf between the town and the cemetery. The living don't appreciate the dead; the living don't even appreciate the living. For me, that's not sentimental—it's unbelievably tough. The play presents us with a difficult truth, and forces us to take a long, hard look at it.

I think also there's a question of the artistry with which Wilder pulls this off. One of the things that makes sentimentality sentimental is that you see it coming. This play, I think, is sneaky. It makes you think this is a familiar, friendly world, where everybody is basically kind and sweet and not too curious—and then it sucker-punches you with this brutal, cosmic truth. This element of surprise or unexpected emotion is different from sentimentality, which I think of as formulaic emotion being elicited in a predictable way.

I wonder at what point I became aware of how deeply *Our Town* influenced the way I thought about *The Leftovers*. Once I started to deal with these questions of loss, and remembering the dead, and figuring out how to keep living in the wake of this loss, I was clearly in dialogue with Wilder in a way I didn't fully understand. As a writer, I would rather not be consciously aware of everything I'm doing at each moment. It's a play that has imprinted itself so deeply on me that it can exert that kind of subtle, unconscious influence.

But, at some point, I did become aware of it and slipped in a few overt nods. My character Jill, for instance, is neglecting to read *Our Town* in her English class. In the same way that Wilder's living can't really appreciate their lives, the students who are made to read *Our Town* in English class—high school kids—are too caught up in what they're doing. They probably haven't lost enough yet to understand what's profound about the book—just like Wilder's living haven't lost enough to see what's profound about their lives. There are a few direct shout-outs like that.

But there are other ways that the play informs *The Leftovers*, and my work more generally. I have a very democratic sense of literature, for instance, that stems in part from Wilder. I get a little nervous when I read novels about extraordinary people, or privileged people. I've always tried to make a principle out of writing about ordinary people and ordinary things—and this play, to me, is one of the great democratic products of American literature. It gives you the sense that the same profound and horrible truths hold true whether you're a sophisticate in Paris or a farmer in Grover's Corners.

There's a kind of political corollary to this. We've all heard the expression "one person, one vote," used to promote the idea that every human being deserves a voice in the political process. Well, I like literature that's "one person, one truth"—that each person's experience, no matter how marginal, has the power to tell us something vital about what it means to be human. It's true that, in many ways, fiction has not been universal: It's probably been a middle-class form, and there are definitely forgotten people whose lives have not been chronicled. I don't think writers should be self-congratulatory. But one of the important ideological things that the novel form helped accomplish was to expand literature's focus. The novel tends to show us that the lives of "ordinary" people are as full of drama, emotion, and even political significance as the lives of the great. This play is one of the building blocks I'd use to make that case.

If this idea—that ordinary lives are as important as extraordinary lives—is at the heart of my values when I try to write fiction, it also helps express my relationship to details. In writing, the power is in the ordinary details. It's the small stuff that allows us to build up to the scenes of great drama, or to the big important truths. My impulse as a writer is this: The bigger the stakes are in a moment, the smaller I need to go to make those moments real. This approach goes back to the heartbreak at the center of *Our Town*, the fact that what overwhelms Emily is the great beauty of the *small* moments she overlooked. As a writer, I try to find ordinary moments with that kind of power, and present them to the reader.

This was part of the challenge of *The Leftovers*, as I wrote about characters left behind in the wake of the disappearances. The last moments of the disappeared people became supercharged with significance—even though that was not a special day, even though they disappeared while doing ordinary things. You might say the line from *Our Town*—"Choose the least important day in your life. It will be important enough"—helped inform these histories, because I looked to simple, everyday moments. Nora's daughter spills some juice, so she goes into the kitchen for some paper towels—when her daughter disappears. Jill is in the room with an old friend of hers watching a YouTube video, and suddenly the friend is gone. So, cleaning a spill or watching a dumb video: It's through the minutiae of everyday life these moments come alive.

I don't think I planned this consciously, but I'm realizing now that when these people disappeared, the characters with them weren't watching. It's that sense—*we don't even look at each other*—that we're so brutally reminded of in *Our Town*.

I've written a bunch of screenplays over the years, and I've adapted my work for film before—I cowrote the script for *Little Children*, which was based on my novel. But this was a different project, because we weren't turning my book into a two-hour feature film—we were turning it into ten hours of television. That meant we really got to open it up, using the book as a jumping-off point. One way that the series is different, then, is that the town becomes more of a character than it is in the book. The book really works in microcosm, remaining focused on the family. But the show does use the town like a kind of collective character—and here, for cues, I looked again to *Our Town*.

To write dramatically about any group, you need some kind of conflict and division. A subculture, even a cult of some kind, that threatens the dominant way of thinking. In *Our Town*, that division occurs between the living and the dead. The living are actually pretty harmonious; it's an idyllic portrait of an American backwater. But the dead are deeply separated from them, and radical perspective shift causes us to see the whole town differently. In *The Leftovers*, the rebellious faction, the cult, also is dead—the disappeared who have completely separated themselves from the living. (Though they make pests of themselves, constantly reminding the living, through their absence, that life isn't what they think it is.) I would say this dual perspective in *Our Town* is transferred to *The Leftovers* in this funny way—the group of people who have *left* life give us a fundamentally different sense of what life is.

Finally, I looked to the play for the way it beautifully represents the passage of time. *Our Town* captures the cruelty of time's brutal swiftness in a way I think is singular. And this was crucial for me in *The Leftovers*, because so much of my book is about how the disappearance divides time into this distinct "before" and "after"—with an unbridgeable gulf between them. One of the reasons I chose to start the book three years after the event is because that's a kind of murky period of time—enough time has passed that the characters can no longer agree how to respond to the mystery. For some people, those three years feel like forever—*this thing happened three years ago, I don't know what, but now I'm getting on with my life.* For others, it's as if some new era started—they see those three years as the steps in a new timeline of a brave new world. For still others, it's as if no time has passed—they are stuck in the moment of the disappearance, and can't accept that others have started to move on. The various subjective, mutually exclusive ways that people view that three-year span becomes a major source of the story's conflict.

Our Town divides time into the stark "before" and "after" of life and death, exploring that gulf from the perspective of the dead. I think I was influenced by this approach, in my story of the before and after of a widespread disappearance, exploring the aftermath from the perspective of the living. It's my unconscious answer to Wilder in some ways—if *Our Town* is about the cruelty of time, *The Leftovers* explores how time's passage can mean so many different things to different people.

One is responsible to life: It is the small beacon in that terrifying darkness from which we come and to which we shall return.

—JAMES BALDWIN, *The Fire Next Time*

AYANA MATHIS

Against Unreality

I WAS PROBABLY nineteen or twenty when I read James Baldwin for the first time. By then, I'd stopped going to church after attending regularly my whole life—but I was still trying to make some kind of sense of the fierce and intense religiosity of my upbringing. I read Baldwin's *Go Tell It on the Mountain* in that context. It was incredible and powerful and illuminating: the story of a boy in 1930s Harlem who has a religious conversion experience on his fourteenth birthday. I've read it over and over again through the years, and it always yields something different.

In Baldwin's long essay "Down at the Cross: Letter from a Region in My Mind," the second of two nonfiction pieces collected in *The Fire Next Time*, he revisits the same material—this time, in the form of autobiography. James Baldwin himself had a religious conversion when he was fourteen years old. In the essay he describes how he became an adolescent preacher at a church in Harlem, where he preached until he was about seventeen, and then he stopped and went out into the world.

"Down at the Cross" is about any number of things, but it begins with Baldwin talking about his experiences as a young religious man, focusing especially on the fear he noticed in the people around him and in himself; a kind of terror of the world composed of many things: in part it was a terror of evil, as seen through the lens of the church, but more particularly the evil of the world as seen through the lens of race.

If you were black in pre–Civil Rights America, even if your body was alive, your intellect, your soul, your psyche, your financial and economic potential—all of that was in grave peril. Baldwin felt the Civil Rights movement was an opportunity for revolution, but it would mean the country, white America in particular, would have to acknowledge the hideous realities of racial persecution and violence. It meant making a critical choice between moving forward as a nation, or maintaining the white supremacist status quo—and succumbing to a kind of national decay and death, the inevitable by-products of the rot at the heart of American society.

In a crucial passage, he investigates what it is about human beings that makes us so susceptible to destructive terror, cowering in the shadows of our fear:

Behind what we think of as the Russian menace lies what we do not wish to face, and what white Americans do not face when they regard a Negro: reality—the fact that life is tragic. Life is tragic simply because the earth turns and the sun inexorably rises and sets, and one day, for each of us, the sun will go down for the last, last time. Perhaps the whole root of our trouble, the human trouble, is that we will sacrifice all the beauty of our lives, will imprison ourselves in totems, taboos, crosses, blood sacrifices, steeples, mosques, races, armies, flags, nations, in order to deny the fact of death, which is the only fact we have. It seems to me that one ought to rejoice in the *fact* of death—ought to decide, indeed, to *earn* one's death by confronting with passion the conundrum of life. One is responsible to life: It is the small beacon in that terrifying darkness from which we come and to which we shall return. One must negotiate this passage as nobly as possible, for the sake of those who are coming after us. But white Americans do not believe in death. . . .

He discusses death in the most literal sense, the end of our lives—"the fact that life is tragic . . . the sun will go down [on each of us] for the last, last time." And he goes on to say that denying that fact leads to death of a different sort: political death, spiritual death, psychic death, all of them fates *worse* than literal death. Baldwin characterizes this refusal to accept reality, a life spent clinging to unreality, as perhaps "the whole root of our trouble, the human trouble"—terror of the ultimate reality can frighten us into squandering the thing we cherish most, our too-short lives. While one is alive, Baldwin argues, one ought to confront life with passion. We are, he writes, "responsible to life," because our lives are just a small beacon between end points—a bright space between the nothingness that precedes our existence and the nothingness that follows it.

Baldwin ends this passage by saying a thing that I have never read anywhere else: "white Americans do not believe in death." (At the time that this essay was written, the term "whiteness" was not in use; Baldwin used "white America" and other substitute terms for "whiteness.") Whiteness, of course, informs what America is—it's the dominant hand. Foundationally, white supremacy shaped this country. And since whiteness informs American society, politics, law, and so on, this notion that it doesn't believe in death—Baldwin is using this as a metaphor to illustrate whiteness's denial of reality, racial and otherwise—tells us a great deal about why the country cannot own up to its most crippling and foundational problem: racial injustice.

That is to say: The country is prey to nostalgia, which is the ultimate, backward-looking unreality. And also prey to a kind of preservation of a status quo that is also based on a fantasy of the past: a moment in time in which you could keep your factory job forever, pull yourself up by the bootstraps, and life was all baseball and Cracker Jacks. Well, that was never the reality of America, certainly never for all Americans. But we move forward, politically and psychically, as though that nostalgic unreality was in fact real.

All of this is exacerbated by our refusal to even admit that we're operating in an unreality. We say things like, "We're not really racist," or "We don't really have problems with xenophobia," or "There is no poverty in our midst." We pretend these things are not informing every aspect of our society. And because we refuse to admit that they're there, we can't correct them. And so our worst impulses continue, entirely unexamined and unchecked. What has happened? The refusal to believe in death has condemned us, as a nation, to death, and has condemned us also, as a nation, to an utterly corrupt and corrupting mode of moving through our lives and through our nationhood.

One of the most interesting things James Baldwin holds true about art—which has become one of the ways in which I think about my work—is that writing is a way of working against belligerent unreality.

In part that work is done through affirming one's existence, and right to exist, and affirming the fullness of one's humanity in a context that seeks to deny those things. For me, as a writer, one of the ways to do that is to put my characters, black characters, in the center of the fiction I write. Usually, in Western literature, race is unremarked upon until someone of color comes along. Then, they're Samoan or black or Puerto Rican or whatever they are. I very consciously did the opposite in *The Twelve Tribes of Hattie*. I'm not interested in having to identify my characters as not white because white is the standard, and therefore they become an other, a deviation from the standard. I'm interested in black characters as the standard. Because for me, they are. Given the ways in which race works in this country, and in the West in general, it actually becomes a radical political statement to introduce blackness into the consciousness of the reader without explanation or announcement. In this way, my characters are not measured over and against whiteness, or understood as a reflection of whiteness. They are simply themselves.

The hardest thing about writing, I think, is observing properly. But more and more, I think, it's what makes a piece of writing good—what I respond to in Baldwin. He gives us reams and reams of wise observation. It is so difficult to be attuned enough to describe experience with that kind of accuracy. It is the most difficult thing, I think, and the thing to which I aspire.

I think Baldwin would say that art, in describing reality, also becomes an antinihilist force, an antidenialist force. And this notion of looking at reality and attempting with passion, and rigor, to describe it—it's an act of love, actually. It doesn't mean it's easy. Quite the contrary. In Baldwin, and in the discourse around the Civil Rights movement, love was invoked all the time as a difficult generative force—not a feeling, a *force*. That kind of invocation of love as a force requires discipline and sacrifice on the part of the person doing the loving, and requires rigor on the part of the party that is receiving the love.

I think Baldwin's art requires that kind of love from us. He holds up a mirror that allows us to see ourselves. We may feel some revulsion at what we see there in the glass. But it isn't a condemnation. I think that's why Baldwin has stayed with us for so long, will continue to stay with us: As difficult as he is, he's holding a mirror and saying, *Look, I'm showing you this so that you are not condemned to death*. There is always hope for betterment.

When I do my work, I try to think about love in that context. I certainly don't think that I have the kind of generosity that Baldwin had. But one of the things that aids me, and which he helped teach me, is this: Fundamentally, I do not believe in despair as a real aspect of the human condition. There is great confusion, there is great pain, there is suffering, all of those things, yes. But despair? I don't believe in despair, and I don't write from despair. I write from difficulty, absolutely. I write about people who are in great pain, who are desperate and sometimes even miserable. But despair, to me, means an absolute absence of hope.

It is a nothing. Despair is a grave. And if that were a steady and truly defining aspect of the human condition, then we would have all killed ourselves a long time ago. Since I don't believe in despair, it's easy for me not to succumb to it.

At the end of "Down at the Cross," Baldwin remembers the Harlem of his youth, as it was when he was growing up. He remembers the guys hanging out on the corner, the guys in the urine-soaked, wine-soaked hallways—these doomed young men who will not become who they wanted to be, or who they could have been. You sense the great tragedy of these people, and the squandered potential of their lives. But then Baldwin goes on to say the most startling thing in the world:

What will happen to all that beauty?

As tragic as these young men are, there isn't really quite such a thing as pure tragedy and pure despair and pure doom. There's also beauty in these young men standing on the corner, even in their sadness. It's not the noble beauty of the poor—that horrifying, patronizing way of looking at things. There is beauty because these men are fully human. When we look at a human being as fully human—regardless of the circumstances—what we will see is a strange, horrible, inviolable creature.

Baldwin's young men are beautiful, too, because they are unlike the whiteness that surrounds them—the whiteness that is doing its best to seek their death. Despite the fact that these young men are the objects of the belligerent unreality, they themselves are living in a kind of reality, as difficult as that is. There is something precious and true about the fact that one isn't living inside a strange lie, despite the price these young men will pay for that.

Baldwin is capable of an utterance like this—*what will happen to all that beauty?*—because he is a generous, broadly and deeply seeing observer, which is what an artist must be. It isn't just that writers shine a light on dark places—on corruption, on immorality (not the Christian right finger-wagging iteration of immorality, but true immorality, which

I understand to be the devaluation of the human being). That's part of it, of course. But they also recognize what is beautiful in places where others might not see the beauty. There is something in that, in those two things together, that makes art the wild, unbridled, prophetic language that it is.

"She would of been a good woman," The Misfit said, *"if it had been somebody there to shoot her every minute of her life."*

—FLANNERY O'CONNOR,
"A Good Man Is Hard to Find"

JIM SHEPARD

No One Ever Changes

WHEN I FIRST encountered "A Good Man Is Hard to Find," I read it the way many people do when they first encounter the story—a kind of social satire that veers over into random violence, plus a little spasm of hard-to-sort-through theology at the end. But when you spend more time with it, it becomes clear the story is a hugely powerful acting-out of a theme O'Connor said was crucial to her work: the action of grace in territory held largely by the devil.

Writers talk a lot about epiphanies—what O'Connor, in her Catholic tradition, called "grace"—in short stories. But I think we're tyrannized by a misunderstanding of Joyce's notion of the epiphany. That stories should toodle on their little track toward a moment where the characters understand something they didn't understand before—and, at that moment, they're transformed into better people.

You know: *Suddenly Billy understood that his grandmother had always gone through a lot of difficult things, and he resolved he would never treat her that way again.*

This kind of conversion notion is based on a very comforting idea—that if only we had sufficient information, we wouldn't act badly. And that's one of the great things about what The Misfit tells the grandmother in the line I like so much. He's not saying that a near-death experience would have turned her into a good woman. He's saying it would take somebody threatening to shoot her *every minute of her life*.

In other words, these conversion experiences don't stick—or they don't stick for very long. Human beings have to be reeducated over and over and over again as we swim upstream against our own irrationalities.

(There's a great line in Orson Welles's film *Citizen Kane*, where one of the protagonist's enemies says to him: "You're going to need more than one lesson. And you're going to get more than one lesson.")

Now, O'Connor really believes that we can flood, momentarily, with the kind of grace that epiphany is supposed to represent. But I think she also believes that we're essentially sinners. She's saying: Don't think for a moment that because you've had a brief instant of illumination, and you suddenly see yourself with clarity, you're not going to transgress two days down the road.

I find this idea enormously useful in my own work. My characters are all about gaining an understanding of the right thing to do—and avoiding it anyway. That sense that we can be in some ways geniuses of our own self-destruction runs, in some ways, counter to the more traditional notion of the epiphany—which tells us that stories are all about providing information to characters who badly need it. Epiphanies are, in some ways, staged and underimportant.

But you still don't want to write them off. The fact that there's a brevity to human connection and human empathy—the fact that it goes away—might make you feel that we should not make a big deal that it was there at all. But of course we can't do that. We have to value the moments when a person is everything we'd hoped this person would be, or became briefly something even better than she normally is. We need to give those moments the credit they're due. The glimpse of this capacity is part of what allows you to write characters who are so deeply flawed. Given that so much great literature is about staggering transgression, knowing that that capability of striving for something better is crucial for keeping you reading.

O'Connor's view of humanity in these stories is that almost everybody's going to be found wanting much of the time. And we are. But you still want to cherish those moments when someone shows you they have the capacity to be better.

What has thou done? The voice of thy brother's
blood crieth unto me from the ground.

—GENESIS 4:10

KARL OVE KNAUSGAARD

Lose Yourself

I FIRST HEARD the Cain and Abel story at school, when I was seven or eight. My teacher told it to our class, and it very much made an impression on me. I returned to it later when I was writing a novel which is set in the Bible, so to speak, and I reread all those stories again. I was struck by how extremely small it was, just twelve lines or something. It was almost shocking to see that this little story could have such an impact, and become the big story about killing, violence, jealousy, brothers—so many huge topics within the culture.

I need 300 or 400 pages to say something significant. I need space to express simple, banal truths—I don't have the ability to express them without that space, and a novel for me is the way of building that space. But Cain and Abel always surprises me in the way it manages to be both extremely powerful and extremely short.

In some ways, this concision is typical of the Old Testament. If you look at other very important texts—say, *The Odyssey*—it's often different. *The Odyssey* is very loose and very long, and it's a completely different way of storytelling. You have that looser, longer form in the Bible, too, but not in this story. In the Bible, if it's very important, it's very short. If it's not important, it's very long. That's a rule in almost all texts.

I was invited to be a consultant for the New Norwegian Bible translation of this story. They made lots of different bibles available to us—the King James, of course, but also Swedish bibles, Danish bibles, old Norwegian bibles. The fun and most interesting thing for me was that we had a bible-translation computer program that made all these different editions available. We could click on a single word and get a translation of it. This helped me get closer to the Hebraic original, which was extremely useful during the work with the text.

The Hebrew text is very raw and very direct—almost impossible to translate. I tried to keep as much of that intact as I could. That version has tremendous power because it's so simple, with the same words coming over and over again in this short passage: *earth, blood, faith*. The language is so archaic and interesting. Though I haven't shown this to anyone who's mastered the language, so I may get everything wrong, this is my sense of the Hebrew original, when Cain has seen his sacrifice rejected by God:

> It burned in Cain and his face fell.
> Jehovah said to Cain: "Why do you burn, and why does your face fall?"

The simplicity, and the complexity in the simplicity: It's bottomless. These are texts people have written about for thousands of years, and keep having different kinds of understandings about. The text is so rich and complex that you can take out one element and look at it, and find it expresses something deeply true. It can support all kinds of different interpretations depending on the way you live, or when you live, or who you are.

For instance, I became very interested in the way looking is described in the text. Jehovah looks down at Abel instead of Cain, and that's when the jealousy begins. As a result, Cain's face falls—another way of looking down. Jehovah then tells him, "Look up, because if you don't look up evil will creep at your door." I interpret this as being about the obligation of looking up at others, of facing the other. To look down is to not face your community—to be alone, to exist outside of society—and, as we see in this story, that is dangerous. I wrote about this when I wrote about the killing in Oslo and Utøya in 2011. *He* looked down. And if he planned this massacre with someone else, it would have stopped him. It would have been impossible. He could only do it because he was alone.

All those kinds of relevancies exist in this text. You may say that you reduce it when you use it as a psychosociological thing, but I don't see it like that. I see it as the opposite. You can take one element out and look at it, and let it express something deeply true—without diminishing other potential interpretations, or the text's overall richness and complexity.

This piece could also be about a basic moment in human history: the first murder, and its connection with sacrifice. The story shows us that sacrifice is meant to take the place of violence. The sacrifice Jehovah wants to see is the sacrifice of Abel's sheep, which is blood—not the vegetables Cain grew. The next thing you know, Cain's killed his brother—which is not just blood, but his *own* blood, spilled on the earth. This brings us in a direct circle back to the sacrifice. When he wrote about this story, the French philosopher René Girard wrote that sacrifice—symbolic violence—is an act meant to replace transgression against life. It unites us as a "we." Without it, there is no "we"—and Cain turns against Abel, brother turns against brother. Symbolic blood becomes real blood. Inside a society, that's a very dangerous thing.

Of course, it's a story about family, too. And though I don't reflect on themes when I'm writing, it's obvious to me that I've always been writing about family. I think it's because I'm interested in identity—and the family is the first group of people who form your identity and sense of self.

When my last daughter was born, I saw what happened when she was lifted up in the first seconds of her life. She was just by herself. She hadn't met anyone. But she was lifted, held on to by the neck, and looked at by my wife, and by myself. Those kinds of bonds are the first you have, and you'll always define yourself in relation to those few people.

Later, you've got your larger community. You've got your nation, and your profession. But it's all layered on top of this core. The core is the same, no matter what.

I wrote my own version of the Cain and Abel story because I wanted to write about brothers. There's a lot of me and my brother in that re-telling of the story. I've always been interested in writing about all those mixed feelings brothers have: your jealousy, and hatred, but always a kind of unremitting love. My brother could do anything he wants—but no matter what kind of horrible thing he does, he would still be my brother. And I think it's the same way with him.

Part of it is because it's always been us against our parents—the bond there of coming from the same place, but still being very, very different. When so many qualities are the same, but so much is differ-ent, it allows for the kind of compression you see in the Cain and Abel story. It's a very good place to write from. It's also a story about losing complete control. Because losing control is the worst thing you can do, and no one wants to do it—I'm sure about that. What is it to lose control so completely?

In a completely different sense, writing *My Struggle* has been an exer-cise in giving up control. Every morning now, I write one page. I get up early and write one page in two hours. I start with a word. It could be "apple" or "sun" or "tooth," anything—it doesn't matter. It's just a start-ing point—a word, an association—and the restriction that I write about that. It can't be about anything else. Then I just start, without knowing what it's going to be about. And it's like the text produces itself.

I'm not talking about quality. For God's sake, no. It's not like this text ever looks good or anything. It's just sitting there writing. Not thinking, and writing. I think it's a state of mind, one I usually compare with music. When you watch musicians, they're not thinking about what they're doing, they're just playing. Well, the same thing can be with writing. It's just writing.

When you are not aware of yourself, you start to write things you have never thought about before. Your thoughts do not take the path they would normally have followed, and the thinking is different from your own. The language is in you, but it's out of you, and it doesn't belong to you. That's what literature can do—when you throw something in, something else comes back.

This approach was something I discovered very early on, when I first started to write with ambition. I was seventeen, eighteen. I just wrote. I didn't think. It wasn't hard, because I was so naïve and innocent. But what I mostly did was spit out clichés.

Later, I had many years when I couldn't write because I felt I knew too much—suddenly, I had a notion of quality. But when I was twenty-seven or twenty-eight, I had a new experience for the first time: I just disappeared somewhere. I just wrote and followed the text. It was like reading, basically. I knew I was onto something because I couldn't predict what was coming and I couldn't identify it with myself when I read it—it was outside my normal reach, in a way. Not that it was better. But it was different.

This is what makes my work so difficult for me to read and see again. The first thing I think is—*oh, Jesus, it's naïve.* But in that naïveté there is something that's very direct and true, in a sense.

There's a difference between writing naïvely now and when I was twenty. When you've been writing for twenty years, you know something about writing. You don't have that knowledge present as you work, but it is still there somewhere and kind of directs you.

For *My Struggle*, the revision process developed during the process of writing those six novels. I edited the first novel with my editor—we did it like a classical novel, more or less. It wasn't hard. There were some bridges made, and then it looked like a novel. But the second book we hardly edited at all. Much of the editing I'm doing while I'm writing, so when I reached the end—we just kept it, basically. We took out some pages, of course, but it was mostly there. The other books were written in a similar way, with the exception of Book Six—that was so long we needed to take out 150 pages. The others are more or less left alone.

But now I have to learn to write differently. I can't repeat what I did in *My Struggle*. It's become a kind of technique: I write a little bit about how I feel about something, a little bit about failure or shame or something, and then there is a reflection of a more essayistic kind, and then there is a description of something ordinary, and so on. I can't write that way for the rest of my life. It would be less and less satisfying for me because there's nothing new in it. Or, the subjects can be new, but the insights are exactly the same.

What I'd really like to do is *think* differently, but that's impossible.

Starting to write differently will be very difficult. Maybe it will create a kind of vacuum where it will be impossible to write. That has happened before. It will happen again. And it will pass again.

The privilege of a novelist is that you're able to sit for three years by yourself, and no one's interfering with anything if you don't want them to. If you have faith in your writing, it's easy. It's when you remove that faith that things become difficult—when you start to think, *this is stupid, this is idiotic, this is worthless,* and so on. That's the real fight: to overcome those kinds of thoughts. When you start a novel—well, ninety-nine out of a hundred novels start in a stupid way, I'm sure. You need to go on so that it can become something. Maybe it will take fifty pages, or a hundred pages, but it will be okay.

When I go to bed, I look forward to the next morning because I know I have these two hours to write. It's a magical place. And I know it's going to happen. I can trust it.

When Law left I felt so bad I thought I would die.
This is not uncommon.

—ANNE CARSON, "The Glass Essay"

LESLIE JAMISON

On Commonness

A PRIMAL PART of me feels spoken to by the poet Anne Carson. It's the part of me that loved Tori Amos and Ani DiFranco, and then Jeanette Winterson, when I was younger—the hungry open mouth inside of me that wants to hear desire and heartbreak spoken about in certain ways. I came to need more nuanced, self-aware voices on these subjects, but the impulse is the same: a longing to hear somebody utter extreme expressions of painful feeling. I stand behind wanting to find company in that, and somehow Carson validates those prior versions of myself, the attraction to the old heroes of my youth.

Carson's "The Glass Essay," one of her strange, nongenre prose poem masterpieces, confronts a huge and terrible heartbreak. In snapshots, you see the poem's speaker visiting her mother in this desolate, moorish locale. (The piece is very much in conversation with Emily Brontë and *Wuthering Heights*.) She's trying to make sense of a love affair that's fallen apart, spending time with her mother inside this state of loss.

I've taught this piece so many times that now I can hear student voices layered over my experience of it. I remember being in a classroom in France, looking at a section where the narrator is remembering her love affair:

I can feel that other day running underneath this one
like an old videotape—here we go fast around the last corner
up the hill to his house, shadows

of limes and roses blowing in the car window
and music spraying from the radio and him
singing and touching my left hand to his lips.

I felt like I was up there trying to make a case for how the things we might think are sappy and sentimental can actually become part of a totally nuanced vision. But one of my students didn't think Carson gets away with this nostalgic depiction of love. "I think it's just sappy and sentimental," she said. That ambivalence is at work inside the poem, too. "The Glass Essay" resonates with passionate feeling, but also resonates with an awareness that's ashamed of having or courting too much feeling. At one point, the mother acts as the voice of that awareness:

You remember too much,
my mother said to me recently.

Why hold onto all that? And I said,
Where can I put it down?

Why hold onto all that? There's a shame around staying too long in a feeling of pain. But I love the speaker's response—"Where can I put it down?"—which feels like a good one to keep in your back pocket if you're ever accused of being melodramatic. "It pains me to record this, / I am not a melodramatic person," she writes, later, which is another articulation of the same idea: *I want to tell you how much it hurts, but I'm also going to tell you that there is a voice inside of me, dogging me at every moment about trying too hard to tell you how much it hurts.* Experiencing intense feeling, and at the same time processing those voices shaming you for having too much feeling—both are part of the experience of the poem, and they don't necessarily detract from each other.

Carson's mode of self-awareness doesn't apologize for its emotion. She simply acknowledges that, whenever we feel, we do so in a way that anticipates the gaze of others—as well as anticipates the empathy or lack of empathy we'll encounter there. I feel some version of this happening when she writes:

When Law left I felt so bad I thought I would die.
This is not uncommon.

These lines feel willfully melodramatic. It's almost like saying: *I'm not going to dress up this emotion for you in original language, or in a cool metaphoric formulation.* Carson's language is so surprising—you already know she can take any feeling and give it to you in some crazy, stylized way. Instead, she says, "I thought I would die." It's so willfully plain. There's something moving to me about saying it so embarrassingly straight.

The following line, "This is not uncommon," can be read so many different ways. The tone might be clinical or dismissive, as in, *this is not an uncommon symptom of the disease of heartbreak.* But it's also an acknowledgment that what she's going through is in no way extraordinary. It's something that's been felt before, and it'll be felt again. Yet she owns this commonness, without apologizing for it, relinquishing it, or dismissing it.

I really believe that there are extraordinary things to be said about deeply ordinary experiences. When I teach nonfiction, the biggest student conundrum around personal writing is: Why would anybody care about what happened to *me*? There's a shame around just having lived an ordinary life. And it's not like they're wrong—it *is* going to be harder for them to get a book deal, say, for their memoir of living in the suburbs. But the paralyzing anxiety I hear students articulate, and also feel in myself, is what "this is not uncommon" speaks to: the experience of trying to find words for an emotion that mattered so much, even while recognizing it's the most common thing in the world.

I think I have an obsession with recuperating commonness. The fact that something is frequently articulated or frequently felt is not a reason to back away from trying to articulate it, or express it, or own how intense it is.

Of course, if "I felt so bad I thought I would die" was a piece of deeply familiar, ordinary language in a sea of ordinary, melodramatic language, it wouldn't have the same impact. But we're in the hands of a writer who uses figurations like "blue and green lozenges of April heat" or "the videotape jerks to a halt / like a glass slide under a drop of blood." Disrupting that lyric, super-cerebral voice to say something so bluntly—that's part of how she pulls this off. The collision of the lyric voice with the plainspoken "I thought I would die" is part of the electricity for me.

The whole poem feels like a self in conversation—not just with other, external voices, but with different parts of itself. There's the section where a part of the speaker that wants to linger inside nostalgia bucks against the part that wants to let go:

> I can feel that beauty's
>
> heart beating inside mine as she presses into his arms in the high
>   blue room—
> No, I say aloud. I force my arms down
> through air which is suddenly cold and heavy as water

That dash, and then the *no*, is so emotionally charged for me. It rings so true to that experience of getting lost in nostalgia for something that was, and then telling yourself to stop. You reexperience the grief in that moment of the dash—*no, it's not there anymore.* These lines illuminate the actual psychological conflict of wanting to remember, but at the same time calling upon yourself to stop indulging in that remembrance.

When I write, I sometimes feel a kind of self-awareness that draws me out of an emotion, or a moment, that can start to feel like apologizing for what's just been said, or ironically scare-quoting it. That can have a detrimental effect, especially on first drafting. I've learned the first draft in my process has to be the part where I don't say no to anything, where I let myself write deeply into a feeling, spend as long as I want on a scene or emotion, follow as many associations as I want—even if some part of me knows my editing self, three drafts from now, will think it's facile or self-indulgent. The "no" self definitely has a role to play, but for me it comes in afterward, in later drafts, where I'm asking harder questions about what really needs to be there.

I've found it's important to risk saying too much. In my students' work, I can see the moments when they offer an extremely condensed version of something out of an anxiety that it's not compelling, or that it's trite. But what I often find is that, in condensing it, they have made it precisely the trite thing they feared it would be. "I had broken up with a guy and it was hard to get over": Often giving just one sentence stems from a reluctance to go on and on about ordinary heartbreak, but the sentiment is made totally uninteresting by being stated in an extremely general way. "The Glass Essay" is a refusal to stop at vague summation. By going so deep, the poem allows a familiar emotion to become something you haven't ever seen before, not quite like this.

My teacher Charlie D'Ambrosio once told me something I've thought about many times, something it always feels like he's re-saying to me again because the advice comes alive in a different way in relation to each particular situation: *The problem with an essay can become its subject.* It's the idea that if you hear a critical voice in you saying "no," it doesn't necessarily mean you shouldn't go there. It just means that you should also make the piece about the resistance itself. "The Glass Essay" does that in powerful ways, bringing the resistance into the body of the text rather than just capitulating to its harsh editor critiques. You see it in the "no" moment, in "I am not a melodramatic person," in the moment where the mother says, "Why hold onto all that?" It can be telling to leave the process of overcoming shame as something legible on the page, rather than dissolving the shame completely—as if it had never been. Especially when shame stems from a fear of being marked as a bad or damaged person, of looking weak or self-indulgent. Those constricting forces can be worth punching through, even if they leave a trace on the page—to see what kind of expression is possible on the other side.

I usually revise personal pieces of writing over a much, much longer period than reported or critical pieces because time permits a more nuanced gaze, more usefully complex. The more time you have away from something, the easier it is to let go of stuff that seems unnecessary. When you're in the immediate aftermath of reporting or writing something, so much still seems luminous or precious. I think there's an additional layer of use when it comes to personal experience: You just see the events of your own life so differently after more years have passed. That doesn't mean that the truest version of an event is going to be the version you write when you're eighty. But your perspective keeps changing. I would be so interested in a book that worked like a series of tree rings: Take an incident and write about it a year afterward, five years afterward, ten years afterward, fifteen years afterward, and the book becomes all those narratives accumulated.

The summer that I spent the most concerted time with "The Glass Essay" was the summer of 2012, when I was writing an essay called "Grand Unified Theory of Female Pain." It was mammoth and unruly and chaotic. In my heart, I knew I was after something urgent—something deeply connected to these questions of pain and its articulation, deeply connected to feeling shame at that articulation—and I had all these pieces I wanted to arrange, but no idea about how to arrange them. I was eventually saved by an idea that Carson keeps coming back to in her poem: the Nudes.

Each morning a vision came to me.
Gradually I understood that these were naked glimpses of my soul.

I called them Nudes.

Nude #1. Woman alone on a hill.

She stands into the wind.

There are thirteen Nudes in the poem, female self-portraits posed in various attitudes of pain, and they became an organizing principle for me—helping me to experience the essay not just as a beautiful object in its own right, but as a beautiful tool that arranges its chaotic material in a series of snapshots of woundedness. Part of what I love about the Nudes in this poem is how they break down the binary between pain and beauty. They're raw soul, but also totally crafted and made. The self in the center is completely exposed, but it's also the product of artifice. That's the heart of what I love in Carson: Her stuff feels so emotional and artistically rendered at once. The craft and the feeling don't come at the expense of one another—they fuel each other. That's what I want to do when I write.

Leopards break into the temple and drink to the dregs what is in the sacrificial pitchers; this is repeated over and over again; finally it can be calculated in advance, and it becomes a part of the ceremony.

—Franz Kafka, "Leopards in the Temple"

JONATHAN LETHEM

Letting the Leopards In

WHEN I FIRST read Kafka's *The Castle*, I think I was fifteen. The copy I had was an old Schocken hardcover edition I found in the library of my high school, Music and Art—New York City's public school for musicians and visual art students. I was a denizen of the Music and Art library, which was not a very lively joint at that point. It was full of incredible hardcovers of all kinds, many of them moldering. At the same time, I was also going to lots of used bookstores all over the city, which, back then, was still filled with them. Rent was so cheap that these eccentric, clubhouse sort of used bookstores proliferated: whole rooms full of books, manned by some old bookseller who wasn't trying very hard and scared away half his customers with his crankiness.

I was right in the middle of a phase where I just wanted to read as many novels of as many kinds as I could. I had no compass. I was just trying to read everything, and I was hot on the trail of Kafka. I'd been reading science fiction, and I'd already discovered Borges, and in a certain way I associated Kafka with these things—I'd gotten the hint that if I liked morbid, fantastical things, gothic stuff, that he might work for me. So I read *The Castle*, read it fast and in a fury, to find out what happened at the end. I took it as a given that every book was headed somewhere, and obviously this book was headed to the castle. There was going to be a great, grand finale up there—because what book called *The Castle* wouldn't have some incredible culmination up in the castle? As I read, it was total cathexis. I was with K., every inch of every paragraph, waiting for revelation. And when the story falls off the cliff at the end, I was enraged. I wanted my money back. (Except I hadn't spent any money.) I couldn't believe there could be a famous book that was so radically unsatisfying. I remember thinking, *How can he even be a famous author if he fucks you over this badly?* It just seemed like a disaster.

And then—at some point not shortly after this violent sensation of having been misused by the book—I guess I wanted more. I needed to be in that headspace again. So I read *The Trial*.

The Trial was one of the key reading experiences of my teenage years. It made me a writer; it made me who I am. And if I never encountered another book by Kafka—if I hadn't then gone on to learn about the short stories, and the aphorisms, and the diaries, and the letter to his father, all of which I eventually devoured in my twenties—even if there were only *The Trial*, and *The Castle* lurking there in the background, I would have talked about Kafka as one of my favorite writers for the rest of my life anyway. I was just his.

But the other part of my incredibly deliberate program was that, if I liked a writer, I had to read every word. (I'd already done it with Graham Greene, Shirley Jackson, and Philip K. Dick.) I didn't necessarily do it right away—of course, sometimes I couldn't even find all the titles right away. But I knew I would exhaust their shelf. I think I was probably done with everything I could find of Kafka's by the middle of my twenties. I would have encountered the leopards aphorism around then.

> Leopards break into the temple and drink to the dregs what is in the sacrificial pitchers; this is repeated over and over again; finally it can be calculated in advance, and it becomes a part of the ceremony.

It would have been one of the last things of his I read, just because of my nature as a reader. I dig narrative. I wouldn't have been shopping for aphorisms, which have nothing to do with what brought me to literature in the first place. I was a very literal reader. I wanted stories with characters, lots of occurrences and situations. That's what I was reading for, and how Kafka first netted me: with this extreme, perverse, but very compulsive narrative. Borges writes about Kafka in a way that turns the Greek philosopher Zeno into his precursor, because Kafka's narrative is all based on Zeno's paradox: the idea that you're always closing half the distance to your target, but you never fully arrive. It's a consummately frustrated form of narrative progress, but it is one, and it has a labyrinthine, compulsive, hypnotic quality to it. That narrative quality is what gets me in a position to become a reader of Kafka's language and someone who identifies with his philosophical implications (though it's hard to say just what those are). It begins with story.

In its way, the leopards in the temple is a tiny little story. There's a violent and exciting plot that takes place over a certain amount of time. But one of the things that's entrancing is—well, how long does it take to incorporate the leopards into the ceremony? Did it take hundreds of years of civilization to incorporate the leopards our forefathers once bemoaned? Or is it—well, last Wednesday we thought it was a problem but this week we decided to work around it? However long the span of time is, there's a sort of intensely embedded kind of narrative situation with characters who make a decision to resolve a kind of conflict in favor of incorporating chaos into their worldview.

But it also looks to me like an M. C. Escher drawing, which is another thing I thought was extremely cool when I was fifteen years old. In some oblique way, this topological quality is still what I respond to in Kafka. The leopards are a piece of the outside that ultimately fit on the inside. Somehow, they complete a shape that initially seems like it's meant to be a negative space, but actually the negative space becomes essential to the completion of the positive space. The temples and the chalices are like the drawing that Escher would render in lighter colors with cutout shapes of negative space that you begin to see look like a leopard, and then you realize—wait a minute, the leopard is the drawing. There's a yin-yang quality to it, the way these two things become interdependent spatially.

To me, the leopards in the chapel are a beautiful allegory of high and low culture. I wear on my sleeve a definition of the literary project of the novel: Its signature is the incorporation of the demotic. The novel is always gobbling up the language of the street and of commerce and of popular culture—in fact, it's driven by the need to replenish itself by what might seem at first to be its nemeses. People are always wanting to put the novel on a pedestal and make it a kind of exalted art form, as if it's a Mark Rothko painting in a chapel, or a Beethoven symphony. They want it to be a purified high form, which is a meaningful desire, because when novels change your life they make you feel exalted. But in fact novels are just organically made of the rabble of the everyday. You can't purify them. You can't extract the demotic material. So you could take the leopards and the chalices as a symbol of the novelist's impure position—as a negotiator of high impulses and low sources.

Pretty much every generation of fiction writers has to find a way to invite in the leopards: the stuff that's objectionable to the older generations. When I started incorporating so much of the stuff of the vernacular culture and commercial that excited me—advertising, comic books, genre, pulp, rock and roll—even I thought I was, in some way, fouling the nest. But I couldn't keep from doing it. And then I began to become defiant about that project. I thought, *Wait a minute, that's what Dickens did.* And I incorporated it into the ceremony.

You could also read the aphorism as about the folly of trying to protect yourself—as a person, or as an artist—from the things that frighten and threaten you. Because what a boring ceremony without the leopards, right? Who wants to see the ceremony without the leopards, once you know that they might come? I was saying this to students last night in a fiction workshop: The impulse to make the ritual safe, to put characters in play who are ultimately admirable and can be redeemed, is extremely boring and also suspect. There's something that you're protecting yourself from—and why bother? Damage is in the mix, and it should be. What was the ceremony *for* before the leopards came along? It was probably for hoping the leopards wouldn't come along. But you don't really want it to succeed. Your damage and your dismay are the best things you've got going, and you've got to open yourself to it.

I learned that, in a way, by writing my two Brooklyn books—*Motherless Brooklyn* and *Fortress of Solitude*—which manage the anxiety and the trauma associated with where I was from. I took my most turbulent and confused feelings about that, my defiance and pride and embarrassment, as well as a proprietary feeling that I could never justify, especially since I'd run fast and far away from the scene. So what was it that I was entitled to claim as my own? But I opened that door—and I did it accidentally, in a way—by introducing Brooklyn into this cute, clever postulate I'd come up with about a detective with Tourette's syndrome. It needn't have been a Brooklyn book, and I hadn't ever written one before. But by putting him in that environment, I found myself tapping those anxieties, and in that book I managed them pretty completely. That was how I announced to myself that the leopards really needed to drink the chalices.

Fortress of Solitude is where I let the leopards in. Ever since, for me, disappointment and embarrassment are among my most vivid subjects. (And I might say that disappointment and embarrassment are primary in Kafka as well.) One of the things that happens in the aphorism is that the chalices are drained, which again raises the question of: Who was supposed to drink it originally? And if it was just going to waste, what were you saving it for? It's partly a parable about this foolish notion that you have anything to protect in the first place.

Despite all these symbolic and metaphorical layers, I love that the aphorism features real animals. It's not ghosts. It's not gargoyles, or a golem. They're leopards—and this isn't inconsequential. That's something that connects to a curiosity of mine, one I had never articulated until recently, that probably starts with *Alice in Wonderland*, which is the

first book I fell in love with, at age eleven, and was really my doorway
out of children's books and into literature. It was also there in Jack London, and Philip K. Dick's *Do Androids Dream of Electric Sheep?*, some of
the books that meant the most to me shortly thereafter: this presence
of the real animal as a mystery or rebuke or cipher for the human to
contemplate. The animal is an uncrackable code, and yet carries a message that we have to abide in some way.

I was slow to notice how much animals meant to me as a literary
emblem. Of course my first novel, *Gun, with Occasional Music*, is full of
talking animals. (It's very much a hard-boiled detective/*Alice in Wonderland* mash-up.) And then, in *Chronic City*, the presence of this tiger in
New York City seems to have some kind of leopards-in-the-temple kind
of message: the creature making all of these intrusions on the life of the
city. He represents a message no one can translate. Almost my favorite
Kafka of all is "The Burrow," with this mole-like creature, whom the
narration totally transubstantiates. He becomes the mind of the writer
lurking in a tunnel, both inside and outside of life, underground and
terrified to come out, and at the same time guarding some cavern of
incredible, indefinable value. Kafka's also got the ape in "A Report to an
Academy," and "Investigations of a Dog," and then the cockroach in
Metamorphosis. Kafka was an animal writer. Against all odds. He was
an animal writer like Jack London or Thornton Burgess. It's the compulsion of an urban mind toward what's been pushed to the periphery,
to what's lurking at the farthest edge. I don't think it's a projection to say
the leopards here are part of the world of our animal cohort, whose indifference or hostility we're permanently excluded from—but feel we
must understand, because it must hold some key to ourselves.

All this, in these three short lines. It's the kind of thing that sounds
almost biblical, once you read it. How could this belong to one writer?
That's true of a number of Kafka's aphorisms—they seem somehow
emblematic of consciousness itself, and they just carve themselves into
the human source code. I don't have a feeling of first reading this. I have
a feeling of having always known it.

'Twas brillig, and the slithy toves
Did gyre and gimble in the wabe:
All mimsy were the borogoves,
And the mome raths outgrabe.

—LEWIS CARROLL,
"Jabberwocky"

JESSE BALL

The Edge of Sense

WHEN I WAS a child, my father would read out loud to my brother, my mother, and me. Several times in the course of my childhood, he would read *Alice's Adventures in Wonderland* and *Through the Looking-Glass* over a few weeks. They were a great favorite with all of us.

We had a very tight-knit little family, and we lived on the outskirts of a Long Island town by these train tracks. My brother and I would run around in the woods all day, and when my father came home it was always a big event. We were pretty poor, and my mother always tried to turn little things into big events—so my father coming home from work would be a big thing. As we ran out of the woods to meet him, he'd come up and would always say:

And hast thou slain the Jabberwock?
Come to my arms, my beamish boy!

This was very exciting for my brother and me. I don't think I thought I was a "beamish boy" per se, but I certainly liked to think I'd been out slaying jabberwocks in the woods.

I had a lot of trouble in school to begin with. I got left back in kindergarten, and I was in special education. My teachers didn't have very much faith in me. At one point, there was a psychological evaluation—which I actually saw about a year ago, when we were going through boxes at my mom's house. It was a very lengthy test, and it scored all my different attributes and proclivities and possibilities. I scored very low indeed. In fact, the assessment was that potentially I had some kind of cerebral damage, which—well, luckily, if it's true, I've managed to carry on all this time.

But there was one attribute that I scored extremely high on, in fact, exceeded all adult levels for: the repeating of long, nonsensical phrases. I guess I was not only above my age group but above all possible results on the test. That was very notable for me looking at this now, because nonsense has been at the heart of my lifelong, ridiculous endeavor.

There's a misunderstanding about what nonsensical things are—the idea that they're just funny, and that's the beginning and the end of it. Nonsense is not "not sense"—it operates at the edge of sense. It teems with sense—at the same time, it resists any kind of universal understanding.

I believe Carroll first wrote "Jabberwocky" as a stanza of Anglo-Saxon poetry. (Nonsense tends to play off and puncture some known landscape.) Here, he's playing off the language of all these wonderful things from *The Canterbury Tales* to *The Pearl* to one of my personal favorites, *Sir Gawain and the Green Knight*. As well as older texts like the *Exeter Book* riddles. He's tapping into those wonderfully alliterative verses, that rich history of sound, within the Old English and Middle English traditions. What comes out is this:

> 'Twas brillig, and the slithy toves
> Did gyre and gimble in the wabe:
> All mimsy were the borogoves,
> And the mome raths outgrabe.

It's not in favor of some other sensical thing that could be said. In fact, it's very precise. You couldn't supply another object that would do a better job of what it's doing in its place. The poem preserves a truth Carroll feels within himself of the sounds of those Anglo-Saxon words, their color and direction.

There's a question of what master are you serving when you write something. If you want to tell someone that they have to go unplug the toilet, that's a very specific sentiment: Go, and unplug the toilet. It can succeed, or not. But what if the master you want to serve is to somehow communicate the entirety of your experience of Anglo-Saxon poetry, in a single poem? That's when something like nonsense comes into its own. The wonder of it is not that it makes something out of nothing, or that it is without sense—but actually that it's exploding with sense. It's not for when you have nothing to say, but when you have many things to say at once.

At the same time the poem provides this very specific insight about the sound of Anglo-Saxon poetry, it also evades clear interpretation. Many times, when someone writes something, they hope for some precision of communication—they want to provide some precise statement that exists in one mind, and make it exist in your mind. But I think Carroll's understanding of communication was more interesting than that. He understands that the text that you create is an object that collides with the mind of the reader—and that some third thing, which is completely unknowable, is made. He was completely content with that, and that contentment allows him to make this object "Jabberwocky" as interesting and beautiful and lovely an object as it can be. The poem's construction allows you to be sent somewhere along the vector of "Jabberwocky," though no one but you can say just where.

But this experience requires trust. That's why the poem veers between sense and nonsense: With the heroic tale of this hero who goes out to do battle with a wonderful creature, Carroll gives us some solid ground to stand on. That's sufficient to give the reader a confidence and sureness of interpretation of what things mean. It works because you've developed an enormous trust that you're in the most immaculate hands with Carroll. He's such a logician, a lover of games, and an extremely—probably even exhaustingly—exacting person. Then, when he decides to be nonsensical, you give him the entirety of your being because he's earned that trust completely.

The crucial thing in any work of any kind is that it must be a gift—the reader must possess it even more than the person who wrote it. It must be given completely. "Jabberwocky" is given in this way, so that you can feel assured that joining your internal world to it is not an error. You should have no fear you have made an error. It's your poem, that's the important thing.

When I write, it isn't so important to me that the page itself be beautiful to look at or somehow unimpeachable. It's simply that it gestures in the right direction, such that something happens within the mind of the reader. In the other direction, unfortunately, it's possible to create page after page of beautiful, perfect-looking prose that is kind of tepid. It's hard to say anything against it because it all figures out perfectly. You look through it, and it's all there, it's all correct, whatever. But something that is ragged and strange-looking might in fact be completely practical and efficacious as writing, because it causes the explosion that's necessary in the mind.

For me, a central principle of writing comes from Daniil Kharms, who said:

A poem, if thrown at a pane of glass, should break the glass.

The effect is the crucial thing. That's the approach I try to take: not to be vain with the success of the writing as writing, but rather its effect.

This is a practicality of means, based upon the immense shortness of time that we have. Imagine I said to you, "Your grandmother is going to die in five minutes. You have to go in and just tell her something wonderful: She wants to hear a beautiful thing." You're not going to try to create a prose object that can be judged by some committee of your peers, something perfectly in harmony and well-balanced and wry and witty and correct. Or something someone writing an essay in *The New Yorker* would pronounce a good work. You're just going to—within the language that's shared between your grandmother and yourself—attempt to burst all bounds and create a resonance. That resonance is your only aim. Anything that is not the resonance, you discard. That's the real work.

In this, thinking about words as sound is essential. When you read, after all, you hear the words in your head. Sound provides a good test for what is artificial and geriatric about written language, and what is essential and real. If you read some work and much of what is there is lost to the listener, then it may be necessary to have as a buttress all these tablets of culture to decipher what is meant. But there's no excuse to say a person needs to read fifty other books in order to appreciate this one. A work must contain all of its tools, and sound gives us clues about what is necessary and real.

I think when I'm writing in the first place, when I really get going, I'm murmuring what I'm writing in a half-breath as I'm working. It's probably embarrassing if I'm in some public place, sitting there ranting to myself. (Usually I try to sit far enough away from other people.) They say that after you write a work, and finally look at it, you can't tell what's there anymore. How can you actually see the work in order to judge it? One way is to read it out loud to somebody who you're a little afraid of, whose opinion matters to you. When you read it aloud, there are parts you might skip over—you find yourself not wanting to speak them. Those are the weak parts. It's hard to find them otherwise, just reading along. But you can judge the work more clearly when you hear and feel its sound.

My father's use of "Jabberwocky" as a means of strengthening and celebrating this daily moment of his homecoming to my family—it was a wonderful way to use poetry. There's no right way or wrong way to use literature. But to use sounds that are passed down, spoken and re-spoken to create beautiful moments of ritual: This is an excellent use of the poem. Maybe it's something we all can strive for.

Mouths don't empty themselves unless the ears
are sympathetic and knowing.

—ZORA NEALE HURSTON,
Mules and Men

ANGELA FLOURNOY

A Place to Call
My Own

I FIRST READ Zora Neale Hurston's *Mules and Men* when I was in the early stages of writing *The Turner House*—the story of one family's relationship, over the span of fifty years, with a house in the city of Detroit. At the time, one of the things I was struggling with was: Who do you think you are to be writing this book in the first place? I mean, who do you think you *are*?

My dad's from Detroit, but I'm not from there. And I have certainly never seen a haint—the specifically Southern-tradition ghost that's in my book—in my whole life. In my research, I found many helpful nonfiction books about Detroit but not much fiction—certainly not a lot of fiction about the everyday, working-class black people who make up 80 percent of the population of that city. So I immediately felt the burden of representation: If I write this book, this will be the book that people look to. Who knows when the next novel set in Detroit and focused on working-class black folks will be? When I realized that, I felt more pressure—and more doubt.

But it wasn't just writing convincingly about an unfamiliar city and its people. I was also concerned about the supernatural element of my story. I didn't understand the folkloric background of it; I just knew the kind of stories that had been told in my own family. So I started reading everything I could about African American folklore. One of the books I turned to was *Mules and Men*, which I checked out of the Iowa library.

The book is the result of Hurston's anthropological research in the South—she went back to transcribe and collect the stories she heard growing up—as well as an account of her time as an apprentice for "hoodoo" practitioners in New Orleans. It's important to consider the context in which the book was written: At the time, as far as black literature and black scholarship were concerned, there wasn't much interest in this material. This was the height of the Great Migration. People were leaving the South and trying to prove themselves "worthy," whatever that might mean, in the North. Part of that meant not being what someone might describe as superstitious. Not having any spiritual beliefs that fell out of the accepted norms. Not being at all messy. But *Mules and Men* is a book that's unapologetically messy.

To me, that's one of the most appealing things about Zora Neale Hurston's fiction: She's never been big on cleaning up black lives to make them seem a little more palatable to a population that's maybe just discovering them. She's just not interested in that. Even today, I know a lot of writers probably struggle with wanting to represent us in a "good light." The fact that she didn't care, eighty years ago, is just amazing.

One line from the book, from an early section where Hurston is explaining her methods for collecting folklore in the South, stuck with me especially:

> Mouths don't empty themselves unless the ears are sympathetic and knowing.

This line changed how I thought about the work I wanted to do. It's not about having a background that lines up with the characters you're writing about, I realized. That's not the responsibility of the fiction writer. Instead, you have the responsibility to be sympathetic—to have empathy. And the responsibility to be knowing—to understand, or at least desire to understand, the people you write about. I don't think the quote means you need to handle your characters with kid gloves—I think it means you have to write something true by at least having a baseline of empathy before you start writing it.

I immediately put that line on an index card and stuck it on my corkboard. It lived above me for the four years it took to write the book. It was a daily reminder that I would never be able to access these characters, or make them feel real, if I didn't have in the back of my mind that my job is to be sympathetic and knowing. And it reminded me that, if I managed to be sympathetic and knowing, I would be free to do whatever I wanted.

Readers only balk at writers depicting people who aren't like them when it feels like the characters are types. It's when you've somehow failed to make fully nuanced and three-dimensional characters that people start to say, *What right do you have?* But when the characters transcend type, no one questions the author's motives. Characters' backgrounds, their gender—these things are only aspects of their personality, just as they are for real people. If the writer pulls it off, if they make you see the humanity in the character, that stuff falls away—no matter who you're writing about.

Of course, it's hard when you're worried about representation, or whether or not you have the right. But at a certain point, you have to be kind to yourself as a writer and trust your own motives. You have to have confidence that you're coming from the right place. You have to allow yourself to let loose, pursue a good story, and create people who feel real. Not good, not bad, certainly not perfect—just real.

It's also about following the story, no matter how hard it gets, so that the characters have time to go where they need to go. You have the right to write the characters you choose, but you also have the responsibility to see those characters through—to give them time to become nuanced and real. Once you've started you have to go all the way. You can't go halfway.

I've found that, if I focus on doing the work every day, the imagination part starts to take care of itself. The beautiful thing about imagination is how it keeps opening doors for your characters to walk through. You'll be surprised—they'll walk through these doors, if you free yourself to allow that to happen.

I spent four years with my characters in this novel. The ones I felt I did not know the most were the ones I tried the hardest to know. People always say that, in order to get to know your characters, you need to know what they want, what their needs and desires are. But, in this novel, I went about it in a different way: I was very interested in what they *didn't* want, and making them contend with that. I thought about the music they dislike, the people they dislike, how they would never act in a crowd. Maybe that's a negative way to think about people. But I think, in fiction, the magic often happens when the thing you don't want to happen happens to you.

It's interesting because, now, when people tell me which characters they felt they knew the best—they tend to be the ones I felt like I knew least. There were certain characters that I was chasing, trying to get to know better. Even though to me they were always hiding, peeking around a corner, readers say they felt they understood them best. Somehow I was able to transmit more than even I understood about them. I guess, because I was conscious of those characters feeling elusive, I tried harder on the page.

The biggest challenge for me, though, is to not take this understanding too far. I'm someone who errs too much toward the sympathetic. Even when my characters, based on their actions, could probably be called "bad" people, I still try to find the good in them, know it, and communicate that. In revision and editing, that was one of the things I kept trying to take out. Readers come to the book with all sorts of backgrounds, and they don't need me to communicate how they should feel about a character. They don't need me to suggest a character should be excused for his actions because of X, Y, and Z. They'll make their own decisions. So I've always challenged myself, especially if I'm writing from a third-person narrator, to editorialize less about the actions that are happening.

People are still reading Zora Neale Hurston because she knew how to strike that balance. She has empathy for her characters, she is deeply knowing, but she never sanitizes or romanticizes them. She lets them be real, and we see ourselves in them as a result.

"This must be a simply enormous wardrobe!" thought Lucy, going still further in and pushing the soft folds of the coats aside to make room for her. Then she noticed that there was something crunching under her feet. "I wonder is that more moth-balls?" she thought, stooping down to feel it with her hand. But instead of feeling the hard, smooth wood of the floor of the wardrobe, she felt something soft and powdery and extremely cold. "This is very queer," she said, and went on a step or two further.

—C. S. Lewis, *The Lion, the Witch and the Wardrobe*

LEV GROSSMAN

Into the Wardrobe, into the Self

I CAN'T SAY with total accuracy when I first read *The Lion, the Witch and the Wardrobe*. I wasn't a particularly early reader, so I couldn't have been much younger than seven or eight years old. But the Narnia books had a kind of special place in our family. My mother's English; she was in London during the blitz, when she was about Lucy Pevensie's age. To stay safe from the bombing, like Lewis's fictional children, she was sent from London to the countryside. The book opens with the Pevensies arriving from London, so you have this strange, dark background—this sense of war going on, which the characters have only just narrowly escaped.

Of course, unlike the Pevensies, my mom failed to find adventures in a magical land accessed through a wardrobe. But, in fact, she claims she was so badly behaved that her host family actually had her deported back to London. I don't know what she did—but apparently it was so naughty that being bombed by Hitler was a preferable fate. The cultural divide between poor urban Londoners and the country English was very great, and it was hard for the two factions to find common ground. I guess, in her case, they never did.

So the Narnia books had a special place for my mom. I think she must have presented them to us with a special flourish. And I'm fairly certain that *The Lion, the Witch and the Wardrobe* was the first book that I ever was transported by. I think it's the book that taught me what novels are supposed to do. It's the book that taught me how books work, and what—if they're good—they do for you. It was the template for all the great reading experiences I had ahead.

Why is Lewis so important to me? In part, it's because—technically, from the point of view of craft—he tells the story with truly exemplary economy. By the time we're only six or seven pages into *The Lion, the Witch and the Wardrobe*, we already know all four Pevensies, we know how each child feels about the other three, and he's gotten Lucy through the wardrobe and into Narnia. With incredible speed, he acquaints us with the characters—just one or two well-placed details, and we're able to know each one—and delves right away into the adventure.

Even more than that, it's the way he uses language—which is nothing like the way fantasists used language before him. There's no sense of nostalgia. There's no medieval floridness. There's no fairy-tale condescension to the child reader. It's very straight, and very clean—there's no Vaseline on the lens. You see everything clearly, not with sparkles or a flowery sense of wonderment, but with very specific physical details. Look at the attention to detail as you watch Lucy going through the wardrobe:

"This must be a simply enormous wardrobe!" thought Lucy, going still further in and pushing the soft folds of the coats aside to make room for her. Then she noticed that there was something crunching under her feet. "I wonder is that more moth-balls?" she thought, stooping down to feel it with her hand. But instead of feeling the hard, smooth wood of the floor of the wardrobe, she felt something soft and powdery and extremely cold. "This is very queer," she said, and went on a step or two further.

Next moment she found that what was rubbing against her face and hands was no longer soft fur but something hard and rough and even prickly. "Why, it is just like branches of trees!" exclaimed Lucy. And then she saw that there was a light ahead of her; not a few inches away where the back of the wardrobe ought to have been, but a long way off. Something cold and soft was falling on her. A moment later she found that she was standing in the middle of a wood at night-time with snow under her feet and snowflakes falling through the air.

She feels the softness of the coats, she hears the crunching under her feet, she bends down and feels the snow, she feels the prickliness of the trees, and just like that she's through the wardrobe and into Narnia. There are no special effects in the passage. He's making magic, but he's making magic out of very ordinary physical impressions. It's very powerful, and it's very new. I don't think anybody wrote this way before he did. He came up with a new way to describe magic that made it feel realer than it ever had.

It works because he's writing fantasy—but he's working with the tools of realism. Even though he had this wonderful romantic yearning nostalgia, he writes like a modernist. He writes like Hemingway, like the Joyce of *Dubliners*. Though he was writing shortly after the time of the modernists, he observes reality in the meticulous, almost disenchanted way they did—but he puts those tools in the service of a totally different effect.

As far as the modern fantasy novel goes, this is ground zero. You're seeing the atom being split for the first time. So much of what's written afterward comes out of that simple moment, just emerges from Lucy going through the wardrobe.

The Lion, the Witch and the Wardrobe is a powerful illustration of why fantasy matters in the first place. Yes, the Narnia books are works of Christian apology, works that celebrate joy and love—but what I was conscious of as a little boy, if not in any analytical way, was the deep grief encoded in the books. Particularly in the initial wardrobe passage. There's a sense of anger and grief and despair that causes Lewis to want to discard the entire war, set it aside in the favor of something better. You can feel him telling you—*I know it's awful, truly terrible, but that's not all there is. There's another option.* Lucy, as she enters the wardrobe, takes the other option. I remember feeling this way as a child, too. I remember thinking, "Yes, of *course* there is. Of course this isn't all there is. There *must* be something else."

How powerful it was to have Lewis come along and say, *Yes, I feel that way, too.*

But I bristle whenever fantasy is characterized as escapism. It's not a very accurate way to describe it; in fact, I think fantasy is a powerful tool for coming to an understanding of oneself. The magic trick here, the sleight of hand, is that when you pass through the portal, you reencounter in the fantasy world the problems you thought you left behind in the real world. Edmund doesn't solve any of his grievances or personality disorders by going through the wardrobe. If anything, they're exacerbated and brought to a crisis by his experiences in Narnia. When you go to Narnia, your worries come with you. Narnia just becomes the place where you work them out and try to resolve them.

The whole modernist-realist tradition is about the self observing the world around you—sensing how other it is, how alien it is, how different it is to what's going on inside you. In fantasy, that gets turned inside out. The landscape you inhabit is a mirror of what's inside you. The stuff inside can get out, and walk around, and take the form of places and people and things and magic. And once it's outside, then you can get at it. You can wrestle it, make friends with it, kill it, seduce it. Fantasy takes all those things from deep inside and puts them where you can see them, and then deal with them.

The thing about the Narnia books is that they're about Christianity. I grew up in a household that not only lacked Christianity—there was very little Christianity in our house, even though my mom was raised Anglican—there was almost no religion of any kind. Religion was, and to some extent has remained to me, a totally baffling concept. I wasn't experiencing the book in any way as stories about religion: I experienced them as psychological dramas. This sleight of hand in which an apparent escape becomes a way of encountering yourself, and encountering your problems, seems to me the basic logic of reading and of the novel.

In this way, the portal in *The Lion, the Witch and the Wardrobe* becomes a magnificent metaphor for reading itself. When she opens the doors to the wardrobe, it's like Lucy's opening the covers of a book and passing through it to somewhere else—which is just the same experience you're having at the moment you're reading the passage. You're watching Lucy do the same thing you are, just in a way that's dramatized and transfigured.

I think the standard psychoanalytic reading of the wardrobe has to do with a return to the womb—you know, passing through these furry coats back into a safe place. But that idea, while perhaps supportable on the grounds of textual evidence, never really seemed paramount to me. For me, the wardrobe's doors open like a book, ushering Lucy—and the reader—into a new imaginative realm of imagination. That's the kind of writer I aspire to be: one that helps the reader make that seamless passage, from the real world to the land of fantasy, from real life to the realm of reading.

It's funny, because Lewis was in some ways a very sloppy writer. The world he created for *The Lion, the Witch and the Wardrobe* doesn't really add up. It's not like it has a working ecology. If he wanted fauns he put fauns in. If he wanted Santa Claus—well, here comes Santa Claus! Let's have him in, too. He took from everybody, and when he saw something shiny, he thought, "Ooh, shiny!" and put it in the book. This drove Tolkien crazy, because Tolkien was very meticulous in his world-building; Lewis didn't care, and wrote in this exuberant, improvisational way. As sloppy as it is, people—myself included—believe in it utterly.

This flies in the face of conventional wisdom as it stands among fantasy writers today—which is that you have to be very, very careful. Today's fantasy writers feel as though the fictional worlds they create have to be full-scale working models. People talk a lot about the ecology of Westeros, for instance: How do the seasons work? What are the climate patterns? How does it function as an ecosphere? You have to think about the economy, too: Have I got a working feudal model? It's gotten so extreme that when characters do magic, it's very common to see fantasy writers talk about thermodynamics: *Okay, he's lighting a candle with magic. Can he draw the heat from somewhere else in the room so that equilibrium gets preserved?*

This is the school of thought that extends from Tolkien, and his scrupulously crafted Middle-earth. Lewis was of a different school from that. Magic, to him, was a much wilder, stranger thing. It was much less domesticated. And when I reread *The Lion, the Witch and the Wardrobe*, I feel as though we've wandered too far from the *true* magic, the kind Lewis wrote. Maybe we want to worry less about thermodynamics and work harder to get that sense of wonder he achieves with such apparent effortlessness.

And then, there are things that he does that are simply not replicable. The lamppost in the woods: There's something indescribably strange and romantic about that image, which recurs at the end of the book. In some ways, you read Lewis and think: I can learn from this guy. But sometimes you have to sit back and think, *I'll never know how he did that.* You know, I've seen the lamppost in Oxford which is alleged to be the Narnia lamppost. To me, it looked like an ordinary lamppost. I would not have seen that lamppost, and gone home to write *The Lion, the Witch and the Wardrobe.* You had to be Lewis to see it for what it was.

I should put on the record my mom's other C. S. Lewis anecdote, which goes like this: After she went back to London, wasn't blown to bits by Hitler, and grew up, she went to Oxford for college. It was her senior year, and she was on her way to her final exams, which were oral exams. As one does, she stopped into a pub to have a pint and stiffen her resolve. There was this old guy at the other end of the bar. They started chatting, and he said, "If you're taking your exams, you should really have a brandy first."

Well, up until that point in her life, my mom had never had any brandy. And the guy at the bar, of course, was C. S. Lewis. He bought her a brandy. She drank it. And she claims to have no memory of anything else that happened that day. She passed her exams, at least, so it can't have been that bad.

Portia had learnt one dare never look for long. She had those eyes that seem to be welcome nowhere, that learn shyness from the alarm they precipitate. Such eyes are always turning away or being humbly lowered. . . . You most often meet or, rather, avoid meeting such eyes in a child's face—what becomes of the child later you do not know.　　　—ELIZABETH BOWEN, The Death of the Heart

YIYUN LI

Strangers on a Train

THOUGH SHE'S NOT very well known in the United States, Elizabeth Bowen is a first-rate novelist, a writer at the level of Virginia Woolf and Katherine Mansfield. I've always been intrigued that she's not as widely read as she should be. Her Anglo-Irish heritage may be one reason she's not better known.

I have read almost all her novels and stories. *The Death of the Heart* is one of her better-known books, though it's not Bowen's favorite—she thought it was overrated among her novels. She did not love the book, and claimed it was more like an inflated short story. I have to say, I disagree: It's a beautiful novel. To me, it's about people being afraid of living their real lives, and choosing to live a life more like a game. Several characters in the novel keep saying to themselves and each other: *It's just a game, it's just a game.*

I like to think you write a book to talk to another book. Or write a story to talk to another story. Often, my short stories talk to stories written by William Trevor, another Irish writer. And when I wrote *Kinder Than Solitude*, I had *The Death of the Heart* in mind, even though the plot and settings are completely different. Especially important to me was a passage that describes the eyes of one of the main characters, Portia Quayne, a sixteen-year-old orphan.

> Portia had learnt one dare never look for long. She had those eyes that seem to be welcome nowhere, that learn shyness from the alarm they precipitate. Such eyes are always turning away or being humbly lowered. . . . You most often meet or, rather, avoid meeting such eyes in a child's face—what becomes of the child later you do not know.

My book concerns orphans, too, people whose status as "welcome nowhere" is reflected in their eyes. My characters are not orphans in the literal sense of having no parents: They've orphaned themselves more than they are orphans. Two of the characters have done so by moving to the United States from China, by leaving the homeland behind (perhaps forever). Another character has not experienced much parental warmth in his life.

This passage describes an averted gaze—eyes we "avoid meeting" because they are so revealing, so full of feeling, and the way these eyes themselves learn to turn away because they cause such alarm. I think it's a very cutting insight into human nature. How often do we turn away from knowing another person as fully as we could, avoiding even the eyes of the people we're closest to? And how often do we hide ourselves, afraid of being really looked into and seen?

This passage sums up *The Death of the Heart* very well—it's a book about looking, after all. It's about a person, whose orphan status puts her on the margins of society, looking at the world—as the other characters avoid looking back. They choose not to meet her gaze, symbolically (and, in this passage, literally).

I relate to this because I'm a starer; I'm interested in looking at people very closely. I look at people I know, but I also look at people I don't know. It does make strangers uncomfortable—which, of course, I understand. I've noticed that, in New York City, you're not supposed to stare at people. No one has enough space, and when people are in public, they're trying to maintain anonymity. But I stare at people all the time, because I like to imagine their lives by looking into their faces, looking at their eyes. You can tell so much just from a person's face.

When I was studying fiction at the Iowa Writers' Workshop years ago, Marilynne Robinson used an example to demonstrate the inexplicableness of human beings. I forget the context, and I'm paraphrasing, but she would say something like this:

Sometimes, when you get home and your mother looks up, her eyes are so unfamiliar, and for a moment it's as though she's looking at you as a stranger on the New York subway would do.

I loved that idea—your eyes surprise your mother's eyes, and for that split second everything is there: a whole emotional world that you don't know well, so foreign and hidden that she briefly becomes a stranger. Then she transforms, she becomes the mother you know again, and life goes on. But, in that brief instant of eye contact, something is caught. This is what we learn by looking at another person's face—and also what makes us want to turn away.

When I try to look at my characters, I see mostly their eyes. In *Kinder Than Solitude* there's a character—she's an orphan, too—who is a starer, like Portia Quayne. What strikes me as very specific to her character—more than anyone else I've ever written—is how she never turns her eyes away. In any of the scenes with her, I can clearly see her eyes staring at people. She looks and looks. She's very smart, and she sees through people, and she knows it. Whether she's taking care of a dying old man, or sitting with a girl her age, or staring at a woman's ugly, expensive shoes, more than any part of her body I can see her *eyes*—taking in the world and forming judgments about people.

Writing fiction is this kind of staring, too. You have to stare at your characters, like you would a stranger on the train, but for much longer than is comfortable for both of you. This way, you get to know characters layer by layer, until any dishonesty is stripped away. I believe all characters try to trick us. They lie to us. It's just like when you meet someone in the real world—no one's going to be 100 percent honest.

They're not going to tell you the whole story about themselves; in fact, the stories they *do* tell will say more about how they *want* to be perceived than how they actually are. There's always a certain resistance with being known, and that's true of characters and real people. People don't want to tell you their secrets. Or they lie to themselves, or they lie to you.

In *Kinder Than Solitude*, one of my characters lied to me from the very beginning about how solitude was best for her. She was articulate about that solitude, and so part of me thought maybe she was right. But as a writer, you shouldn't believe what your characters say about themselves. When they avoid being looked at, they avoid being studied, you need to push them and push them until they admit, or relinquish, or confess. I got stuck with this character, with her belief in her solitude so beguiling. My friend Brigid, who is an early reader of my work, marked the passages with fierce comments and many question marks, so I knew I didn't get close enough. Eventually the character (and I) found out it's not solitude she has: It's a never-ending quarantine against life.

That's why I stare at my characters. Not physically—I can't really see them physically—but in an act of imagination that's similar to the way I stare at people in real life. It can be harsh, but I think I like the harsh, true things you see when you don't turn away. The writer must never look away. You can feel it in a book when a writer flinches away from seeing too deeply into their characters. I think you have to look beyond the characters. You really have to strip your characters naked, every single layer, to finally understand them.

We see that turning away here, in Bowen's passage. "What becomes of the child later you do not know," she writes, but I think she could have written, "you don't *want* to know." The child's future is written in her eyes, it's there for us to see: Her eyes will get her into trouble, and when she feels too much or looks too long, people will turn away from her. All of that is contained within the passage. So when the "you" of the passage turns away, it's a decision to not face the painful fact of this, a decision to deflect what can be glimpsed there in the eyes.

That's why when one writes about young characters—as I do in this book—I think one should know some of the moments in their future. When I write a child character, I have to include a second reference point later, to force myself to reckon with what becomes of him or her. I don't want to say "what became of the child later you do not know"; I want to say "what became of the child later you *must* know." To follow a person beyond a single point in time, to remain with them on the longer course of their life's path, is a way to continue looking.

Let the wind blow; let the poppy seed itself and the carnation mate with the cabbage. Let the swallow build in the drawing-room, and the thistle thrust aside the tiles, and the butterfly sun itself on the faded chintz of the arm-chairs. Let the broken glass and the china lie out on the lawn and be tangled over with grass and wild berries. —VIRGINIA WOOLF, *To the Lighthouse*

MAGGIE SHIPSTEAD

Time Passes

In *To the Lighthouse*, Virginia Woolf writes:

> Let the wind blow; let the poppy seed itself and the carnation mate with
> the cabbage. Let the swallow build in the drawing-room, and the thistle
> thrust aside the tiles, and the butterfly sun itself on the faded chintz of
> the arm-chairs. Let the broken glass and the china lie out on the lawn
> and be tangled over with grass and wild berries.

If there are such things as universal truths about how we experience life, "time passes" is one of them. (I'd suggest its harsher relative "everybody dies" as another.) Time is the medium in which we live, the thing that separates each heartbeat from the last, the axis against which the distance between birth and death is measured. Time is also a necessary conductor for literature. Reading, the basic act of moving eyes over words and allowing sense to penetrate the mind, takes time, even if during the best and most transcendent reading experiences the forward tick of time ceases to register.

Or perhaps, reading, we don't so much forget about time as give ourselves over to an alternative, artificial version of it, one manipulated by an author to suit the needs of a narrative. Time within fiction is a malleable thing. I might speed my characters' clocks along, spinning the hands into a blur, or I might stop them entirely to dwell on a suspended moment. This is the power of a god, and, as far as my characters are concerned, I *am* a god, the only god.

To me, Virginia Woolf's *To the Lighthouse,* a masterpiece if there ever was one, is defined and spectacularly elevated by its middle, those twenty pages of expansive vision and extreme beauty called "Time Passes." The novel's other two sections, the much longer "The Window" and "The Lighthouse," each take place over one day at the Ramsay family's summer house on the Isle of Skye. Their pace is measured; in them, Woolf's attention stays trained on the psychology of her characters and the complex emotional resonances set off by offhand remarks and minute gestures. "Time Passes," in contrast, makes a majestic, impersonal swoop through ten years, a period when the Ramsays don't come to Skye, three of them die (their deaths noted briefly and parenthetically), and nature—fertile and insensible, as Woolf puts it—creeps in among the family's abandoned possessions, inhabiting and reclaiming the house. Only the last-minute intervention of the caretakers, Mrs. McNab and Mrs. Bast, saves the house from total disintegration.

In a purely structural sense, the section is unnecessary. It's awful to imagine such a loss, but Woolf *could* have transitioned from "The Window" to "The Lighthouse" with a few sentences explaining that a decade has passed, that Mrs. Ramsay, Prue, and Andrew are dead and the house fallen into disrepair. If plot means dealings among the characters, there is no real progression of plot here, but, at the same time, what plot is grander or more essential than time passing? In and around the Ramsays' vacant house, the seasons pass and pass again; the sea advances and retreats; new life and decay cycle endlessly into each other. The confrontation of life's persistence with death's inevitability is thrilling.

As a reader, I want the house to be saved and repaired, made habitable again, but I also want it to crumble away, as everything must. I want to see it *all.* Yes, *let* the wind blow; *let* the swallow build; *let* the broken glass be tangled over with wild berries. "Only the Lighthouse beam entered the rooms for a moment, sent its sudden stare over bed and wall in the darkness of winter, looked with equanimity at the thistle and the swallow, the rat and the straw," but I want to go with it, to be the human gaze where there is no human gaze.

The planet is indifferent to the beginning or end of any individual life. Mrs. Ramsay's death devastates her husband but means nothing to the house where she once lived, now occupied by "the trifling airs, nibbling, the clammy breaths, fumbling." Not one of us makes any difference to the waves, the thistle, the rat, the wind. Knowing that the only important thing about my single, finite life is my experience of it, I can't help but want to squeeze more into its confines than is actually possible, and my best idea for how to do that is to read, to scoop a profusion of vicarious experiences into my lap like poker chips. My second-best idea is to write, although I vastly prefer reading because it's easier, more satisfying, more fun, and much, much faster. Writing is a geologically slow process, the drip-drip of a stalactite forming, and I am not a naturally patient person.

I come by impatience honestly. My father is a change-jingler and knee-jiggler for whom every commute is a road rally and who watches sports on mute because he can't endure the commentators' blather. My mother, on the other hand, spends most of her time making quilts: sewing together tiny bits of fabric, tearing out her work if the corners don't align perfectly, ironing every little seam, adding embroidered embellishments by hand. She loves baseball. When I was little, she used to listen to spring training on the car radio, and the indolent crowd noise and the announcer's leisurely calls bored me to the point of rage. Clearly, in this case, my father's genes had shoved past my mother's, determined to get there first.

What pleasure I derive from writing arrives and departs unpredictably, like some shy, nocturnal animal, but frustration is always there, an underlying constant. In a single day, even a banner day, I can only produce a horrifyingly small portion of a book, and, in all likelihood, what

I write in any given day will be deleted and sent into oblivion, maybe the next day, maybe not for a year, but probably sometime. The sentences and paragraphs and chapters that eventually fall away are as necessary to the project as those that survive: I know this intellectually—I *believe* it, even—but I still catch myself thinking, as though the idea were perfectly plausible, that maybe this time I'll just sit down and unspool one perfect first (and last) draft.

My brain presents this fantasy to me as though avoiding the prolonged, tedious, swampy struggle of writing might only be a question of willpower, or luck. As soon as I write the first word of a novel or story and realize that the process, again, will not be enchanted and effortless, I start longing to write the first word of a different novel or story, one that will come with breathtaking ease and speed and is only a mirage, of course. A mirage of fiction—nothing could be less real.

But, as more of my own time passes, I'm better able to discard my foolish wish to accelerate through the in-between parts of my work and life. The thing to long for is the impossible thing: for time to slow, for the chance to loiter in a moment. A novel offers such a chance; it is a portal into a preserved wedge of time, a past, present, and future that can be revisited in a way our own can never be. A novel also offers an opportunity to rocket through more time than any person could ever live, to knock off ten years in twenty pages or twenty words, to follow generations, to experience versions of the distant past or future. It's a trade: The writer sits at a desk (or somewhere) and expends many, many quiet, solitary hours of her finite life in exchange for the opportunity to build more lives, imaginary ones, cantilevering them off her own and out into the ether. The reader trades hours, too—for access to those lives and the irregular chronologies on which they are stretched like flesh over a skeleton. Woolf cut her time short. I don't think I'll ever understand how she could look at death with such clear eyes and then choose it, but we all make our bargains.

Don't be sad, I know you will,
But don't give up until,
True love will find you in the end.
　　　　　—Daniel Johnston,
　"True Love Will Find You in the End"

JEFF TWEEDY

Translating the Subconscious

I FIRST CAME across Daniel Johnston's cassettes in the late '80s or early '90s—I don't remember exactly what year. We were touring through Austin, Texas—where Johnston lived and performed at the time—and Waterloo Records carried them in their store.

From the beginning, I loved the way he records his material. There's so much potential evident in his songs, but it's rarely fully realized—and that's kind of the beauty of it. It can be like listening to a Neil Young demo tape or something, like hearing an early, stripped-down version of a great song. For a songwriter like myself, hearing this music in such a raw state is exciting. There's so much to draw you in. You can get lost in the potential, in how much he leaves open to interpretation.

Around then he started getting a little bit of national attention with that Shimmy Disc record, *1990*, which includes what's become one of his best-known songs, "True Love Will Find You in the End." That song has an incredible line that says so much—much more than what you should be able to say in so few words.

> Don't be sad, I know you will,
> But don't give up until,
> True love will find you in the end.

This captures a very real internal moment. I think it's a window into the way someone really thinks and feels when they're telling somebody else not to be sad. The speaker tells the subject to feel better—it's even an order, "Don't be sad." At the same time he knows that's impossible. In fact, before the line is even over, he's retracted it.

I love, too, how the line doesn't have a "but"—the more obvious thing to write would be "Don't be sad, but I know you will." The way Johnston wrote it is so much more powerful. It means it's not an either/or. It's an all of the above. "Don't be sad" *and* "I know you will"—two contradictory emotions, experienced at the same time. It captures a profound feeling: the desire to comfort someone, and the impossibility of doing so, all at once.

It's heartbreakingly real. It's heartbreakingly accurate. And I think it demonstrates why we need poetry, why we need songs—to say the things that can only be expressed in this kind of elegant, inexplicable way. Things that, if you could explain them straightforwardly, you wouldn't have to have poetry, you wouldn't have to have songs. I'm very drawn to Daniel Johnston's real gift for tapping into this depth of feeling—there are lines like this one littered throughout his recorded output.

I've thought about Johnston a lot in my own work with words and lyrics. Lyrics are a very tricky thing to write, because songs, in my mind, are ruled by melody. I really believe that melody does all the heavy lifting emotionally. When I write lyrics, or when I adapt a poem to a song, what I really want to do is not interfere with the spell that's being cast by the melody. Basically, I just don't want to fuck it up. I just want to stay out of the way. At the same time, I hope—at best—that the words enhance some meaning, or clarify somehow what the melody makes me feel.

I think that's partly why I usually don't bother with lyrics for a long time, because I don't want them to get in the way. In fact, one of the primary ways I write lyrics is to sing and record vocal sounds without words, vowel and consonants that *sound* like language but don't actually mean anything. I'll even double vocal tracks of these sounds without words—I call them "mumble tracks." A lot of times people will hear them and think I'm singing real lyrics there, but I'm not. I mix them low so you have to struggle to hear, but loud enough so you can get the sound you want and get the melody to come through. With this approach, you can work on a song and finish it without even having the lyrics done.

Then, I'll take the recordings out to our summer log cabin and sit around for hours listening to them, taking notes. I translate them—I guess that would be the best way to describe it—doing my best to hear what it sounds like I'm saying. Once I've transcribed and translated the mumble tracks into words, I look at what I've got. The lyrics at that stage are often pretty meaningless and nonsensical—though sometimes they're not, which is kind of crazy. The second step after translating is to add one more round of editing and shaping so that the final product has some coherency. Usually, there has to be an image in my mind that guides me through the song—some narrative, even when it's impressionistic or fractured. For me, that visual connection is important—I have to be able to see something to remember it.

I don't think this is an unprecedented process. Keith Richards has done that on demos for years, and Mick Jagger's translated his mumbling. I think it's a pretty common approach. And it works because our brains are wired to make sense of things. If you listen to a mumble, your brain really wants to hear words. You listen to one line at a time, over and over again—well, a lot faster than you think. It's hard to stop hearing the words. For me, I often get the feeling "That's obviously what I'm singing there"—which is strange, and wonderful, because no words were intended at all.

I think I'm attached to this process, too, because it keeps me attached to the song in its early state, the way it was before I'd thought it through and figured out what it was. I don't trust myself to make conscious choices. I trust myself to make stuff and respond to things that I can feel and intuit, but I don't really trust when the ego gets involved. This way of working means I get to preserve that felt, wordless melody until the very end—and when I do write lyrics, they're a way of listening and responding to the song, instead of imposing a vision on it. It keeps the observing ego out of the way as much as possible.

For the same reason, those early demo takes can have such magic: They're closer to the subconscious. That's why I like to include elements of early recordings on the finished records when I can. Almost every song on *Sukierae* has the original element somewhere in there. A lot of my iPhone acoustic demos became the basic tracks we overdubbed to, and they're still there in the finished record. (That's why we listed the iPhone as an instrument in the track notes.) The song "I'll Sing It" includes a cassette recording from a *Being There*–era demo of that song. Stuff lies around forever, and for this record it was fun to make some use of it.

It's a totally different process working with an ensemble. Wilco is a six-piece band, and its members have varying degrees of interest in the finishing touches. As a collective, we always gravitate toward something much more fully realized—and that's the pleasure of it. Working on my own, I always hope to abandon something before I feel like I've made all of the choices that could be made. If I commit too much to one approach, I mourn all the choices that *weren't* made when I get to that point. I think that's one way *Sukierae* would have been different if it had been recorded by Wilco. I can still hear possible overdubs on every track, I can still hear things I could have done, and that's the most enjoyable part for me. It's the same thing I love about Daniel Johnston's music—all that unrealized potential.

This may sound strange, but as a person who's spent a lot of time in the studio, and who's written a lot of songs, I can hear those finishing touches even when they're not there. And they're just as enjoyable as they were. At this point in my life, I can have a certain amount of confidence that I know how to put a record together, that I can make it sound a certain way, and that there are a certain number of people that will respond (or not). But that's not the part that's satisfying to me. The part that's satisfying to me is how it sounds way before that happens, when I can still hear all the different potential pathways that are being laid out.

When a song is still new, it retains a mysterious quality that it's hard to take ownership of. I'm proudest of my music when I come to a song after the fact and think—*how did that happen?* It's a much more enjoyable thing to appreciate something that you made, with some sense that it wasn't you who made it. Even though I sometimes have feelings of pride when I listen to stuff—*you did good, Jeff; that's great*—I would rather enjoy my music the way that I enjoy other people's records. If you don't let the observing ego get too much in the way, this really can happen. My favorite songs I've written move me in a way that I can't allow myself to claim with pride—it's as though I didn't write them.

Writers tend to get pretty mystical and metaphysical about these things. You hear people talking about "channeling" something like it's coming through you, or being "given" a song. I think that's all bullshit. It's obviously coming from *you*. But it's your subconscious. The gift, I think, is the ability to be able to go into your subconscious, come back unscathed, and present something from it.

That going in and coming back again is Daniel Johnston's gift, what he does best. There's an added element of mental illness, I think, that makes one feel a little bit uncomfortable discussing it. But basically what comes across, most of all, is this incredible bravery. Bravery in the face of more than most people could bear. For him, I'm assuming there really isn't another option. Music is the mode of communication that he has found for himself that's the most conflict-free, the way he can experience aspects of his subconscious and make them palatable or perceivable to someone else.

This is the sustaining and consoling part of what artists do, even the ones who aren't fighting mental illness. I know that's the part that most matters to me: being able to disappear into something that's bigger than you, and returning from it with something to show. Music in general is a thing I've disappeared into, as a listener, since I was a little kid. And making my own music takes me to an even richer and deeper place, as far as how it can console me and be a comfort to me.

The stone which the builders rejected has become the cornerstone.

—PSALMS 118:22

NELL ZINK

The Long Game

I FIRST HEARD Psalm 118 in church. I was raised Catholic, and as a child, I couldn't miss it: It comes up in all four gospels, plus Acts and the first letter of Peter, and is the responsorial psalm at Easter mass. Sadly enough, a lot of the more violent passages appealed to me when I was young. *I will look down upon my foes as their heads are dashed out against rocks*, that kind of thing, which I would read in eighth grade to get up the courage to go to school. My parents were always pressuring me to fight back—I was supposed to slug people and say mean things. But instead I would be really submissive and just let them beat me, and think of the martyrs. (I was a weird kid.)

One line from Psalm 118 made an especially profound impression on me:

The stone which the builders rejected has become the cornerstone.

This is a very strong statement. The builders, the people who put me here, reject me—but one day, the city will be built on my foundation. It's a lovely, constructive sort of revenge fantasy. Of course, this was presented to me in the context of Jesus, who in the Bible is always saying this avant-garde stuff: "Blessed are you when they revile and persecute you," or, "A prophet has no honor in his own country." To me, this fit right in with that. I thought it was expressed in an especially poetic and musical way. It still sounds good to me.

You hear all these fairy tales, when you're a kid, about the ugly duckling, and Cinderella, and the littlest snowman: people who are overlooked and then have to be discovered. And that's how this line is often interpreted, though in that reading both the originality and insight are gone, along with the suggestion of power. I think the message Jesus conveyed was different, at least subtly different. The stone that the builders rejected became the cornerstone, but it doesn't say the stone *changed*. The stone didn't grow up to become a swan. It was the same rock, and later, the builders said, "Oh, yeah—that thing is useful."

I guess that was my dream.

When you're raised in a family that's religious—not like we were fundamentalist freaks or something, but I was taught religion—you learn you're supposed to please one person. Your audience is God. And if you do what God wants, it totally does not matter what anybody else thinks. I think there's a link between that and the anarchic individualism that's so normal for Americans: the antisocial willingness to defy the group. The Protestant ideal, of course, is that ethics are between you and the higher power. This idea was omnipresent in my childhood, and I know it was important to me. When you're an unpopular kid getting beaten up in school, the idea that your behavior is somehow pleasing to someone . . . I think I found it comforting for that reason.

I think this is part of why, for many years, I didn't seek out readers: My career was lying low. I wasn't Jesus—I was the early Christians hiding in caves. I was like, okay, I'm not going to get out there and try to tell people what I'm about, because they will crucify me. That's what Heinrich Heine said about images of Christ on the cross, which are all over the place in Catholic countries: "He's put up as an example and a warning." *This is what will happen to you if you act that way.*

When I was writing little stories for my zine, *Animal Review,* in the early nineties, I was conscious that I couldn't think of anyone who was going to like these stories or approve of them, except me. I remember vividly just writing for myself, and how each one just had to be right. Like a lot of people, I trust my own superego. I think one can make good ethical judgments if one takes a little time to think about it. Editorial judgments for me feel ethical when I'm making them. I want to say what's *right*. I've always felt like writing is a little bit like drawing: If you get certain details to be accurate, then the full picture will be accurate. Like with that facial recognition software that, because of nine dots that it computes from your features, can tell it's you. You'll have a recognizable picture if you put the dots in the right place.

It was a special state of mind I had put myself in to write. At the time when I was writing little tiny stories, I was living in New York, working as a secretary. It's not like I went around in an idealistic trance—I would have been run over. I had to be more aware than that. (In the time I lived in New York, I saw five bodies in the street of people who had been hit by cars—they weren't all dead, but it happens.) But when I sat down to write, which I did Saturday mornings, it was a very pleasant experience of putting myself into this mental state where my concerns mattered. It was just between me and these stories. Just a paragraph, looking back at me on the page.

I guess it's like flower-arranging or anything else. To tweak a text and say, okay: It's good now. Sometimes you discover that there are people who agree with you—*yes, it's good now*—though, of course, that came late in life for me, and was a very cheering experience. For years, I had only the sensation of making something I loved, and having the privilege of being my own favorite writer.

I do regret that I suffered so much doing terrible jobs, when possibly I could have been making money writing. At the time, there weren't that many creative-writing programs. There was Iowa, and nobody ever mentioned any other program. In Williamsburg, I knew one guy who got into Iowa, and it was as if he had ascended into heaven. People wanted to touch the hem of his garment. Of course, even then I wanted to do journalism—but I think the avant-gardism that was serving me so well would have been drilled out of me. I knew people who did journalism, and I watched it being drilled out of them, and I thought, *Nah, that's not for me.* I don't know. I was a little odd, my social behavior was weird. Maybe I wouldn't have made any money anyway.

When I got out of college I went to work for a bricklayer. Today, it's considered so politically incorrect to say this—you have to be reading Pierre Bourdieu to have someone admit that the work that women do in a system of masculine domination tends to be routine maintenance, while the men create and construct. But my mom was a very feminist person, and it was clear to me that in this system you did not want to be on the female side of the equation. There was absolutely nothing genderqueer about it—I was just saying, if we have a system where men skim the cream off the top while women drink the dregs, I need to move up. That, and I loved Irving Stone's book about Michelangelo, *The Agony and the Ecstasy*, which I read when I was eleven or twelve, which made me want to work with my hands on stone, a big hunk of Carrara marble.

Well, I immediately got $8 an hour instead of the $4.50 you got doing women's work. But going to work as a bricklayer was not the smartest thing I ever did. It was punishingly hard work. The weekends were more like convalescence than like time to relax. I wouldn't say I'm a physically frail person, but I have little tiny bones like a bird. I did not belong on construction sites.

The first time I published something (besides my stories in *Animal Review*) was a little piece on the *n+1* website, and I was sort of terrified emotionally. I knew it wasn't true, but the feeling was as if everyone was going to read it, and they were all going to hate me. It was not a good feeling at all. I wrote it in a way that was completely coded and very indirect. It's funny: I think that might be part of what people find interesting about my writing even now. If I ever lose my fear of the mass audience, maybe I'll just become a banal crank or something.

Of course, we've long had the idea that art is supposed to be subversive or unpopular. You see it all the time in interviews with artists—even people like Bob Dylan, who traces the idea of the avant-garde to the French symbolists Verlaine and Rimbaud, the feeling that art is supposed to appeal initially to only ten people and then twenty years later maybe to fifteen, and then maybe you're famous after you're dead. That was the avant-garde ideal from the nineteenth century. Today, though, it's more common to hear people stomping their foot and saying, *Why didn't I get a Booker nomination?* It's funny, because even in the fifties and sixties, self-respecting artists were turning down prizes. It was a sort of popular mass appeal they didn't want. People associate that kind of thought with people like Cocteau, but I was picking it up as a two-year-old, sitting in church: that the best kind of person to be is the kind of person being nailed to the cross. It's such a weird message, but it shaped me.

Whenever you put yourself in the public eye you're going to be looked at, and people are going to make judgments about you, and they're not all going to be positive. If you care what people think, you'll do what I used to do: hide. We're now in a societal phase where caring what people think is just a way to completely lose your mind. So I don't do that. You put those people out of your mind. It's not possible to care what people think and do what I do.

Young man I think I know you—I think this face is the face of the Christ himself,
Dead and divine and brother of all, and here again he lies.

—WALT WHITMAN,
"A Sight in Camp in the Daybreak Gray and Dim"

CHARLES SIMIC

Lifting the Blanket

LIKE ANYONE MY age, war has always been part of my life. I was born in 1938 and was three years old when the bombs started falling on my hometown of Belgrade. When the city was liberated in October 1944, I was six, living in the center of the city. My parents always being busy with—well, who knows what they were busy with—we kids used to just run in the street. And we saw a lot of stuff. Stuff young children are not supposed to see. Including, you know, dead people.

There is a story told in my family that I remember only vaguely. I came home wearing a trooper's helmet on my head. This was after the Russians had liberated the city. There was a church nearby where I lived, and I went in the churchyard and inside there were some dead Germans. The helmet had fallen off, kind of to the side. I remember distinctly that I did not look at him in the face—that was too scary. But I took the helmet. The reason the story is repeated in my family is not because of what I did—that I took it off a dead German. More awful things than that happened during the Second World War. They told the story because I got lice from the helmet, and they had to shave my head.

When I first got to the United States, I was sixteen, and as soon as I arrived people started telling me—"Oh, Charlie, you're going to Korea!" But

I didn't, of course. I was too young, but there was always that fear. I remember working for the *Chicago Sun-Times* when I was young—a lowly job, going in in the morning into what was called the composing room, where they put together the paper on Saturday mornings. I was in a pretty good mood because I'd gotten paid the night before. One of the workers yelled out to me, "Hey, Simic, you're going to Lebanon!" They were sending Marines there at the time. It scared me—ruined my day. I thought, "I don't want to go to Lebanon!" On and on, for the rest of my life. I was in the army before Vietnam, then my brother was in Vietnam, and then the first Gulf War and my son thought that he would be in that . . .

As you know, we no longer see carnage from our wars. But during the Vietnam War, if you stayed up late at night—which I did in those days, certainly—and turned on the TV around eleven o'clock or midnight, they would show documentary footage of the war. They were really graphic pictures that are just impossible to forget. Dead Vietnamese. Machine-gunning dead Vietnamese from a helicopter, or our soldiers lying dead or wounded. Vietnam was the last war where you could see those things, and they learned their lesson. This is sort of the context for my interest in this poem.

I don't read it that often, but every time I read "A Sight in Camp in the Daybreak Gray and Dim," I sort of choke up. I tried to read it to a class this fall and found myself being immensely, immensely moved by it—even though I know the poem very well and knew what was coming.

The Civil War was a big break in Whitman's poetry. Sometimes, he'd drive you nuts before that with his *oh, what a great country we are, marching toward this glorious future!*—all that Emersonian optimism. He saw this vision of collective humanity in this country that he really believed in. He expected all good things would happen from this very energetic and attractive people. And then, boom—the war.

In 1862, his brother is wounded, and Whitman goes down to find him. He then becomes a wound dresser, as they used to call them, in the hospitals around Washington, D.C.—helping to attend to the sick and dying. At this point, a tragic note enters his poetry. This is not the same Whitman. In "When Lilacs Last in the Dooryard Bloom'd," the great Lincoln poem, for instance, there's no jingoism at all—just tragedy.

"A Sight in Camp" begins with the narrator waking up, leaving his tent, and seeing a row of covered bodies:

> A sight in camp in the daybreak gray and dim,
> As from my tent I emerge so early sleepless,
> As slow I walk in the cool fresh air the path near by the hospital tent,
> Three forms I see on stretchers lying, brought out there untended lying,
> Over each the blanket spread, ample brownish woolen blanket,
> Gray and heavy blanket, folding, covering all.

It's just so matter-of-fact. There is not an extra word. Everything is completely pared down to the essentials. The whole thing is so understandable, vivid, poignant, troubling. "In the cool fresh air": Right away, we're there. We know what it's like to be there with the "sleepless" narrator, who has seen these kinds of things before. And those shrouding army blankets— that detail is so interesting. Nothing is sticking out—no foot, nothing. Everything is completely covered. We don't want to lift those blankets.

But Whitman does. There's a kind of choreography in the poem. One by one, he lifts the blankets to take a peek.

> Curious I halt and silent stand,
> Then with light fingers I from the face of the nearest the first just lift the
>   blanket;
> Who are you elderly man so gaunt and grim, with well-gray'd hair,
>   and flesh all sunken about the eyes?
> Who are you my dear comrade?
>
> Then to the second I step—and who are you my child and darling?
> Who are you sweet boy with cheeks yet blooming?

Whitman had compassion. He understood these were unique lives that had been extinguished, three examples among countless others. Empathy is one of the strongest things in Whitman from the very beginning. And as I read this, I really feel sorry for that old man. And of course, for the kid—young guy, who goes to war to be a hero and gets killed. The whole poem is a live wire vibrating with feelings. It manages to be both restrained and emotional as the speaker uncovers those bodies and looks in horror at their faces.

And then we reach the final, shocking stanza:

> Then to the third—a face nor child nor old, very calm, as of beautiful
>   yellow-white ivory;
> Young man I think I know you—I think this face is the face of the Christ
>   himself,
> Dead and divine and brother of all, and here again he lies.

We keep killing Christ, or someone Christ-like, over and over again. It's a vision of our collective madness. Of course, in Whitman's time there were a lot of people who read that poem and felt this was blasphemous—the idea of putting Christ there. But this is the power of the poem. I'm not a person who gets teary-eyed reading poetry—other people's poetry, or my own. But my eyes were moist, and my students looked at me with some discomfort, as I tried to explain to them what I was feeling.

In a larger sense, there are other blankets we don't want to lift and see what lies underneath. There is a kind of truth—that's a big word—that we hate to look at. It could be a face in the street, someone who looks in pain, someone who's suffering. We turn away—we can't look at everything. But I like poems that occasionally do that to the reader: make them look.

Whitman was good at that. Being a city person, and a journalist, he was a noticer. He's always alert, catching these little dramas that other people don't see. He has a beautiful poem about kids watching a knife-grinder on the street—their eyes growing bigger and bigger as they watch sparks fly.

For the last forty-two years, I've lived in New Hampshire, in the ti-niest little village. Surrounded by woods and mountains—what they *call* mountains; they are really hills. When I'm in the city, I notice every-thing. When I'm in the country, I really don't notice that much. Though I have time on my hands up here, I look—but I may as well be blind. When I was young I never learned about different kinds of trees, differ-ent kinds of birds, and on and on. So my abilities to notice are pretty limited in the country. I very often take long walks along small little dirt roads or paths, but I miss much of what goes on.

I guess it has something to do with the fact that I grew up in cities. My imagination is totally connected to the city. If I see a person walking down the street—the way they look—I start speculating what they do or what sort of person they are, about them. In the city, I'm a noticer, happy to spend hours doing nothing but that.

When I wrote my early poems "Knife," "Fork," and "Spoon," in 1964, I lived on 13th Street and University Place in a little dump of an apart-ment. It was summer, and I'd eaten something. I was looking at the table at the knife, the fork, and the spoon. And I noticed, how interesting these three were. I'd stolen one from a greasy spoon, and another from somewhere else. I remember thinking, "Well, Mr. Simic, let's see if you can write a poem about this." Because no one had ever written a poem about a fork, or a knife, although we have to use them every day.

So I wrote them, and I sent them to a magazine called the *Quarterly Review of Literature*. The editor wrote to me and rejected the poems, saying, "Dear Mr. Simic . . . you obviously sound like an intelligent young man."

Which sort of puzzled me—I thought, "What the fuck does he know?"

He said, "Why do you write poems about these things? Why do you write about such inconsequential things as silverware utensils?"

I came into the library with that letter, feeling both annoyed—I mean, thinking, *You idiot! Should I write about sunsets in June?*—and at the same time I felt triumphant. I thought, *Well, this is what I'm going to do from now on. This is my thing.* I felt I was on the right track. There's pleasure in that.

To me, the ideal poem is one a person can read and understand on the first level of meaning after one reading. An accessible quality, I think, is important. Give them something to begin with. Something that seems plain and simple but has something strange—something about it that's not quite ordinary, that will cause them to do repeated readings or to think about it. The ambition is that, each time they read, they will get to another level of the poem. This fearsome little ten- to fifteen-line poem becomes something like this poem of Whitman's, which the reader wants to read over and over again.

My fantasy goes like this: A reader, in a bookstore, browsing in the poetry section. They pull out a book and read a few poems. Then they put the book back. Two days later they sit up in bed at four o'clock in the morning, thinking—*I want to read that poem again! Where's that poem? I've got to get that book.*

I know it may sound idiotic, but, on Sunday mornings, when we used to visit
the zoo with my father, the animals seemed more real somehow, the lofty, long-
drawn-out solitude of the giraffe resembled that of a glum Gulliver, and from
the headstones in the dog cemetery there arose, from time to time, the mournful
howls of poodles. The zoo had a whiff about it like the open-air passageways in
the Coliseu concert hall, a place full of strange invented birds in cages, ostriches
that looked just like spinster gym teachers, waddling penguins like messenger
boys with bunions, and cockatoos with their heads on one side like connoisseurs of paintings; the hippopotamus pool exuded the languid sloth of the obese,
cobras lay coiled in soft dungy spirals, and the crocodiles seemed reconciled to
their Tertiary-age fate as mere lizards on death row.

—ANTÓNIO LOBO ANTUNES, *The Land at the End of the World*

VIET THANH NGUYEN

Follow This Voice

IT WAS THE late spring or summer of 2011, and I was having trouble with my novel. For months, I struggled to write the section that would begin the book. I felt I really needed to grab the reader from the beginning. I was thinking of certain books—like Ralph Ellison's *Invisible Man*—that immediately established both the narrator's voice and the narrator's dilemma. I was looking for a sentence that, once it was written, would drive the rest of the novel completely. But as I worked through various first lines and opening scenarios, nothing seemed quite right.

Then I came across this book review of António Lobo Antunes's *Land at the End of the World*. The novel was originally published in the 1970s—this was a new version by Margaret Jull Costa, one of my favorite translators of Spanish and Portuguese literature. The excerpts I read in the review had an incredible effect on me. *I have to go out*, I thought, *and read this entire book*.

I bought a copy, and kept it on my desk the entire time that I wrote my novel. For two years, every morning, I'd read a few pages of the book until my own urge to write became so uncontrollable that I finally had to put the book down and start writing myself. Two or three pages at random every morning before writing, until I felt my own creative urge take over.

My interest was partially due to the content of the book: Lobo Antunes was writing semi-autobiographically about his experiences as a medic in the Portuguese army, fighting brutal colonial warfare in Angola. That was happening roughly around the same time as the war with which I was concerned, the Vietnam War. The perspective of his narrator—someone who was bitter and disillusioned with his country and the conflict—was something that led to the direct development of my narrator.

But the language of the book was the most important thing to me. It was so dense, so rhythmic and beautiful. The sentences just go on and on in unpredictable ways, often leading from the present into the past all within one sentence. This effect really served the purposes of my book, because the novel takes the form of a written confession. The narrator's concerns at the time of writing always bring him back into the past—his own personal past, but also the history of his nation, the history of colonization, the history of war, all of which are unescapable to him. There was something incredible about the ways these sentences were constructed, in terms of the languidness of their rhythm, that would engulf me and pull me back into the past of my narrator's own time.

And then, the images—throughout, the novel is filled with great, indelible pictures. Take this short passage, for instance, from the opening of the book:

I know it may sound idiotic, but, on Sunday mornings, when we used to visit the zoo with my father, the animals seemed more real somehow, the lofty, long-drawn-out solitude of the giraffe resembled that of a glum Gulliver, and from the headstones in the dog cemetery there arose, from time to time, the mournful howls of poodles. The zoo had a whiff about it like the open-air passageways in the Coliseu concert hall, a place full of strange invented birds in cages, ostriches that looked just like spinster gym teachers, waddling penguins like messenger boys with bunions, and cockatoos with their heads on one side like connoisseurs of paintings; the hippopotamus pool exuded the languid sloth of the obese, cobras lay coiled in soft dungy spirals, and the crocodiles seemed reconciled to their Tertiary-age fate as mere lizards on death row.

I love how precise, and how unexpected, these images are. And the way that Lobo Antunes doesn't just give us one image in these sentences—he gives us several in a row. That's excessive, I think, for a lot of people. Having one great image in a sentence is oftentimes more than enough. But here he's giving us a whole sequence: The ostriches look "like spinster gym teachers," the penguins look "like messenger boys with bunions"— the list goes on and on. There is something in this method about not wanting the reader to move on, wanting the reader to stop, look, and luxuriate in these kinds of images, that I personally found seductive.

I think some readers don't want to be stopped in their tracks—they want to be carried along by the language to whatever destination it wants to take them. But because my book was deeply concerned with how you can't get away from the past, I wanted that reflected in the way you couldn't get away from beautiful or dramatic images, either. The way that Lobo Antunes was able to extract these incredible pictures was something I wanted to emulate—something I feel I actually failed at, in writing the book. I couldn't do what he did. Still, it served as a high marker for me to aim at.

When I say I'm attracted to this passage because of its rhythm and its images, there's still a logic to these things that is separate from the more rational process of saying, *I need to construct my story or my characters in such and such a fashion.* The language itself had some kind of impact on me that was more emotional than intellectual. The book acted as a condensed, compact, extremely powerful substance that woke me up to what I needed to do, each day, as a writer. I thought of it as espresso. It wasn't coffee—I couldn't drink it all day long. I could only take small doses, and that was enough. With caffeine, how do you quantify what's happening with that? You just know you need it. The process was mysterious, and it worked.

One day, a line came to me after reading *The Land at the End of the World*:

I am a spy, a sleeper, a spook, a man of two faces.

It just came to me. And I thought, that's it. All I have to do is follow this voice for the rest of the novel, however long it takes.

Immediately, that day, I wrote to one of my friends who was going to read the manuscript and said: *I found the opening line to the novel!* That was true. It enabled me to start writing without hesitation, after that.

One of the challenges of the novel's prose was: I created a character who is going to be a spy, and a double agent, and was inevitably going to do bad things. I knew in advance what some of those things were, although not all of them. My protagonist does kill people and betray people. These are not things I've done—things the majority of people haven't done—and yet you have to get readers to follow this person, for a very long time. So I felt that the whole book would be dependent on the seductiveness of our narrator's voice and character.

One of the reasons why I paid so much attention to the narrator's voice was that he needed an ability to persuade or seduce simply through the way he spoke. I needed him to be able to draw the reader in, and accept that they were going to follow him, regardless of his actions—which might be objectionable in many different ways. His seductiveness—if that's what it is for some readers—is partly due to his beliefs, his politics, his character, but also a lot to do with how he uses the language.

Another part of the seduction was an effect I wanted: a sense of high dramatic and emotional stakes from the very first page. In an interview, Tim O'Brien said his fiction always begins with a big moral question he wants to answer. It also happens in *Invisible Man*: We're told first paragraph, the first page, what the major theme of the book is going to be. This is a tricky thing to do—you don't want your fiction to come off as didactic, or polemical, right from the very beginning. And yet I wanted my novel's first paragraph to announce to the reader that this is a narrator who is very intent on meditating on certain important issues. It was difficult to know how to do that in a way that was dramatically interesting as well.

The question he arrives at, I think on the second page, is: *What is to be done?* That was always a question I encountered in college reading Lenin and other Marxist variants, and it's something I was never able to adequately answer—it was the question I wanted to wrestle with through the writing of the novel. The book itself, writing the story about this person, and what he encounters, and what he does, was a way of forcing myself to answer that question.

At the same time there's a big, existential, political/moral question, I also wanted to present the reader with a difficult problem of plot: put a character in a situation he can't get out of, and watch what he does. I wanted the book to be entertaining, given its literary constraints, despite the very serious questions and issues the narrator confronts.

Through it all, I had *The Land at the End of the World*. There's something very mysterious about my attraction to the book—and that is one of the powerful things about writing. As someone who's a scholar, I try to rationalize and think about why I make certain kinds of artistic choices. But there's also the part that's intuitive and emotional. Whatever happened with this book, it was a decades-long process of osmosis: the product of reading hundreds and hundreds of books and authors, absorbing all their styles on conscious and unconscious levels. Some of them mean more to me than others. There was a short shelf of books that I kept near me of writers whose styles and stories I felt I wanted to try to emulate or take something away from. Then I came across this book—somehow, it seemed to be the work that spoke most intimately to how I saw myself as a writer, and how I saw my narrator as a character. It seemed to be the culmination of all these years of influence and inspiration.

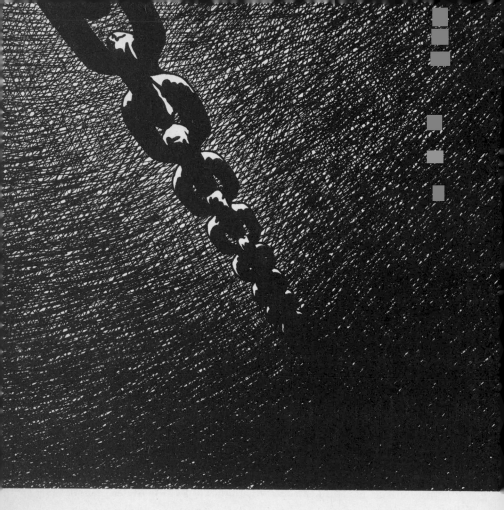

Rowing in Eden—
Ah, the Sea!
Might I but moor—Tonight—
In thee!
                    —EMILY DICKINSON,
      "Wild Nights—Wild Nights!"

EMMA DONOGHUE

You and Me

My mother was a teacher of English, and is a book lover, and she used to quote Emily Dickinson to me. I think she remembered Dickinson because the poems were short, easier to recall than something with big wodges of text. The first one I can remember was "I heard a Fly buzz—when I died—" but there were others. I was even meant to be called Emily, at first, before I was born. That's what my father wanted—he was working on a book on Dickinson that year. But my mother held out for Emma, even though she was a huge fan of Dickinson the poet.

I think we should have gone with Emily, personally—I'd have preferred that. But what can you do? Emily Dickinson was not exactly known for her personal happiness and fulfillment. Maybe my mother thought it would be like naming me Sylvia, after Sylvia Plath.

One of the poems she used to recite to me, "Wild Nights—Wild Nights!," became very important to me in my teens. I probably sought it out again once I knew that I was in love with a girl myself at fourteen—because there I was, in 1980s Ireland, realizing that I was a lesbian and couldn't tell a soul. It was as if there was nobody around in Irish culture at the time who I could see myself in. So I used Emily Dickinson. On the basis of her poems and letters, it seemed like she had strong passions for women in her life as well as for men. I remember thinking, "Well, I may be a freak in my social context, but I can be like Emily Dickinson. Who needs to be normal?"

Most of the writing I did at the time were lyrics addressed to a "you" beloved, the way this poem is. They weren't all love poems, but when they were it was always "I" addressed to "you": It frees you from the necessity to specify the gender of the person you're speaking to, so it's a closeted lesbian's best friend, this pronoun. The lack of specificity makes it a really attractive form, and the intimacy of the "you" helps draw the reader in directly. (That's one reason the "you" form is used all the time in pop songs.) It allows readers to imagine someone speaking to her beloved, but to use their own imagination about who the beloved might be.

The poem begins like this:

Wild Nights—Wild Nights!
Were I with thee
Wild Nights should be
Our luxury!

I find the whole poem to be viscerally expressive of romantic and erotic love. What comes across most is this sense of overwhelming yearning. It's actually quite a demanding overture: She's saying she wants to "moor in" somebody, a very physical and intimate image.

At the same time, you don't know who she's addressing—it's very unspecific, and not just in terms of gender. It's hard to determine the relationship between the narrator and the object of affection. Is the speaker someone who has experienced a cozy life with the beloved, and has been sadly parted from that person? Or is the narrator pining for an acquaintance from afar? "Were I with thee"—that could even be a stalker talking. It's very ambiguous.

What makes it all work is the slight edge of hysteria we sense in the speaker. One minute you're thinking, oh, she's a wonderful, romantic hero- ine; the next minute you're wondering whether she's a stalker. The slightly unhinged feel to her adds to the reader's thrill. She appears to be offering images of safety and comfort and home, but there's this crazy edge.

One thing I loved about Emily Dickinson is that there are always vivid images to grab hold of, even if you're not quite sure what each one means. There are so few words and yet you could spend hours discussing each one because she doesn't put much down, making room for a huge amount of rich ambiguity. At first glance you see those lovely concrete images—the winds of the port, and the compass, and the chart—and you think you know what this poem means. But it's not a poem saying, "Oh, lovely to be at home with you." When you start to tease it out, you're thinking, hang on a minute. You think you're moored, then the next thing you're sailing again, and then you're rowing instead of sailing. The images don't quite fit each other easily, and she seems to go back and forward between those seas and the harbor. How are we rowing in Eden—which is usually thought of as an earthly, agricultural paradise—and are we moored or not? There isn't a clear progression from the seas to the harbor. She's got a lovely hidden complexity.

I love concrete images and I have no brain for philosophy at all. I hang out with a lot of academics because my partner's an academic and my dad is one, but when they start discussing Derrida or something, my brain just seems to get woozy and I'm always needing to say to them, "Oh, is that a bit like . . . a banana?" I seem to think best in concrete images.

We all want to put big ideas into our books, right? But when you're writing a book, you're exploring the subject so deeply that, of course, you end up with your head full of big theories about what's going on. You don't want to just cut all that out, but nor do you want to weigh down the book by putting in a conversation in which people discuss things in very abstract or stodgy terms.

One example would be in my novel *The Wonder*, when I was trying to have the protagonist finally realize that her people, the English, had to bear some responsibility for the Irish Famine. But I didn't want that just to be presented as a political argument. So I have her walking along a road in the country and then she eventually learns that this particular road was built as a workfare exercise by the starving and that as they died along the way they were buried just under the surface of the road. The scene begins in a pleasant way, everything green and pastoral— and then we watch as she begins realizing that the bumps of the grass under her feet are not clods of soil, but skulls.

This approach makes her feel something in a visceral way, not just in an informational kind of way. I could have gotten the same idea across in a conversation about theology or politics or who's responsible for the Irish Famine, but if you give the reader a vivid and concrete image, that will hook their attention, making it easier for them to understand and remember the details longer.

For me, the writing is about the basic thrill of making something out of words that never existed before. That hasn't changed since I was a child. I really love writing, I'm not one of these writers for whom it's a crippling task. Not that I always write beautifully, but I just love that business of dreaming up new things that never existed before and then endlessly fiddling with the words to get them right.

I used to love the idea of your poems being discovered after your death. As a child I remember thinking that *The Diary of Anne Frank* was a pure text because it was written in the moment without any concern for publication. The same with Dickinson—as a child I loved the fact that she tried to publish one or two poems, and got rebuffed, and then just put them away. She was unpublished until after her death, and I found this deeply romantic. That was what I wanted. I sort of assumed that the way to be published is, you hoarded up your best poems, and then you died and somebody found them. It was quite a weird model I had for the writing life.

But something about that idea has stayed with me, nonetheless. Dickinson was a crucial role model to me as far as: Just follow your own passions, write your own poems. Don't even care if they get published or not. Write them for the bliss of writing them.

Who is Emily Dickinson talking to in "Wild Nights"? A stranger? A lover? A friend? Nineteenth-century women friends quite often addressed each other in these terms, so they didn't draw that neat line between friendship and lover relationships the way we do. But there are so many other possibilities. Even her poems to death are somehow passionate and intimate, and her poems to God have the same sense of overwhelming yearning. The poem's main image—of the long, difficult voyage and then coming into port—is more traditionally recognized as being about going to heaven than about losing your lover. She was a bit of a mad mystic, so her idea of going to heaven probably did include some wild storms.

Of course, in some ways it shouldn't matter what a writer's life was like, or whom she was writing to—the poem should work on its own. But there can be a wonderful tension between the life and the poems, especially in poems as enigmatic as Emily Dickinson's are. I have her collected poems and if I had to bring a book to a desert island that would be one of the few books I'd bring—even though, in some of them, I haven't a clue what's going on. They can be really, really strange in a way I love. She sounds like nobody else.

These fragments I have shored against my ruins.
—T. S. Eliot, "What the Thunder Said"

CLAIRE MESSUD

Words on Paper
Will Outlast Us

FOR ME, IT was a formative experience reading Eliot when I was younger. *The Waste Land*, in particular. I don't know if schools still assign it so frequently as they once did, but many people my age read "What the Thunder Said" early on, probably first even in junior high school, and again in high school, and again in college. Looking again at the poem now—which I haven't for years—one of the things that strikes me is how much has stuck, even though I have the memory of a sieve. I wouldn't say I know it by heart, but reading it is like reading learned lines from the play you were in last year.

There's one line in particular I have carried around with me for years. It's near the end of the poem:

These fragments I have shored against my ruins.

When I ask myself "What is it all for?" I think of this line.

With death, everything goes. All of it. In our brains are recorded every second of our lives, whether we're able to retrieve them or not—of course, we can't retrieve most of it. But every thought we have had, every smell we have smelled, every change in the light, every embrace, everything is there. When we die, these moments can never be retrieved. They are gone. Forever.

The large portion of human experience will vanish. I remember my grandfather, when he was quite old and in his nineties—he lived to be ninety-four—sitting in the window of his apartment. He was French, and he lived in an apartment overlooking the Mediterranean in the south of France. I remember him staring out the window at the vast open sea. I was in my early thirties, and I assumed, "Oh, he's thinking about my grandmother. Or he's thinking about death." But when I said, "*Grand-père*, what are you thinking about?" he said, "I'm recalling my visit to an oil well in the Sahara in 1954."

I hadn't known he'd been to an oil well in the Sahara. It's just proof that we live so many lives, contain so much experience, that even the people who know us best don't know. When someone dies, all that goes. All of it.

Things we write down are the fragments shored against our ruins. They outlast us, these scraps of words on paper. Like the detritus from the tsunami washing up on the other side of the ocean, writing is what can be salvaged. Of course, there are other ways to make your mark. If you're rich, you can leave a library, a building, or a hospital wing. But writing leaves behind a visceral sense of what it was like to be alive on the planet in a particular time. Writing tells us what it meant for someone to be human.

Every art form is a version of this. A painting lets us know how somebody literally saw things. A piece of music is another language that transmits a whole wealth of emotion and wordless experience. But writing is special in the way it allows us to temporarily enter another person's world, to step outside the boundaries of our own time and space. I teach at the MFA program at Hunter College, and earlier in the term we read Tolstoy's *Childhood*. You read *Childhood* and you know exactly what it was like to be an aristocratic child on a rural estate in 1840s Russia. You don't know it in an intellectual way—you know it in an absolutely visceral way. In a way that no painting could ever give you, no piece of music could ever give you. You are there. You're in that room. You're with those kids. This is a power specific to literature—the power to acquaint us intimately with a world that no longer exists on earth.

And yet we have so little. Only fragments survive. We know about Tolstoy's childhood because he wrote about it—but so much of his experience, his surroundings, his epoch have vanished for good. And he is just one person among the millions who shared his moment on earth, some of whom we know about, countless more we don't. We cannot know what isn't written down. To salvage only what is in books is to retain an infinitesimal portion of what was.

It reduces still: Though there are as many books as shells upon a shore, in a lifetime you can only pick up so many.

And still: Even of what you *do* read, you only recall so much—a feeling, a thought, an image, or even a single line like the one we're talking about now. In one beautiful long rant, the narrator of Thomas Bernhard's *The Loser* laments how great philosophers become grotesque, shriveled versions of themselves on our bookshelves: All of Kant, he says, reduced to a single shrunken head!

Even our daily lives reduce this way as we live them. We know so little about even the people we know and love best. We know their gestures and their habits and their responses—I know what my kids will order in a restaurant, and I know what they look like asleep, and I know what they like to read—and yet so much of their lives is unknown to me. And as they grow older, of course, they will become only ever more so. There will come a time when I know only the tiniest things.

And so much of what we *do* experience vanishes without a trace from our memory. Even under "normal" circumstances, we forget so much, but our ability to remember can change rapidly. Toward the end of her life, my mother lost her memory fairly quickly. I remember one day I said to her, "Mom, what are you thinking about?" And, for a moment, she really did become sort of like the Delphic Oracle. She turned to me, and with this sort of lovely smile she said: "Shards of memory, and new worlds discovered."

Just because we lose so much does not make the small fragments we *do* preserve less valuable—quite the opposite. Storytelling is a human impulse, and making meaning is a human impulse. We want to make sense of things, and we will always try to tell the fuller story from the fragments that we've got. If you think of something like Pompeii, with so much destroyed and so much never found, we still create the story based on the pieces that we have. Look at that Malaysia Airlines flight. We want to make sense of it. We want to know what happened. There is always a world to discover within the shards we have.

In the absence of much—we'll take little. And that's what fiction is, too—distilling your whole life into the shards you'll leave behind. This principle of reduction—of shoring fragments against an encroaching ruin—is a useful metaphor for the writing process. Every time you're trying to squeeze some experience down into words, you're reducing it, and you're losing something—even if you're able to make something beautiful of it, you're losing something, too.

I'm aware that I don't have an infinite amount of time. I will get to write a few books in my life. I will only be able to address so much of what I've seen and what I know. And so I have to try to choose wisely. So it's like the moment when you're walking along the seashore: You want to pick up all the shells, they are so beautiful, but you can only carry so many. I get a few. And each shell might be the last one you get.

But as you do write, something strange and wonderful happens. I often feel that there is something that cannot be articulated about what we do when we write fiction—but I know that it is magic. When I'm working on something and it's going well, I am so far in that world that I look up and I think, "Where am I again?" You achieve a real distance from your life and enter a different place—and that world has a reality, those characters have a reality, even if they've never exactly existed. When I write I am condensing the broad scope of my experience into something narrower but longer-lasting, reducing myself into something that does not contain *all* of me but will outlast me. If we are very lucky, those fragments will add to the broader conversation of what it means to be human.

As a writer, how do you choose which fragments to shore? In a first-draft situation for me, it's a visceral rather than an intellectual process. Though I'll generally have a vague outline in mind, I'll feel it through rather than take a preplanned course. I don't think, "Okay, I need a scene to do X." And while trying to be as efficient as you can, you generate a great bulk of material. In revision, you begin a kind of creative destruction. If you've written three scenes and each of them does a different thing—explores a different facet of a character, or shows her in relation to different people, or whatever it is—well, if you could have one scene that would do everything at once that those three scenes are doing, then that would be better. To have a more efficient and more intense fragment is going to be better. So you compress, the same way that to make something very tasty you might reduce a sauce.

You hope that as you boil down what you have seen and known into your writing, you reduce the best of yourself, too.

Of course, almost none of this will last in the long term. I heard a frightening program on the radio where a scientist was asked: What's going to happen in the long term? In a millennium, say, down the line, what will survive of our world? And his answer: Concrete. Maybe some glass. Well, what about paper? It will be carbonized, any book will be a black oblong object, the contents will be lost forever. All that literature and art and music, that's going to be gone. Of course, what we have from Pompeii is pots and pans—frescoes, too—the hard goods. All the softer stuff is gone.

But for as long as they do last, books give us something else: Literature reminds us that we're not alone on this planet. You're not alone in this time. You're not alone in this experience. And not only are you not alone in your city, your nation, your moment—you're not alone in *history*. Sappho felt the way you feel. Or Shakespeare, or John Donne. We have this connection. And we are able to have a kind of conversation. The fragments we shore against our ruin—everything that we have read, whatever little fragments we retain—are part of our understanding of the world, the way we see the world, and our conversation that we have with ourselves and with the world.

It's almost the last line of "What the Thunder Said": You see, the poem presents fragments from many voices—Kyd and the Vedic texts. All these allusions are part of the human conversation. And Eliot now is one of those allusions, too. He's referring to the fact that we live with these fragments, that they chatter in our heads long after their authors no longer exist. That's why I've quoted Eliot's line in all my books, in one form or another. It's a reminder that literature is a conversation, and it continues.

Up came the sun, streaming all over London, and in its glorious impartiality even condescending to make prismatic sparkles in the whiskers of Mr. Alfred Lammle as he sat at breakfast.

—CHARLES DICKENS, *Our Mutual Friend*

JANE SMILEY

Nobody Asked You
to Write That Novel

I READ OLIVER TWIST in seventh grade, and *Great Expectations* in eighth, and I hated them both.

So when I was assigned *David Copperfield* in ninth grade, I put it off for as long as I could. Finally, of course, a deadline forced me to get started. I went down to the basement and read the entire thing in one weekend. And it caught me off guard—I adored it. This was where my love of Dickens started.

When I got to college, I didn't read any Dickens. I was an English major, but I focused mostly on medieval stuff. I don't know why I picked up *Our Mutual Friend* during my senior year, over Christmas vacation. But I remember how I sat out by the Christmas tree, just reading and reading, completely absorbed by it.

Of all of the Dickens I've read, including everything I studied for the biography I wrote, *Our Mutual Friend* remains my favorite. There are so many interesting things about the book. First of all, it has one of the greatest portraits of a stalker you could ever imagine. And he plays with the novel's conventions in fascinating ways. The standard romance ends with the happily married couple, for instance—but here Dickens moves beyond the wedding into the marriage itself, exploring how a successful love story works itself out with time. By this stage of his career, Dickens was old and successful, and he knew he could do whatever he wanted. You can see him playing with established elements of the genre, subverting them, and it's part of this novel's greatness to me.

But there was a more immediate, straightforward connection—I simply loved his descriptions. Though I had read lots of books before *Our Mutual Friend*, this was the one that made me think: I've got to do this. I've got to try to write novels. It's just too interesting to pass up—I can't go on and be a lawyer now. (Not that I ever wanted to be a lawyer, but I might have gone on to be a vet or something.) After *Our Mutual Friend*, other careers were no longer an option. I had to try this novel-writing thing, because the images Dickens uses are so great and riveting.

Dickens's descriptive powers are on display throughout *Our Mutual Friend*, but one of my favorite examples concerns the bad guys. Not the really bad guys, but the sort-of-bad guys—Mr. and Mrs. Lammle, two small-time swindlers who marry each other for money. On their honeymoon, they each find out the other person has pretended to be wealthy, so they're forced to go on swindling other people together.

Mr. Lammle is sort of a villain, but he's enjoyably villainous. In the last section of the novel, Dickens describes him in a way I love:

> Up came the sun, streaming all over London, and in its glorious impartiality even condescending to make prismatic sparkles in the whiskers of Mr. Alfred Lammle as he sat at breakfast.

I've always remembered the image of Lammle's beard sparkling in the sunlight. I can see the little breakfast nook. I can see him sitting at the table. I can see his beard, and I can see the sunlight sparkling in his beard. We already know by this time that Lammle is extremely mercenary, so Dickens is highlighting the impartiality of the sunlight—the way it can beautify anything, good or bad. We know Lammle's a scammer, but there's still this beautiful moment anyway. And there's a kind of magical foreshadowing at work, too: The way the sun shines down, making his beard sparkle, signals that something unusual is coming, some unusual plot twist—as indeed it does come.

As a reader, and as a writer, I love images and sentences that are so striking that you remember and cherish them. Because they're embedded in a huge amount of language, such standout lines and descriptions must truly be extraordinary. *Our Mutual Friend* is probably a 200,000-word novel; there are probably 10,000 sentences. Yet as the reader goes along reading this abundance of sentences, from time to time one grabs and holds on. To me, that's the essence of the novel: the tension between wanting to linger in appreciation of an individual line, and wanting to see what happens next. You must move on, if you're ever going to finish the book—especially one as long as *Our Mutual Friend*—and yet certain details capture you, slow you, ask you to pause. It's because of this experience that I love novels most among the art forms. When you're reading a poem, you're asked to linger. If a poem is 100 words long, you're asked to pay attention to each word. But when you're reading a novel, you're asked to keep moving—yet you resist this forward motion when certain lines demand your attention.

The moments are what come to mind when I think about the books I like best—moments that stick in my mind as pictures. When you're deep into reading a book that you're very fond of, the images pass through your mind and leave a permanent impression. I don't tend to remember the ideas as strongly. For me, a novel's conceptual framework generally takes a backseat to the images that tell the story. Ultimately, these images are more important and enduring than what the writer believes.

There are novelists I love who have advanced their theories about how the world works, how life works, and so on. Some of these theories have been very detailed—one of my favorite examples is Émile Zola. But though the theories may motivate the novel, and they may help structure the novel, they fall by the wayside almost always. The enduring things are the story, the characters, the scenes.

The reader has to have images in order to feel oriented in the world of the novel. We must be able to see our way around. Your images may not be the same as my images—different readers will perceive a novel's world differently, depending on what they notice and respond to in the descriptions—but the visual details are our entry into the story.

It's fascinating that readers can have images of places he or she has never seen. Recently, I met someone who grew up in Russia. One of her favorite books had been *Huckleberry Finn*, while one of my favorite books was Dostoyevsky's novel *Crime and Punishment*. There's a scene in *Crime and Punishment* where a horse and carriage are going down the road, and the driver whips the horse so badly that it falls to its knees in the street and dies. I remember being fifteen and reading that, and imagining that I could see all St. Petersburg, and within it that horse dying in the middle of the street. Simultaneously there was somebody in Russia imagining Huckleberry Finn going down an American river she had never seen. I believed in my images, and she believed hers. These mental images—created in collaboration with the author—are what give one's love of a story a base.

Dickens was extremely observant. People who knew him or met him were sometimes taken aback by how he seemed to be scanning them. He was observant not just visually, but aurally—he was a practiced eavesdropper. Many moments that the rest of us might pass over, he would note, and they would filter into his work.

I think he created his images both consciously and unconsciously, as all novelists do. By the time writers are old and practiced like Dickens was, the choice of imagistic details is not really a conscious thing. As you sit there, starting a new chapter, your mind goes hmmm—and then, bingo. It's on the page. It's not like you've sorted through every image in your brain and picked the best one. It's more that you knew what the theme of the chapter was going to be, and this thought or image cropped up as one way in. It gave you energy, and off you went.

Often the story details we choose have an unconscious, unintended power. For example, in *Our Mutual Friend*, the stalker is a young man who's a teacher; born poor, uneasy about his social mobility. During the day, he attempts to do a good job with his teaching—but during the night, he stalks the gentleman Eugene Wrayburn. It's this social uneasiness that makes him more and more aggressive as he stalks his aristocratic target. I don't think we can read *Our Mutual Friend* without seeing this stalker as a kind of weird self-portrait of Dickens and his social rise. But it's very possible Dickens didn't intend this at all. Maybe he just drew upon his own life—his experiences as a kind of social weirdo in the class system of England—in order to portray a stalker's obsessiveness.

This unconscious power is often tapped through the act of description, and unexpected story revelations can spring out of the physical details of a scene. The images themselves, in other words, can contain clues about where the story needs to go. When I was first starting my novel *Moo*, for instance, I was describing some abandoned buildings that my character Chairman X was looking at. Suddenly, he saw a young man going inside, though he didn't know why anyone would enter an abandoned building. Well, I didn't know why either! But this man went in, even though I had never thought about those buildings or that man before. Suddenly, I had to find out what was inside. As it turned out, the giant pig Earl Butz—the hog at the center of the finished novel—was inside. Earl Butz hadn't been part of the plan before that point. But as the book progressed, the secret I discovered in those buildings became essential to the novel.

As a writer, that kind of experience is what I always want: the energy that comes from sudden inspiration. That's what inspiration is to me—the idea that gives unexpected energy to the narrative. Work that is too planned out often doesn't have that kind of energy.

That's why you cannot be judging yourself as you write the first draft—you want to harness that unexpected energy, and you don't want to limit the possibilities of exploration. You don't know what you're writing until it's done. So if a draft is 500 pages long, you have to suspend judgment for months. It takes effort to be good at suspending judgment, to give the images and story priority over your ideas. But you keep going, casting about for the next sentence. I think there are two kinds of sentences in a rough draft: seeds and pebbles. If it's a pebble, it's just the next sentence and it sits there. But if it's a seed it grows into something that becomes an important part of the life of the novel. The problem is, you can't know ahead of time whether a sentence will be a seed or a pebble, or how important a seed it's going to be. That bit of *Moo* turned out to be an important seed. But if Chairman X had turned away and had another thought—had I stuck with my plan and insisted the man entering the buildings was just a pebble—the book might have gone in a different direction.

This is why it's important to remain open to the unexpected. The writing experience is in some ways like riding a bucking bronco— sometimes he's good, and sometimes he bucks you off, sometimes he follows orders, sometimes he spooks. I like that unexpected quality. You have to be able to keep riding whatever comes.

Of course, I don't want to suggest one's ideas and beliefs have no place in the novel. They're important. One's ideas can inspire the story. The writing process is an interplay between the ideas you begin with and the story that emerges despite what you think. The story and the ideas talk back and forth to one another. As I write, my ideas about the book may inform how the characters think, how the story works itself out, what happens. But at a certain point, the characters start to take on their own life—and they begin to transcend the ideas that initially inspired them.

For example: In Volume Three of the trilogy I'm completing, there's a good guy and a bad guy. I thought of them as "good" and "bad." But when I went back for the latest rewrite, I was surprised by how appealing the bad guy was. The idea part of me thought, "Well, maybe I need to make him more of a scumbag." But the novelist part of me said, "No. Ambiguity is always good."

So you learn to expect the unexpected, and make allowances for it. There's a constant back-and-forth between what you planned and what you didn't plan, and how you are going to reconcile the two. I guess that's what drafts are for—negotiating how much plan to preserve, how much newness to let in.

I think all novel writing, and all art, is a form of play—and it's the unexpected that gives it the playful aspect, while ideas give it the serious aspect. When the unexpected crops up, that's like playing a game where your body has to catch the ball you didn't even realize a moment ago was heading in your direction. So, I like this aspect of play, I think it's wonderful—and makes it all worth doing.

When I was a student at the Iowa Writers' Workshop, I remember opening the door to my friend's office and looking inside. Over her desk, above her typewriter, she'd tacked up a phrase: NOBODY ASKED YOU TO WRITE THAT NOVEL. I knew right away this was going to be an important idea for me. The line reminded me that writing was a voluntary activity. I could always stop. I could always go on. And since no one's asking you to do it, I've always seen writing as an exercise of freedom, rather than an exercise of obligation. Even when it came to be that writing was my income, it still seemed like an exercise of freedom. Yes, writing is my job—but I could always stop and do something else. Once writing becomes an exercise of freedom, it's filled with energy.

I remember when I proposed *A Thousand Acres* to my agent, she said, "Are you kidding me? No one wants to read a novel about farming." But no one was going to stop me. "We'll see," I said, and I just wrote it. That's been the case with all my books, successful or not successful. I wrote the books I wanted to write. I know I've been lucky to be able to write this way.

To me as a reader, the greatest thing about the novel—I start sentences this way all the time, but I always say a different thing—is that it gives access to the mind of the writer. *Our Mutual Friend* is a perfect example of this: You have access to the mind of this guy, Charles Dickens. Prolonged access, 880 pages of access. There is no intermediary between you and this guy's mind. There are no actors, there's no stage production. To read a book is an act of humanity. It's an act of connection. And it's also an act of freedom—at any point, I could say, I'm done with *Our Mutual Friend*, I'm moving on to Anthony Trollope. As long as you're reading, you're there voluntarily. To me, that's the essence of the novel: accessing the mind of another human being in a way that combines freedom with intimacy. This is a rare thing. You don't get it through an interview, you don't get that through relationships—other people can always withhold information from you. You don't get this kind of access in any other art—poetry, maybe, but the contact isn't as prolonged. I find it perennially alluring. I've been at this for years and years, and yet this voluntary act of connection still fascinates me in my reading and my writing.

Something that never before existed must have entered the
world. An infernal machine of humanity.

—KARL KRAUS, "Nestroy and Posterity"

JONATHAN FRANZEN

My Favorite
Curmudgeon

By weird curricular accident, I found myself a German major in college. I ended up spending two years in Germany—one in Munich and a second in Berlin on a Fulbright. In the years after that I was very isolated, and one of my main contacts with the world was reading newspapers. I needed them, but I also hated them. I was trying to be a rigorous writer, trying to be a novelist, and the clichés and problematic language even in a good paper like the *New York Times* really upset me. I didn't think the press was paying enough attention to the issues I was passionate about—the environment, nuclear weapons, consumerism— and for a while I felt they were giving Ronald Reagan a free pass. It seemed like everything was wrong with the world and no one could see it except me. Me and Karl Kraus.

I'd encountered Kraus's work in college and then again in Berlin. Here was this guy who was absolutely morally certain, and his critique of Vienna's bourgeois press was incredibly rigorous, angry, and funny. He particularly attacked a corrupt coupling of two things: that a small number of media magnates were getting extremely rich, and that the newspapers they owned kept reassuring their readers that society was becoming ever more democratic and advanced. More empowered, more enlightened, more communal. And it drove Kraus crazy, because he saw these naked profit-making enterprises masquerading as great equalizers—and *succeeding*, because people were addicted to them.

Kraus was so smart and funny and fanatical that he developed a big cult-like following in Vienna, with thousands of people coming to his readings. And seventy years later I became kind of a virtual cult follower of his. His sentences were hard, but they really popped. There's nothing like moral certainty to give an angry edge to the prose, and I fell for it, because I was looking for that kind of angry, funny edge in my own writing, and because I felt so alone with my anger at the press. I was also attracted to Kraus's conviction that we were heading toward an apocalypse. For me, at the time, that meant nuclear apocalypse, because we were still very much in the saber-rattling late stages of the Cold War. As long as I remained convinced that I was right and the world was wrong—basically, throughout my twenties—I was really under his spell.

Then I entered a dark wood in my thirties, and everything that had seemed black and white to me began to seem gray. When newspapers stopped seeming like the cultural enemy, and became embattled as the Internet came along and journalists started losing their jobs, I realized, You know, these are actually hardworking people doing their best to cover news responsibly. They're not pretending to be something they're not. It's wrongheaded to fault them for their linguistic crimes. At the same time, my parents were dying, I was going through a divorce, and you really can't go through those things—if you're honest—and come out convinced that you're right and everyone else is wrong. It was demonstrated to me quite plainly in my mid-thirties that things that I had been absolutely certain of in my personal life, I'd actually been quite wrong about. And once you're wrong about one thing, the possibility is open that you might be wrong about everything.

So I lost interest in Kraus, though I'd been translating him for presumable future publication. I gave up that project and didn't go back to it until a couple of years ago, when I met some people who were Kraus fans. They encouraged me to go back to him, and when I went back I realized that he was more right about our technological and media moment than he was about newspapers in the '80s. That a lot of what he's saying seemed unbelievably prescient. You could apply his critique almost directly to the blogification of the newspaper, to the rise of social media—he really saw all of this coming 100 years ago. Even though I'd outgrown his fiery brand of moral certitude, I decided to return to my translations and try to make his writing as accessible as possible to an English-reading audience.

One of the lines from Kraus that matters the most to me is "Ein Teufelswerk der Humanität," *an infernal machine of humanity.* In the mid-'90s, when I started to feel worried about what was happening to literature with the introduction of the third screen, and with the increasingly materialistic view of human nature that psychopharmacology was producing, I was looking for some way to describe how technology and consumerism feed on each other and take over our lives. How seductive and invasive but also unsatisfying they are. How we go back to them more and more, *because* they're unsatisfying, and become ever more dependent on them. The groupthink of the Internet and the constant electronic stimulation of the devices start to erode the very notion of an individual who is capable of, say, producing a novel. The phrase I reached for to describe all this was "an infernal machine." Something definitionally consumerist, something totalitarian in its exclusion of other ways of being, something that appears in the world and manufactures our desires through its own developmental logic, something that does damage but just seems to keep perpetuating itself. The sentence that summed this up for me owed a lot to Kraus's writing: "Techno-consumerism is an infernal machine."

It's interesting that in the '90s, a number of different writers and thinkers were all becoming alarmed about these things. You can see *Infinite Jest* as a giant book in response to the problem of techno-consumerism—with the cartridge film that, once you start watching, you can never stop looking at. Already, in the '90s, it seemed like machines were beginning to command us with their logic, rather than serving us. Whether we like it or not, Moore's law says that computers are going to be twice as powerful and compact two and a half years from now as they are today. Obviously, twenty years later we're reaching the limits of Moore's law, but at the time it was in absolutely full swing. Applications were developed, and then people had to throw their old machine away because a whole new set of machines and apps had come along. And without our ever giving our active consent, this just became the way we lived. Became the way *I* lived, despite the strong misgivings I felt.

And then there's the second part of Kraus's phrase, "der Humanität"—"of humanity." I didn't pay much attention to it in the '90s, but going back and reworking the translations and starting to think harder about what Kraus was actually saying, I was struck by the strange word "Humanität." He had a different word available to him, "Menschlichkeit," which he didn't use. He was working in a vein similar to Walter Benjamin in "The Work of Art in the Age of Mechanical Reproduction." Benjamin saw that mechanical reproduction and increasing technologization of life could bring real social benefits, but that it would come at the cost of a flattening of life. What I find particularly troubling about our own technological moment is that I hear people saying again and again—happily and proudly and excitedly—that computers are changing our notion of what it means to be a human being. The implication of all those excited people is that we're changing for the better. Whereas, when I look at social media, it seems like a world that once had adults in it is being changed into the eighth-grade junior-high cafeteria. When I look at Facebook, I see a video-poker room in Vegas.

To me, taken as a whole, Kraus's line suggests that the infernal logic of techno-consumerism, which has absolutely nothing to do with being a human being, has been coupled to this rhetoric of freedom and human rights and human self-realization. And there's something that should not be taken for granted in that coupling—because, again, who's profiting from it, and who's being pauperized? Kraus was a bit of a conspiracy theorist. His notion was that it's no accident that these absolutely profit-mad profiteering plutocrats are speaking the language of humanity. At the time, of course, that was on the editorial page, but now it's steeped in the very culture of Silicon Valley: "We're making the world a better place." Or Twitter, for instance, trying to take direct credit for Arab Spring. The grotesque thing for Kraus was not just that the machine was infernal and had its own logic, but that it could only operate with this big lie at its center.

It connects with Kraus's other line: "We were smart enough to build the machines, but not smart enough to make them serve us." And boy, does that ring true. When you look at the actual content of our interaction with computers—plenty of good stuff, but a whole lot of hours spent looking at other people's photos of their stupid parties on a Facebook page. I really don't mean to say it's all bad. I held out until 1996 against email, but now it's part of the way I live and I actually appreciate it—I prefer it to phone calls. I don't have a complete hard line on this. What I object to is the idea that just because we *can* do something, we automatically will do it. Now everyone is armed with a camera 24/7. Is that a good thing? A bad thing? There's not really any discussion of that. This potential exists, and so it will be exploited. It will be marketed, it will be sold, and we will buy it. That's the infernal machine.

Kraus was very suspicious of the notion of progress, the idea that things are just getting better and better. In 1912, when he was writing the essays that are in my book, people were very optimistic about what science was going to do for the world. Everyone was becoming enlightened in a straightforward scientific sense, politics was liberalizing, and the world was going to be a much, much better place—the story went. Well, two years later the most horrible war in the history of humankind broke out, and was followed by an even worse war twenty-five years after that. Kraus was right about something: He was right to distrust the people who were telling us that technology was going to serve humanity and make things better and better. In the context of the crazy techno-utopianism and crazy techno-boosterism we're now living through, it seems worth taking a look at a writer who was there at the birth of modern media and tech, being suspicious of the language of the people who were talking about how everything is getting better. I'm not convinced that I'm right about the things that I distrust in the new techno-media world. But I'm also not convinced I'm wrong, and so I'm disturbed by a rhetoric that aggressively dismisses people who are raising what seem to me quite reasonable objections—I see these dismissals a lot.

Are we getting better, thanks to the Internet? My position is this: The Internet is fabulous for a lot of things. It's a fabulous research tool. It's great for buying stuff, it's great for bringing together people to work on communal things, like software, or people who share a passion or are all suffering from the same disease and want to find each other and communicate. It's wonderful for that. But the Internet in general—and social media in particular—fosters this notion that *everything* should be shared, everything is communal. When it works, it's great. But it specifically doesn't work, I think, in the realm of cultural production—and particularly literary production. Good novels aren't written by committee. Good novels aren't collaborated on. Good novels are produced by people who voluntarily isolate themselves, and go deep, and report from the depths on what they find. They do put what they find in a form that's communally accessible, communally shareable, but not at the production end. What makes a good novel, apart from the skill of the writer, is how true it is to the individual subjectivity. People talk about "finding your voice": Well, that's what it is. You're finding your own individual voice, not a group voice.

Where Kraus spoke of an imaginative space, or implied that there was an imaginative space, he used the word *Geist*—the good old German word "spirit." He found technological progress antithetical to that spirit. You'd have to be a German to truly buy into that particular formulation, but there are American ways to interpret this that I do think make sense as a critique of the Internet. Not as a useful tool for people, but as a way of life, and as a way of being a human being. Particularly, as I say, for certain types of artistic production for which the electronic world is actually very harmful, to the point of being antithetical.

You don't have to be as extreme as Pynchon in eschewing the Internet's capacity for self-promotion. But if I look around at the really great writers of the recent decades in North America, I think of Alice Munro, I think of Don DeLillo, I think of Denis Johnson. These are people who are not invisible, but they have clearly set up rather strict boundaries. Alice Munro, you know, she's got work to do. She has the work of being Alice Munro to do. Same thing for Johnson, same thing for DeLillo. Pynchon's self-isolation is so extreme that, as with Salinger, he risks producing the opposite of the effect that maybe is psychologically intended—it becomes a kind of reverse publicity to be absolutely publicity-averse. The writers who have become models for me are the ones who manage to have some public life—we're all communal—but a restricted one. Writers have audiences and responsibilities to those audiences. But we also have a responsibility to remain ourselves. It's a balancing act. And again, the Internet and social media are so seductive, are so immediately gratifying in that addictive-substance way, that you can get carried away from yourself rather easily.

I feel we're at a moment when technology has far outstripped other human capabilities. You see this in so many ways—increasing economic disparity, the hatred and conflict and terrorism in the world, our own political dysfunction. It seems to me that, at some point, if we're going to survive, we have to start to identify undesirable aspects of technological development and say no to them. It's extremely unlikely, but it's actually not inconceivable, that after an unintended nuclear explosion and a few more power plant disasters people will say, "We *can* split atoms, but we're going to choose not to. We're going to get together as an entire planet to ensure that this thing we can do, we're not going to do." With GMOs, and recombinant DNA in all its forms, we're already hearing people saying, "Just because we *can* do it doesn't mean we should." But our embrace of the new digital technology? It's been headlong, despite obvious negative consequences. I mean, the Internet has almost destroyed journalism! How can you have a functioning, complicated democracy of 300 million people without professional journalists? The boosters are always saying, well, you can crowdsource it, you can leak it, you can take pictures with your iPhone. Bullshit. You can't crowdsource working the Capitol beat for twenty years. We need to think critically about the consequences of our machines. We need to learn how to say no, and how to support the vital social services, like professional journalism, that we're destroying.

And this is true, especially true, for anyone who aspires to write serious fiction. When I first met Don DeLillo, he was making the case that if we ever stop having fiction writers it will mean we've given up on the concept of the individual person. We will only be a crowd. And so it seems to me that the writer's responsibility nowadays is very basic: to continue to try to be a person, not merely a member of a crowd. (Of course, the place where the crowd is forming now is largely electronic.) This is a primary assignment for anyone setting up to be and remain a writer now. So even as I spend half my day on the Internet—doing email, buying plane tickets, ordering stuff online, looking at bird pictures, all of it—I personally need to be careful to restrict my access. I need to make sure I still have a private self. Because the private self is where my writing comes from. The more I'm pulled out of that, the more I simply become another loudspeaker for what already exists. As a writer, I'm trying to pay attention to the stuff the people *aren't* paying attention to. I'm trying to monitor my own soul as carefully as I can and find ways to express what I find there.

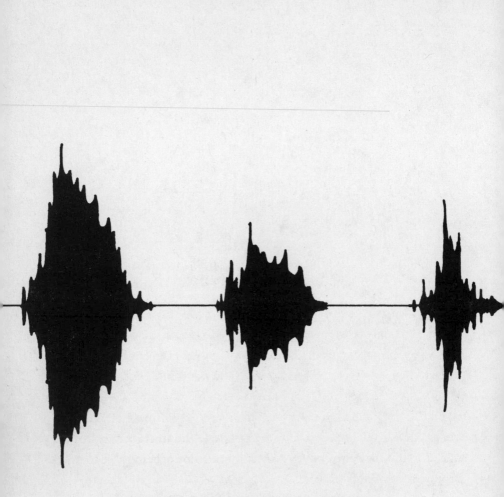

Lolita, light of my life, fire of my loins. My sin, my soul. Lo-lee-ta: the tip of the tongue taking a trip of three steps down the palate to tap, at three, on the teeth. Lo. Lee. Ta.

—Vladimir Nabokov, *Lolita*

HANYA YANAGIHARA

Writing for Right Now

WHEN I WAS thirteen, my father gave me a copy of Vladimir Nabokov's *Lolita*. Certainly in the way he taught me to read it, *Lolita* was never a book about a love affair or about pedophilia. I remember how he'd get annoyed when anyone called it a love story—to him, the point of the book was the language, the obvious delight of a nonnative English speaker basically playing with his food. Yes, the Baroque style and invented adjectives convey the creepiness and the unctuousness of the narrator. But they also convey Nabokov's pure joy of being able to muck around in another language.

That's what I love about *Lolita*, too: this overblown-ness, the rich, self-conscious pretension of language. The Americanisms that Humbert encounters, and mocks, and also delights in, juxtaposed against the clear indulgence of English itself. That excess, his way of manipulating words, his way of rolling around in sentences, was in my father's reading always what this book was about and its true import and genius.

This is a rare ability. I think if a writer doesn't have it, I'd always prefer them to be plainspoken. But *Lolita*'s literary sprezzatura and lack of modesty are just terrifically appealing. Nabokov, of course, was a famous lepidopterist, and there is that sense in this book of how it feels to dissect a language and understand its innards; at the same time, he's able to reconfigure words into something else entirely. It may be why I've never actually finished the book: The story was never the important part. I've gotten to about a third of the way through, right after Charlotte Haze, Lolita's mother, dies in the car accident. Every couple of years or so, I revisit the first 100 pages—but I've never read beyond it.

My father had me memorize the novel's first lines, which, really, contain everything that the book is about. These first couple of paragraphs are meant to be read aloud like poetry:

> Lolita, light of my life, fire of my loins. My sin, my soul. Lo-lee-ta: the tip
> of the tongue taking a trip of three steps down the palate to tap, at three,
> on the teeth. Lo. Lee. Ta.

Reading these lines is almost like watching a gymnast perform: You can see the work and the thinking, paid to the structure and the rhythm of the language. He turns her name into something alive, makes it become a butterfly. To make a name itself a poem is an exceedingly hard thing to do.

Then, that second paragraph:

> She was Lo, plain Lo, in the morning, standing four feet ten in one sock.
> She was Lola in slacks. She was Dolly at school. She was Dolores on the
> dotted line. But in my arms she was always Lolita.

This here is almost an articulation of how a writer chooses a word, how a writer chooses to name things, how something can be known by many names. Why does a writer choose the word "insect" and not "bug," for example, or why does he choose the word "stomach" and not "belly"? It's because of the way it sounds, and how slightly different words that mean the exact same thing can also signify something completely different. This paragraph is almost a mini writing seminar, not only about the importance of language, but the importance of names—how we can transform something in the very naming of it. This is a theme repeated in the book as well, as Nabokov explores the nature of love, the nature of self-gratification, and the nature of the lessons we try to tell ourselves in order to justify what we want.

Then there's Humbert's obfuscations: "About as many years before Lolita was born as my age was that summer," he says, setting up the novel's events within a willfully indeterminate time. It's an example of the self-conscious cloaking that language can do, how it can hide, how it can conceal, how it can reveal, and how it can be manipulated. I mean, everything that you want to know about Humbert's character is in these first couple of paragraphs.

The voice in this book is terrifically present. But you could also see a contemporary editor asking him to do less—to make Humbert not necessarily more likable, but more *palatable*, perhaps more understandable. And that's a terrible thing to happen to fiction. I hope *Lolita* would be allowed to stand alone if it were written now, but I could also see how an editor might want it to be more minimalist, more streamlined. I do think we're in a literary moment in which there is a hunger for less—for something tidier and, I suppose, sleeker. I suspect there would be a winnowing of this language if an editor encountered it today.

And that's too bad, because literature depends upon writers taking large leaps on the page. Whether it's plot, or characterization, or structure, or a voice, or the language, a book has to take risks with at least *one* thing.

Yes, *Lolita* is not a tidy or inert book. But a tidy and inert book is never going to be worth doing. A writer has to try to make something new, and what Nabokov makes new in this book is language. In every single sentence, almost, there is something that's invented, and you can feel it being invented in real time. At the same time, you feel that the writer isn't looking over his shoulder to see what's been done before. Nor is he looking into the future to see what the reception might be. It's that present-tense-ness that a writer must possess, the confidence that what's being done on the page, in real time, is simply all that is going to matter.

So much of being any kind of artist—whether you're a composer, or a painter, or a writer—is a lifelong process of trying to forget everything you've been taught. When you look at Picasso's juvenile work, you can see he was a draftsman: He was someone who had been taught how to draw. But he was also, critically, able to unteach himself. It's the same when you see writers using language in a way it's not supposed to be used or it hasn't been used before. What you're seeing is somebody who has the gift of forgetting (or of selectively ignoring) the rules. Often, this works best when you've been taught how you're *supposed* to do things—so that, when you're actually doing your own work, you can unlearn those lessons. But not necessarily. Nabokov is self-taught in a lot of ways, and he writes the way that a very talented autodidact writes.

The best time to write is after your book is bought but before it's published, because you're able to write in complete ignorance. You must draw a line between what it means to be a writer and what it means to be an author—an author is a performative role, and a writer is not. It's so important to be able to forget your public persona when you work. When you're writing, your responsibility is not to your publishers. It's not even to your readers. It's only to the story.

If you can always keep in mind that your only goal is to serve the story—whatever the story may be, and however the story may be told—then that's all the insurance, all the protection, that you need. It's a pretty basic piece of advice, and it's very easy to forget, but I think you can never go wrong with it. Whether it comes down to a language choice or a plot point, if you keep your focus only on serving the narrative itself—not the book, necessarily, but the narrative, the story, the characters—then that's the very best you can do. You hope that focus emboldens you to make all the right choices for the creation itself, and only the creation.

I say that everything should serve the story. But *Lolita* is the rare book that successfully breaks that rule. The wonderful thing about this book is that you could take its first 100 pages, tear them out, cut them into bits, and scatter them: And just by picking up any one of those bits, a paragraph, or a sentence, or a line, you could have a singular reading experience. When we talk about books being poetic, what we often mean is that there's an indulgence or a fuzziness to the language. This is poetry of a different sort. It's sharp, and it's unpleasant, and it's barbed, but it's also mischievous, and playful, and fanged. It's language at its most fun, at its most enjoyable, at its most delightful, and also at its most wicked and resonant. I wish more people read the book that way, instead of letting it become eclipsed by the scandals and the conversations that have surrounded it. The pure pleasure of reading *Lolita* is what makes it as enduring as it is.

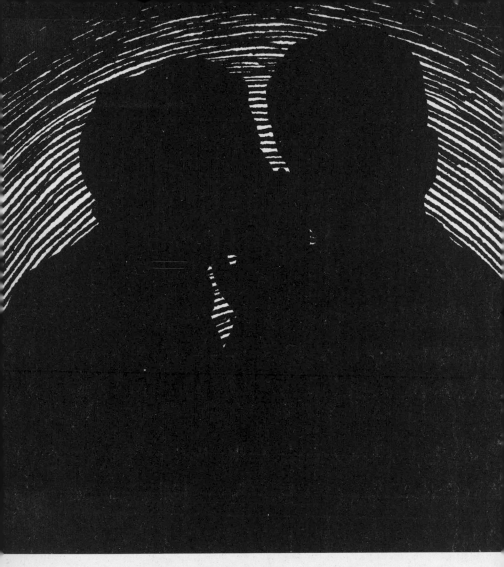

The Emperor—so they say—has sent a message, directly from his death bed, to you alone, his pathetic subject, a tiny shadow which has taken refuge at the furthest distance from the imperial sun. He ordered the herald to kneel down beside his bed and whispered the message in his ear.

—FRANZ KAFKA, "A Message from the Emperor"

BEN MARCUS

Recommended Dosage

I THINK I first read Kafka's parables in a philosophy course in college. It was probably my first exposure to Kafka. Parables are a powerful point of entry to that world of anxiety, fear, and paranoia, but also the yearning, beauty, and strangeness that I connect to Kafka's work. The first parable I read was "Leopards in the Temple"—it's a very brief piece, beautiful and strange and eerily logical. Later on I found "A Message from the Emperor," which became my very favorite.

It starts with a compelling proposition. The emperor, the greatest figure of civilization, is sending a message to "you," the reader. That opening configuration is captivating. An extremely important person has something to tell you, and you alone:

> The Emperor—so they say—has sent a message, directly from his death bed, to you alone, his pathetic subject, a tiny shadow which has taken refuge at the furthest distance from the imperial sun. He ordered the herald to kneel down beside his bed and whispered the message in his ear.

But the piece focuses on the impossibility of that message ever arriving. It turns out that the palace has ring upon ring upon ring of walls, successive outer palaces, and the messenger has to get through one and then the other, and then the other. If he could ever do that—which he never could, the narrator tells us the palace is too vast and impossible— then he'd only be at the center of the city, which is filled with people and garbage, all kinds of difficult obstacles. He will never get through.

The ending is haunting: You will never hear this message that's intended for you alone.

> And if he finally burst through the outermost door—but that can never, never happen—the royal capital city, the center of the world, is still there in front of him, piled high and full of sediment. No one pushes his way through here, certainly not someone with a message from a dead man. But you sit at your window and dream of that message when evening comes.

This breaks my heart. Something important has been communicated to you, but you'll never hear it. And yet you'll sit at your window and dream it to yourself—and so there's immense yearning and hope coupled with the sense of impossibility and futility. These incompatible sensations all assail you at the same time. This is just perfection to me.

It's hard to miss that, on some level, "A Message from the Emperor" is a parable about reading. On the one hand, I'm resistant to say, "This is all about what it means to tell a story!"—but it does seem to really be there. I like thinking of it as a reminder of how desperately we want to be spoken to. We want to be addressed. We want there to be some important message out there for us. And yet: How futile it might be to hope for that. The story goes beyond a mere illustration of the literary paradox: It hints at the supreme difficulty of ever truly connecting to *anybody*. With Kafka, you always have this kind of bleak futility—but the futility never feels flat and pessimistic. Despite the impossibility, we still have that messenger heroically striving to break through. The parable is a great form for capturing that paradoxical feeling.

This piece is a model for how I'd like to feel when I read. And what

I might like others to feel, reading what I've written. What attracts me is the way it puts opposite, seemingly conflicting sensations into motion and makes them feel compatible against all odds. The sense of difficulty, futility, and tremendous obstacle—coupled with searching and yearning desire and hope.

And this is what writing is about for me—the way I can read a short piece and feel transformed within the small amount of time it takes to get from start to finish. There are deliberately cerebral pieces of writing that I think are fantastic and beautiful in their own right—but for me, in the end, I need literature to make me feel things. And not just a little bit. I want writing to be the most intense form of feeling that I can find. As if we're putting words together in order to deeply alter or enhance or trigger our feelings—in order to feel more alive. This is part of why I write a story, why I put words together: because they are, in the end, a tremendous—possibly unrivaled—delivery mechanism for intense feeling. The kind of feeling that Kafka traffics in I find especially appealing because of its contradictions and conflicts, and because of the mixture of fear and beauty, the seemingly incompatible sensations are suspended and held aloft and presented to us.

Without reaching for that kind of feeling I'm just not sure what I would be doing. It's what I tried for in the short pieces in *The Age of Wire and String*. The diction and the syntax and the language I used came out of my interest in what a single sentence can do to our heads and hearts. An individual sentence can be penetrating, almost like a drug when it gets into me. I read, and as I read I find myself rearranged and transported and moved, as if I've swallowed a little pill. I love sentences that instantly hit my bloodstream and derange me.

I think the emotional force of "A Message from the Emperor" is aided by the way it unfolds in an indeterminate setting. The world being described is not our own. We don't have an emperor in a palace with ring upon ring upon ring of squares that someone has to cross through. Kafka's tilted away from his own world, toward something ancient and mythic. At the same time, he puts us in the story with that pronoun "you." He puts us at our own windows, dreaming of what we might be told by somebody important, by God, by some kind of unknowable figure (who he points out is dead now, it's taken that long for the message to arrive).

This is a stunning feat of defamiliarization—we're not in the real world, and yet the world is entirely familiar to us—from stories, from myths, from legends. It's dreamlike. It's not invented to the degree where you have to suspend disbelief—there's a feeling of plain normalcy, this banal particularity that *is* our world, at the same time it's otherworldly. I've always loved that effect, because I very readily start to take things for granted in my own life: I walk down the street, and stop thinking about how strange a tree can be. I stop thinking about how strange it is that you can walk on the surface of the earth, but not fall off of it. Or how strange it is that we built all these things to hide in called houses. But I start to become alert to the world, amazed by the very fact of it, when I try to forget what I know. If I can find a way to strip away my assumptions, forget what I know, it's a way to drop back into the world as if you've never seen it before. It's delirious, it's intense, it's terrifying to try to see the world afresh. But that's a literary space I love to explore.

People want different things when they read, of course, and I respect that. There are some whose first desire is to "understand" the meaning of what they've read. That's a perfectly legitimate thing to want. But a lot of what I love, I love it precisely because it eludes understanding. Now, obviously, you don't just want to read word salad—a text that just means nothing. But I tend to remain enthralled by writing that isn't so easy to pin down, that can sustain contradictory readings, holding up to many rereadings. We can treat literature like a product that's meant to reveal itself in full, right away—and what's great is, we have that. You can go to any bookstore and identify that as what you want, you can get that. It's available. But there's also more enigmatic stuff. I think there's room for all of it.

A good example is *The Childhood of Jesus* by J. M. Coetzee. I've seen some strange and dismissive commentary about the book—many reviewers were not pleased. But I think it's so captivating, so strange, so compelling. Coetzee is another writer, like Kazuo Ishiguro, who can take you into a kind of Kafkan space of indeterminate context: In this case, a guy arrives at a settlement with a child. There's no past, there's no context, you don't get a fucking *flashback*—all explanation is withheld. This is a deal-breaker for some readers. And yet, for me, it's the absence of that stuff that actually rivets me. That makes me feel pulled in and curious.

Curiosity's an interesting thing. In the courses I teach, one of the common things you hear is this: If you're talking about a story, someone will say, "Well, this character John. I wanted to know more about him." This is a common request—to ask for more information about a character. But let's say you know everything there is to know about this character. All the data you could possibly give: Let's give the flashbacks, let's show the childhood. Would that make it a better story? To me, it's not so simple. You can flood the text with *information*, but that doesn't enhance the literary experience of it, the drama. I think there are some readers willing to live with a certain degree of unsatisfied curiosity—the curiosity keeps you pushing forward—but others find such withholding annoying. They want to know, in Coetzee's case, well, wait, is the boy Simon *really* Jesus?

What's interesting about this novel, in particular, is how much work the title does. Because nowhere in the book does it suggest in any explicit way that Simon is meant to be Jesus as a young boy. But the fact that the book is called *The Childhood of Jesus* is constantly there, grabbing you and reminding you that you're reading something very possibly much more deeply tethered to mythology than you might think. The book had an unnerving effect on me. I admire how little context Coetzee uses and yet how compelling his present world is. He takes you to a moment that's so rigorously empty all around it—and to me, that's a very Kafka-like experience.

I don't usually feel the need to know in some critical way what something was "about," and I would much rather be taken through something mysterious. But if I find myself being "certain" that this is what I like to read, and what I like to do—I think that's a terrible place to be. That's exactly when I start thinking, *Now, I need to turn on all of that.* See what I'm missing by throwing myself all in with this approach. I'm constantly correcting course, based on what I've previously written. I'm always looking to try something I haven't done before—and through it, to experience something I've never before experienced. So I get nervous if I start to sound like I'm propagating some single vision of what writing can be. If I've been writing or reading mannered and strange sentences for some time, maybe I need to try very simple sentences that hide in plain sight.

Because there's a degree to which literature's means and methods are unknowable. We don't know what's happening when somebody reads a poem. We know that even if a writer labors and labors to make a precise text, much will be lost in transmission—we'll have no real idea, even, how much gets through. It gives me tremendous respect for the difficulty and variety of language. Writers believe that if you put words in a certain order, you're going to transport readers: You're going to give them feeling, you're going to give them sensation, you're going to tweak deep things in their imaginations. And yet, we can't systematize it. We can't say, *Okay, this is exactly how you write a good short story. This is exactly how you write a novel. Works of literature have to be like this, and not like that.* We can debate these things, but just because something works well once doesn't mean you can repeat it. The way books come together is, to me, ineffable. The fact that I can know so little about this process, and yet feel so drawn to it—well, that's what keeps me coming back.

When I read Kafka's parable, I feel strangeness and beauty, I feel sorrow. It's inventive, and yet the invention is tethered to deep, plunging feeling. These are the important values to me: when something otherworldly gets its hooks in you emotionally. To me, this is a perfect text.

it's not more beautiful, just different. a new beauty. a different beauty.
the other beauty is still beauty. this is new and right now it has the
edge of newness and that snapping fire you sense when you go out
there from the spaceship where nobody has ever been before.

—RALPH J. GLEASON, *Bitches Brew* liner notes

MARK HADDON

Music for Misfits

GROWING UP, I should have been listening to the Sex Pistols and the Clash like everyone else under eighteen in the U.K. But I was sent away to a boarding school as a teenager, so I was pretty cut off from the mainstream youth culture. It was not a pleasant place and I never felt at home, which is one of the reasons why I became a lifelong non-joiner of institutions. In that strange, hermetically sealed little world in the middle of the English countryside, I think I was seeking out a music of my own—something I could like that no one else liked. Outsiders' music, music for non-joiners.

Having heard very little music beyond my father's mild jazz collection and *Top of the Pops* every Thursday night, I hadn't had too many formative listening experiences. But on two occasions, I heard a piece of music that changed the way I saw the world. The first was Benjamin Britten's "Hymn to St. Cecilia," which was performed at school by the choir. And the second was hearing Miles Davis's *Bitches Brew*.

Miles Davis was hugely popular, of course, but not in the English shires of the late 1970s. I think I understood at the time that I was listening to something absolutely extraordinary. The sound of someone inventing a completely new language, but one that was nevertheless totally whole and endlessly articulate.

It wasn't just the music that struck me. It was also Ralph J. Gleason's liner notes, the way the music and the liner notes echoed and explained one another.

There's a passage at the end which moved me then and still moves me now:

> it's not more beautiful, just different. a new beauty. a different beauty. the other beauty is still beauty. this is new and right now it has the edge of newness and that snapping fire you sense when you go out there from the spaceship where nobody has ever been before.

This is the definition of art which has always most excited me, the feeling of being taken to the very edge of the universe then just over that boundary into the surrounding darkness. It's not an experience that happens very often, but I'm willing to wait. I've never enjoyed music in general, or contemporary fiction in general, or films in general, or theater in general. I'm standing on the runway waiting for the next big one to come in, trailing some of that outer darkness in its wake.

Reading the liner notes lines again, I realize there was something else that was clearly important for me about this passage. I was born in '62 and like a lot of kids of that generation, the space program played a hugely important role in my imagination. I wanted to be an astronaut—we all did. Of course, it rapidly dawned on me that I was too anxious and oversensitive to be an astronaut. You had to be a fighter pilot to start with, and be ready to kill people, which I wasn't. Plus I had a lazy eye, so I'd have flunked the medical on day one. Reading this passage, however, is a reminder that there are other ways to get to the edge of the universe.

One other thing. I loved the fact that the liner notes were all written in lowercase. It was the coolest thing. An official printed text with no capital letters! Whenever possible, I still write in lowercase and curse modern word processing programs with their insistence on capitals at the beginnings of sentences, for proper nouns, for "I." When I have the time, I'll go back and meticulously remove them because they look so untidy. And it's all Ralph J. Gleason's fault.

There's only one passage in the liner notes which fails to ring wholly true for me. Gleason writes, "we can always listen to ben play funny valentine, until the end of the world it will be beautiful and how can anything be more beautiful than hodges playing passion flower?" He's saying that new forms don't invalidate the old forms, which retain their power. And maybe that's true for some listeners, but less so for me . . . As I grew older, I stopped listening to most jazz that was recorded before *Bitches Brew*, and quite a lot recorded after it. It took me a while to formulate exactly why. It think it's this: If I can imagine something being played in a hotel foyer, it's not the kind of music I want to listen to. Sadly, a lot of jazz—which was, of course, intimately interwoven with the experience of slavery and the subsequent continuing oppression of black Americans, a music of protest, a celebration of pride and difference—was co-opted by commerce. As most things are, eventually. It's become background music for most of us, and for me it lost that angry beauty. I've come to realize that much of the music I like is music that is going to annoy people sitting in that metaphorical hotel foyer. Not lyrically, but musically. *Bitches Brew* passes that test. It's beautiful, but it's not bland.

When a writing student shows you a piece of writing that's not working, it's relatively easy to help them improve. But it's very hard—if not impossible—to tell someone how to write well. After all, there would be more good writing around if there was a formula. I think it's because the best writing—like the best music, the best theater, the best art—always does something you don't expect. It doesn't have to be radical, it doesn't have to be a wholly new invention, but is has to surprise you in some way. If it's merely an improvement on what went before—that's just craft, isn't it?

I think it was Jean Cocteau who said fashion is what seems right now and wrong later. Art is what seems wrong now and right later. Great art has that slight discomfort to start with. It takes you a while to think, *Yeah, this is right. I just didn't realize that it was right at the time.*

I think art grows out of a place of discomfort, too. For me it does, at any rate. I've come to accept that I'm going to be bored and frustrated for long periods. I've come to accept that I will be regularly dissatisfied and that I will have to throw a lot of stuff away. I have to be patient and slog onward and trust that something better will come along. I'm constantly trying to balance ambitions and withering self-doubt. I spend a lot of time pacing up and down getting absolutely nothing done.

I often say to people when I'm teaching that if you're having fun it's probably not working. And for me, the job of writing is pretty uphill most of the time. It's like climbing a mountain—you get some fantastic views when you pause or when you get to the top, but the actual process can be tough. I'm sure there are people out there who enjoy writing, and I wish them all the best. But I'm not like that. I wish I could enjoy the process more. But I think I've come to accept that for it to work, I have to be uncomfortable.

Becoming a writer is not a decision I ever actively made. It's more like coming to terms with a borderline pathological obsession, an activity I simply have to do regularly to feel human. At root, it's a desire to understand the effect extraordinary books have had on me and then, in turn, to attempt to give other people a similar experience. That, combined with a complete inability to do any other job. I simply cannot turn up at the same place every day five days a week and be told what to do by someone else. Which is one of the reasons why I'm at home writing books and drawing and painting pictures. I'm quite lucky I've been able to make a living in that way.

I think you need two things more than anything to be a successful writer: imagination and bloody-mindedness. You're going to sit on your own in a room for a very long time. If you can't do that, it's not going to be worth starting.

I used to quote Philip Pullman, who when he was asked if he had any advice for young writers, said: "Just don't." It's quite funny, but it also encapsulates a truth: If you have the requisite bloody-mindedness, you're not going to take advice from anyone, even Philip Pullman. (The coda to the story is: I was talking to Philip Pullman and said, "I often quote what you said about advice to young writers." He said, "I didn't say that! But I *am* going to say it now.")

Whenever I sit down to write something new, I just think: "*Please* let me be able to write something—anything—that works." And that's one of the reasons why I've doglegged all over the place and ended up lately with writing short stories. I have an overwhelming desire to write well, but an inability to stick at the thing I'm doing right now. I'll go anywhere to find something that works. That's the only plan.

The liner notes and music from *Bitches Brew* are connected in my mind as they are connected for no one else on the earth: with an illustration which I first saw in a science book I had when I was a little kid. It was a reproduction of an engraving from Camille Flammarion's 1888 book *L'atmosphère: météorologie populaire*, which depicts a fake medieval landscape. A guy in a robe has walked to the edge of the picture, to the edge of the earth. He's somehow managed to poke his hand under the bottom of the smallest of the bounding spheres, and behind it he can see the machinery of the universe: the cogs and the wheels and the smoke and the fire. That's what I want art to feel like, and for me it's always connected with Gleason's image of stepping outside the spaceship.

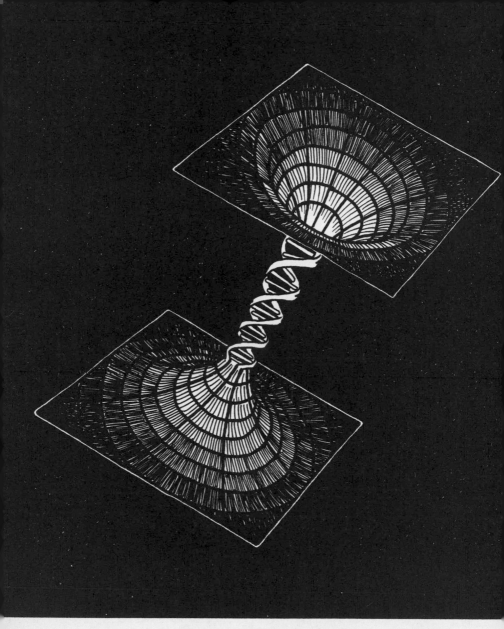

You read something which you thought only happened to you, and you discovered it happened 100 years ago to Dostoyevsky. This is a very great liberation for the suffering, struggling person, who always thinks that he is alone. This is why art is important. Art would not be important if life were not important, and life is important.

—JAMES BALDWIN, interview with Studs Terkel, Chicago, 1961

AZAR NAFISI

Enough About Me

WHEN I RETURNED to America from Iran, in 1997, I hadn't been here for eighteen years—not since I'd been an undergraduate in the 1970s. One thing I love about the U.S. is this: Everywhere I go, red or blue states, ordinary Americans are passionate about reading, about meaning, about connecting. And yet I noticed something here that appalled me, a kind of denigration of imagination in public spaces. The tendency I'm talking about has many manifestations, but we see it everywhere. From our policymakers in education who don't feel that art, music, and poetry are necessary to a democratic education, to our universities and schools, where students are asked to interrogate books before they have a chance to first connect with them, we are told that the imaginative exercise is not important.

It's common, of course, to hear people defend books in nations that aren't free. What I find ironic is that people don't seem to appreciate the relationship between books and freedom in functioning democracies. But tyrants in any country, from the Islamic Republic to the Soviet Union to anywhere in the world, understand their enemies: Their enemies are freedom of ideas and freedom of imagination. Tyrants attack these things first, alongside women's rights and minority rights. So when someone in a democracy thinks, "Oh, why does it matter to read? Why does it matter to imagine and to think?"—well, it's mind-boggling to me.

I believe that literary fiction is a crucial force within democracy itself. In its desire to include many perspectives, to give voice to everyone— not just the privileged, or powerful, or culturally dominant—fiction both exemplifies democratic ideals and promotes them. In America, Mark Twain is one clear example: His whole project bucks against the notion of a single, totalitarian truth. In a bit of writing advice, Twain once said: "Don't say the old lady screamed, bring her on and let her scream." This is more than a command to show, not tell. He insists that we give people their voices, let them talk, let their perspective be seen, heard, and felt.

Twain's classic novel *The Adventures of Huckleberry Finn* has this idea at its core. The main characters are a white urchin child and a black slave—both of whom, in different ways, are repressed by "respectable" society, and continually find their opinions silenced. But they learn to rely on one another for survival. Through this experience, these two outcasts begin to empathize with one another, and start to see each other as fully human.

We see Twain's commitment to this idea in a biting, outrageous speech he gave to the Mayflower Society, a group of people who gathered to celebrate their status as descendants of that first ship's passengers. Twain began by deriding the early Pilgrims, saying they "abolished everybody else's ancestors." He goes on to dispute the very notion of "pure" heritage. "I have the morals of Missouri and the culture of Connecticut," he told them, before claiming that his true ancestors are the Native Americans, the Quakers, the persecuted victims of the Salem Witch Trials, and, finally, the slaves.

"The first slave," he said, "brought into New England out of Africa by your progenitors was an ancestor of mine—for I am of a mixed breed, an infinitely shaded and exquisite Mongrel." By making his main characters a pair of outcasts, Twain dramatized the idea of a mixed, multifaceted national identity famously formulated by Walt Whitman:

"Do I contradict myself? / Very well then I contradict myself, / (I am large, I contain multitudes)."

American literature can have its Aunt Sallys and Judge Thatchers, the novel suggests, but it must also contain the story of the homeless orphan, the subjugated slave. It just took my breath away. And I thought, this is my idea of what it means to be an American: to be an exquisite, many-shaded mongrel.

That is why I deliberately began my book *The Republic of Imagination*—which is about how I became an American through the country's fiction—with Twain. And I ended it with another writer, James Baldwin, to focus on how these two writers became guardians of American morality, so relevant to issues we face today, from race to immigration to the idea of America itself.

Twain's idea of being of mixed origin was also central to Baldwin, who called himself "a kind of bastard of the West." Not by choice, but by force, he had been uprooted and deprived of all his ancestry. When the racists told him, *You're not of us, you're not like us, you're not American,* Baldwin said—*No, you bloody bastards. You took everything away from me. I can't go back to Africa. I'm not an African and yet you don't allow me to be an American. I become an African American.*

For Baldwin, to be black and American was to be painfully aware of the complicated, mixed nature of one's heritage. "When I followed the line of my past I did not find myself in Europe but in Africa," he said,

And this meant that in some subtle way, in a really profound way, I brought to Shakespeare, Bach, Rembrandt, to the stones of Paris, to the cathedral at Chartres, and to the Empire State Building, a special attitude. These were not really my creations, they did not contain my history; I might search in them in vain forever for any reflection of myself. I was an interloper; this was not my heritage. At the same time I had no other heritage which I could possibly hope to use—I had certainly been unfitted for the jungle or the tribe. I would have to appropriate these white centuries, I would have to make them mine.

Baldwin took the best from what was offered to him, and the origins didn't matter—jazz and the blues, or Shakespeare and Bach, he took what he wanted. And this expanded the literary America.

We need to remember this. Because one thing this country does, which I very much resent, is categorize you. If you are a great writer, you're not really a great writer—you're a great *African American* writer. When I came to this country, someone told me, "Oh, you're a woman and you come from a Muslim-majority country. You've got great chances to go into Islamic studies and women's studies." I said, "*You* go into Islamic studies and women's studies. I want to talk about white males." You know? The academics who told me that did so without realizing that literature is about the Other. It is so boring to constantly talk about yourself! And that is the message of fiction—you *can't* talk only about yourself. You have to understand and give voice to everyone, even people unlike you, even the villain—because even if you're fighting the villain you need to understand him first.

In the 1950s Baldwin broke this barrier. He refused to be called a Negro writer. He refused to be called a gay writer. He simply said: "I am a *writer.*" That is the only stance that gains respect, to be accepted for who you are. Writers must refuse to submit to simplistic categories, even though we still have this tendency in our culture to tag everyone by a certain name.

And yet, though Baldwin was very faithful and very fierce in his essays and activities, and in his fight for civil rights and human rights, he insisted on something that I think is crucial. We should revere and celebrate differences and the particular, he said, but we must never forget that the particular is very dangerous if it doesn't become universal. Yes, we are different. Those differences are fascinating, worthy of exploration. But writers, all of us, share a common humanity—and this common humanity contains the best and the worst. No people, no nation is exempt from this. I think that is a great, great contribution.

We need literature to remind us how like each other we are, despite our differences. Baldwin spoke beautifully about this:

You read something which you thought only happened to you, and you discovered it happened 100 years ago to Dostoyevsky. This is a very great liberation for the suffering, struggling person, who always thinks that he is alone. This is why art is important. Art would not be important if life were not important, and life is important.

In reality, in this very pragmatic sense, we all have limitations. There are borders within all of us, things that make us unalike. We come from separate nations. But when you read literature, you enter a republic of imagination that transcends time and space. So you are an African American boy living in New York City, and you discover that the person who best expresses you is a man who lived in Russia and has been dead a hundred years. That gives you a sense of hope, a sense of connection and camaraderie. It is one of those moments when you're glad you're human. This is why so many people will say that one book changed their whole life. Or writers talk about how reading a book made them want to become a writer.

One of the greatest things my father did was when he read a great deal from Persian stories and our epic poets especially and Iranian mythology but he mixed it with all sorts of things. So at the same time that I was thinking about Iran, I was becoming familiar with Pinocchio's Italy or Hans Christian Andersen's Denmark. He installed a sort of cosmopolitanism in us. Not by taking us to foreign places, but by bringing those books to our home. I never lost that. It's why, when I came here, it seemed so obvious that I should be talking about other people's books, even though a lot of people would tell me I am a Westernized betrayer of my culture if I do that.

I believe that when you teach a work of fiction, you should not bring all the baggage that comes with it. You should not fill the minds of the students with the background material. Let the students first connect to the book. Even if that connection is negative, even if they hate it—that reaction belongs to them. Then once they connect to the book and they form their impressions of it, it becomes so exciting to read about how Mark Twain came to know so much about African Americans, how his own childhood was in terms of his relationship with the slaves. What do other people say about Mark Twain, and what are the controversies? All of that should come after the initial connection.

If I love a book, it first strikes my heart. The mind comes in later, as I start to articulate why it is I like it. Both experiences are joyous, but you need that initial emotional link. It's why I don't like theories that espouse interrogation as our primary method of engaging with books. It's as though Alice—instead of just running after the white rabbit and jumping into the hole—would first say, Why is this rabbit white? Why is it running so fast? Should I be following it?

That way, she would never get to Wonderland.

My eyes were still closed. I was in my house. I
knew that. But I didn't feel like I was inside
anything.
     "It's really something," I said.
               —RAYMOND CARVER, "Cathedral"

T. C. BOYLE

How Stories Say Goodbye

I KNEW RAY CARVER when he was hanging around in Iowa City in the 1970s—I lived there for five and a half years, getting my MFA from the Writers' Workshop and then my PhD. He'd just published his first book, *Will You Please Be Quiet, Please?* Before that, no one paid him much attention except us: We all knew how great the stories were, and we followed them in the little magazines.

All the writers whom we revered would come through town at one time or another. Most of them were jerks and drunks and drug addicts who had just been released from the mental hospital. But still, to see them reading was a great thing. Ray, after he became well-known, came and gave a reading. Of course, he was very shy and didn't want to give readings. It was in the horrible lounge on the third floor of the English department building, and he just had one little lamp, and his face was shaded, and he just kind of mumbled. But it was great—it was Ray.

He is definitely a great favorite. When I first began to read Ray's stories, I was doing something very, very different—something with much longer and more rhythmic sentences, certainly nothing that had to do with working-class people or realism or anything else. I had never paid much attention, at that point, to realism. Ray opened my eyes to a different mode of storytelling.

"Cathedral" is a wonderful point-of-view story in which the narrator, a working-class guy, talks straight to us. He's extremely jealous because a good friend of his wife's is coming to visit. She knew this man, Robert, before the narrator and his wife were acquainted; she knew him in the capacity of reading to him, because he's blind. Our narrator—who isn't even named in the story—is prejudiced against the friend and makes detrimental comments about him. For instance: How preposterous it is that Robert had never seen his wife (who has since died). Whether she was beautiful or not—and whether she was wearing purple or red or mismatched clothes—the friend would never have known.

The narrator is groping toward an understanding of what being blind might be like, but in a very crude, antipathetic way. He depersonalizes the friend by referring to him as "the blind man" throughout the story. Of course, underneath it are his own fears and uncertainties about his relationship with his wife, the extent of her relationship with this other man—who is now no longer married—how close they've been, and how much this man means to her. And now, of course, our narrator will meet him for the first time: He's coming for a visit, and to spend the night.

The narrator is baffled by the man who shows up at his door. The blind man has a beard, and he's surprised by this. *How could a blind man have a beard?*—as if a blind man were a completely different species altogether. The blind man lifts his beard and sniffs it, one of his little quirks. The narrator notes this in the way he'd notice a wild animal in the zoo doing something.

And yet, the blind man, even though we're getting him from a prejudicial first-person point of view, seems like a very natural and likable kind of person. He speaks in a big rumbling voice, and calls him "bub." He has no problems with the heat he's feeling from the narrator. Ultimately, he disarms him—which is the beauty of the story.

After seeing a special on European churches on late-night TV, the blind man has an idea. "Why don't you find us some heavy paper? And a pen," he says. "We'll do something. We'll draw one together." Then they hold the pen at the same time and start to draw a cathedral:

> "Close your eyes now," the blind man said to me.
>
> I did it. I closed them just like he said.
>
> "Are they closed?" he said. "Don't fudge."
>
> "They're closed," I said.
>
> "Keep them that way," he said. He said, "Don't stop now. Draw."
>
> So we kept on with it. His fingers rode my fingers as my hand went over the paper. It was like nothing else in my life up to now.
>
> Then he said, "I think that's it. I think you got it," he said. "Take a look. What do you think?"
>
> But I had my eyes closed. I thought I'd keep them that way for a little longer. I thought it was something I ought to do.
>
> "Well?" he said. "Are you looking?"
>
> My eyes were still closed. I was in my house. I knew that. But I didn't feel like I was inside anything.
>
> "It's really something," I said.

The story ends with the narrator refusing to open his eyes—he doesn't see the drawing. And the drawing probably isn't that great, from the perspective of putting it on the wall in the art museum. But that's not what matters. The narrator, by keeping his eyes closed, is finally seeing the way the blind man does. What matters is the union between the two, and the fact of making it—of making art, the way art can transcend their differences and make us mutual in some way. It's very complex, what is said in such a stripped-back and simple form.

At the same time, it's not like the world is suddenly a happy place, and we make a musical out of the end, and everyone gets up and sings and dances. After all, Robert is never referred to by name. He remains "the blind man" even to the end of the story, and there's always a distance between them. The narrator has an experience he could never have dreamed of having—but, for all this, the blind man remains "the blind man," not "Robert." And yet, what matters is—that anybody, especially somebody as prejudiced as this, can have this wonderful moment.

This story—like Carver's "A Small, Good Thing"—makes a kind of metaphorical leap into a place that you could never imagine the story going. A lesser story might not have seen this, or imagined this. Is it believable? Would it actually happen that these men would put their hands together and trace something? The author takes his care to convince us, and I buy it—fully. And yet, if you think about it logically in terms of the world we know, maybe it's unlikely. That makes the story all the more amazing and all the more unexpected. It would not have worked as well had he been sympathetic to the blind man from the beginning. "Cathedral" makes a leap that might not be entirely credible—and yet it seems perfect, it seems right, it transports the story into another arena.

Every story is organic, and every story finds its own ending. And Ray's stories—like anyone else's—are varied in terms of how they find their endings. Personally, I love to find an ending that invites you back into the story rather than closes the story completely. That's what the last line does, here. When the narrator says "It's really something," it tells us that he's feeling deeply, but it doesn't tell us *what* he's feeling. That's the beauty of the story: It's up to *us* to know what he's feeling. The reader wonders, well—what does that mean? How is that? And it draws you right back in.

I think the best endings bring you back in, rather than close things off with absolute finality. I'm not saying they necessarily have to be ambiguous, but we don't always need to know what happens when everyone wakes up tomorrow morning. "Cathedral," in particular, couldn't go a beat beyond this. Maybe tomorrow, the narrator will continue to be kind of a jerk. Or maybe he's going to found the Friends of the Blind Society—it doesn't matter. It remains mysterious. We don't know, and that brings us back in.

When I start a story, I don't know what the ending will be in advance. I very much believe in working organically—that is, I don't know what the story will be or what's going to happen. As Flannery O'Connor said, she didn't know that the Bible salesman would steal Hulga's leg until she got there. Even with an author whose work is as uniform as Ray's, each story is going to work in a different way, find its ending organically, and its structure organically.

This is the beauty of the art of fiction, as opposed to laying out an essay or writing a thriller. You remain open to the possibilities throughout the entire story. When they're lucky, the artist finds one line, one moment that brings it all together. It's hard to say how certain stories just punch us in the heart and the brain at the same time at the end. I suppose that's what we're all looking for. But each story has its own valence, its own way of saying goodbye to you.

For my book *The Harder They Come*, I had the title and the epigraph before I began writing. I discovered those in the process of research, of thinking and reading and seeing things. These bare essentials give me a little framework, just enough structure to hang something on. From there, I just see something and translate it into words and just follow it. I'm not saying that it's a mystical experience necessarily—although there is certainly that element. At any juncture, you have a thousand different choices as far as word choices, sentence choices, structure, the entrance of character, what characters will do.

We've all had days when we're rewriting and rewriting and it's frustrating and nothing happens. And then there are days when gloriously it all comes together and just flows out. Over time, your conscious brain discovers—line by line, day by day—where it's going and what it is and why you're doing it. And if you're very lucky, and very happy, you get to the ending of a story like "Cathedral": You make a magical leap which opens the story out, and then brings the reader back in to wonder about its themes and its characters and what it means.

I only do one draft of everything, and that's it—though it's a draft that's been gone over in the process of writing over and over and over, so that it builds gradually in increments while I make discoveries until the end. I'm not the sort of writer who would shift structure or write scenes out of sequence or anything like that—it just kind of flows as one organic thing. When I'm done, I give the novel a reread in two or three days, push the button, and send it off.

Each time it's different. Each story and each book finds its own way. I have a questing curiosity—stylistically, and in terms of subject matter—although I think you could look back and see what my themes are and how they keep replaying in various books. While my natural line is longer than Ray's, I don't mind taking it up a little bit and trying different things. There are scenes in my first novel, whole chapters, in which I write short, declarative sentences—that can be very, very powerful. Certainly Ray had an influence on me in that way. I had never thought of writing a realistic story in that way, before I read him. But I like to push myself to do different things. In my case, it's a mixed bag: I do anything I like. While Ray had his own territory and that's where he stayed and he was great at it.

There are no rules. You do what you do. All we can do is look at a story like "Cathedral" and have a long discussion over what it means to us and how it's put together. I think that's what art is about: to provoke you. It helps me make sense of a senseless universe because I become the god of the story. I create it and I see it in all its lineaments in my own way, and can control it—in a world in which everything else is out of control. I'm sure all of us artists feel the same way about art, and this is why it's so vital to us.

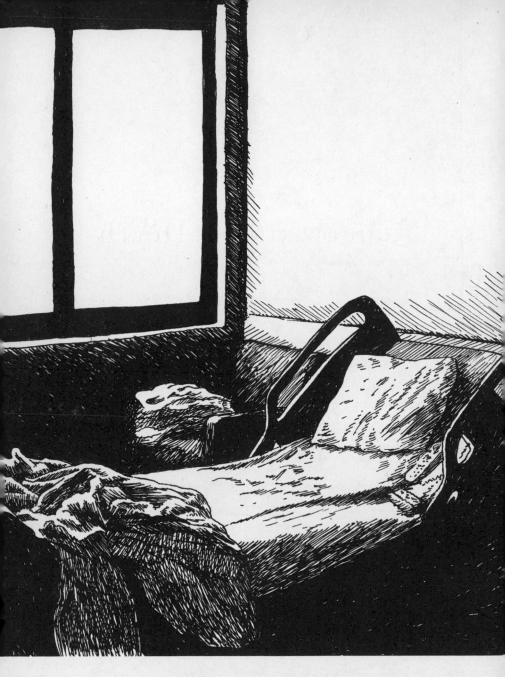

That was how he was.

—SAUL BELLOW, "A Silver Dish"

ETHAN CANIN

Rehearsals for Death

When I went for my medical school interview, I had an old paperback of *Henderson the Rain King* in the pocket of my coat. I was wearing the best clothes I had, a pair of cords and a sport coat—but when I got to the office, all the other interviewees were lined up in their black suits. As they stood there talking about whether they preferred intravenous versus oral chemotherapy, I thought, "Oh my god, I'm about to get myself into the wrong line of work." But when I went in for the interview, the guy noticed I had a book in my jacket pocket. He asked what I was reading, and when I took it out, he said, "Oh, that's my favorite book." All we did was talk about *Henderson the Rain King*. I think that's how I got into medical school.

I think Bellow's the greatest American writer of his century, personally. When I read him, I'm in awe.

One of my favorite works is the great short story "A Silver Dish," a story not too many people seem to know. It ends with, for me, one of the most memorable lines in fiction:

That was how he was.

There are five words in that sentence, each one essentially meaningless: *That was how he was.* Two of them are the same word: "was" and "was." Hardly any *sounds* even, in those words, there's no tilt, no break, no angle to the rhythm—just tap, tap, tap, tap, tap. Of all those words, only "he" and perhaps "was" have any sort of meaning. "How" is technically an adverb the way it's used here but feels more nounish to me, in the sense that I get a little visual spark when I read it, entirely from what has come before in the story. The whole sentence uses only seven distinct letters, and contains only fifteen letters total: three a's, three h's, three w's, two s's, two t's, an o, and an e.

It's an amazingly restrained line from Bellow, who was a poet of the first order. I think he was intentionally restricting his palette. Compare it to some of his other great sentences, like the famous first line of *The Adventures of Augie March*:

> I am an American, Chicago born—Chicago, that somber city—and go at things as I have taught myself, free-style, and will make the record in my own way: first to knock, first admitted; sometimes an innocent knock, sometimes a not so innocent.

You can open that book up to page 400 and find the best sentence you've ever seen. It's an astonishing, volcanic eruption of ideas and language. Or take this section from "A Silver Dish," when Woody takes a streetcar ride that leads him to the story's culminating moment:

> What he heard and saw was an old red Chicago streetcar, one of those trams the color of a stockyard steer. Cars of this type went out before Pearl Harbor—clumsy, big-bellied, with tough rattan seats and brass grips for the standing passengers. Those cars used to make four stops to the mile, and ran with a wallowing motion. They stank of carbolic or ozone and throbbed when the air compressors were being charged. The conductor had his knotted signal cord to pull, and the motorman beat the foot gong with his mad heel.

That passage is full of visceral, Anglo-Saxon words, and every single one of those words means something instantly. I think that's what poets try to do: They try to sidestep neurology and go straight to meaning.

But the last line of "A Silver Dish" is nothing like that. I can't tell you what any single one of those words means. Imagine you're a lexicographer and you have to define the word *that*, or *how*. And on top of this, there's none of Bellow's typical play with rhythm and language—it's almost a nonsentence. And yet, when I get to it in the story, I weep. I've read the story three times in the past few weeks, and each time I arrived at that sentence, tears came to my eyes.

How does Bellow pack so much emotion into those five ordinary words?

I think it's their very blankness that allows them to channel so much emotion. Because they don't bring anything specific to mind, they allow us to feel without thinking. At the end of a story or novel, you do not want the reader thinking. Endings are about emotion, and logic is emotion's enemy. It's the writer's job to disarm the reader of his logic, to just make the reader feel. You'll often see this in the final moments of a film: The camera tilts up, and the movie ends with a nondistinct image of the sky, or the sea, or the coast. Something the eye can't quite focus on, which allows you to focus on everything that's come before. That's how "that was how he was" works, too. It brings nothing else to mind. This sentence would be a nonsentence if it began the story—but, placed at the end, it's packed with the charge of everything that precedes it. Each of those nonwords is nitroglycerin, and the story that precedes it is the fuse.

To me, this line also shows that content trumps style. I have a theory about writing, which is that you cannot simultaneously write something true about character and, at the same time, write something linguistically beautiful. There are too few words to express both truth and beauty, so most empathetic—or another way to say this might be *character-driven*—writers tend to naturally reserve their beautiful constructions for when the content is less urgent. You'll see Bellow get poetic when he's writing about the scenery, like when Woody and his dad take that street-car ride. But when he's trying to write something that really gets to the narrator's deep emotional experience, the prose is mostly very simple: *That was how he was.* Five plain words. At the crux of the story it pays to write what's true, rather than try to write what's true and then dilute that by making the prose beautiful. It's a continuum, of course, but I don't think you can be at both ends of the continuum.

For me, I should also say, this story answers almost every question a young writer could have about fiction writing.

That dialogue is conflict, for instance. Bellow doesn't write down a word of dialogue unless people are fighting. As I always say to my students about dialogue in fiction: If you can't say something nasty, don't say anything at all.

Or that any story about death must be a story about life.

Or how to approach one of the most difficult things for literary writers: plot.

In a way, plot is very simple: You have someone do something wrong. You don't plan out a plot. You have somebody do something wrong, and that engenders other bad behavior. Behavior—especially bad behavior—is what forces character to emerge.

When "A Silver Dish" begins, it's remarkably static: Woody, pierced by the sound of church bells all over Chicago, is mourning his father, a lifetime of old memories and impressions washing over him. But the story snaps into sudden focus when he recalls one of his father's trans-gressions, a betrayal that's haunted the younger man all his life. It's that individual transgression—that memorable instance of bad behavior—that gets the story rolling.

I think of that moment as the story *standing up*. The moment when the black lines on the page suddenly become a story.

I've heard David Milch say (though I might be butchering it slightly) that it's easier to plot your way into an idea than it is to idea your way into a plot. And I think a lot of writers start out making the mistake of trying to write a novel *about* something. Novels are discussed as though they are intentionally about something, but they're not. They're stories. We're taught to think about them that way by literary critics, or by English teachers, who are, in their defense, generally trying to teach you to write a paragraph rather than a novel. But to be a writer, I think, you have to abandon the idea that fiction is "about" something. This concept is bad enough in your reading life. But it's fatal in your writing life.

I've seen plenty of students come in and say, I want to write a novel about *blah blah blah*. But you just can't do it. You can only write a novel about a character who does something wrong, and see what happens from there. Novels are compendiums of bad behavior, and literature is the gossip about it.

In other words, if you're writing a piece of fiction, I'd urge you not to try to show anything—instead, try to *discover* something. There's no way to write anything powerful unless your unconscious takes charge.

The biggest problem for young literary writers, besides plot, is how to characterize: how to make a character seem like a real human being. One of the more subtle ways, which Bellow does beautifully, is to have a character describe other people. The trick is that when characters describe other people, it's they themselves who are being revealed. In this section of "A Silver Dish," Woody's description of his father gives a sense of his own diction, articulation, and philosophy:

> Pop, as he took his sheepskin off, was in sweaters, no jacket. His darting looks made him seem crooked. Hardest of all for these Selbsts with their bent noses and big, apparently straightforward faces was to look honest. All the signs of dishonesty played over them. Woody had often puzzled about it. Did it go back to the muscles, was it fundamentally a jaw problem—the projecting angles of the jaws? Or was it the angling that went on in the heart?

It's physical description and self-contemplation and contemplation of others, all at the same time. As Woody meditates on his father's inherently crooked appearance, we get a sense of Woody, too: that he is in some ways an upright, noble, kind man but also has a sense of his own unworthiness, his own brutishness—a sense that he himself is as crookedly bent as his father.

Writers tend to think that their own prose is the compelling thing. You have to strangle that off, I think. Talk about killing your darlings. It's not just about killing your good *scenes*, it's about killing your instinct to try to impress with witticism and handsome phrasing—becoming, instead, a vessel for telepathy in a way. The less present you can be, the more you can be the character you're trying to write about. Some of the writers I admire most—like Philip Roth or Alice Munro—they're beautiful prose stylists in the sense that their sentences are lovely, but as I read them I'm not thinking about the prose. I'm thinking about the truth. I'm lost in their ability to make me into another human being. That, to me, is the compelling thing.

With characterization, you have to let go. You've got to release yourself from your grandiose intentions, your ambitions, your ideas about humanity, literature, and philosophy by focusing on the being-another-person aspect of it—which, by the way, is freeing, delightful, and one of the few real joys of writing. Stop worrying about writing a great novel—just become another human being.

I should add that, to a remarkable degree, it's a physical thing. I try to do it by pausing for a moment before I begin writing, by taking a few seconds at the beginning to let my self drop away.

I also find that restrained bits of physical activity help. I have a standing desk—which I have to say, I built myself long before it became fashionable. That works for me. I also put in one of those mini elliptical trainers below it, the kind without handrails, so that I have to concentrate a little to not fall off. I'll start to walk. And as I try to balance, trying not to topple to the side, I'm starting to type—somehow the slight physical activity takes the brakes off. In the same way, I often get good ideas when I'm driving a stick-shift car: The shifting requires just enough concentration that it unglues your inhibitions. It allows your unconscious to bubble up.

Ultimately, I read for the sensation of being another character. That's how I know a book is good, when I can no longer tell that I'm reading a book, when I become not a reader but another human being. I read for that sensation of transport, and I write for that sensation, too.

I had this weird experience once. I was on stage, I think at the Kansas City Public Library. Some kind of onstage conversation. And the first question the interviewer asked me was: *What's the purpose of literature?* Imagine getting that question unannounced. And out of my mouth popped: "It's a rehearsal for death." I'd never thought about that before I said it, but in some ways I think it's true. Fiction's about running through other people's lives, running through the great and terrible things that happen along the way, and especially the thing that lies at the end, experiencing it over and over and over. Whether or not a novel actually contains death, it's often about the highlights of a life. Literature allows us to experience thousands of lives, to understand how we might want to live our own.

But back to "A Silver Dish." There's a little mystery in this story: Twice, Bellow slips out of third person and into first. "He wanted me to be like himself—an American," the narrator says, at one point. Is it some sort of meta-fiction, as if Bellow anticipated the current trend of narrators having the same names as their authors? I don't know what to make of those two little shifts in point of view, unless they're little tacit admissions that this story is indeed about him. Some kind of winking admission that this is I, Saul Bellow, and not Woody.

Whatever it is, "A Silver Dish" gives us profound access to the life of another. For me, that's what great fiction is: the window through to someone else's days on earth. *That was how he was.* It's all of literature, isn't it? Or pretty damn close.

For a few minutes his joy was immediate and unspoiled, and then it was smashed and he remembered again what he had said to Molly in the tunnel, for through the quiet—all other noises were suspended for this new sound—came the roaring of the car, tearing along the road with the cut-out open, and he could see it, a scarlet Model A roadster with the top down as it appeared and disappeared in the lacy sarvis berry that grew along the bank.

—JEAN STAFFORD, *The Mountain Lion*

EILEEN MYLES

Happy Accidents

I FOUND JEAN STAFFORD'S *The Mountain Lion* at a thrift in Marfa. I thought, I ought to read some Western fiction, you know? It just seemed like, *The Mountain Lion*—who could be interested in *that*? I almost bought it as a joke. I don't like reading logically. I love having a library of lots of odd books around me, and whenever I'm staying somewhere for a while, I buy a ton of books; I like to reproduce a kind of mini-used-bookstore experience wherever I am. So I picked this book up on a whim.

Right away, I could see what a fine stylist she was, though there were so many things that were of the period, including amazing racism, just casual racism. But as the book proceeded I began to see a doubleness there—Stafford's speaking truthfully about her era without being simply of it. I started to realize that this is an astonishing writer.

The Mountain Lion is a family novel, and it starts with four kids living with their widowed mother, who's been through a couple of husbands. They're in Los Angeles, and then they have this opportunity to go to Colorado to live with their booze-swilling, big-booted grandfather, who their mother disapproves of. The family's sort of divided into two older, perfect, preppy daughters and two confused, skinny, slightly ailing younger kids who are the narrators of the book—Molly and Ralph.

At some point the two of them go there for a whole year, and in that year their very close relationship falls apart. Molly keeps getting weirder and weirder, while Ralph quickens and thickens and starts to become a man. The grandfather kicked off on their porch maybe the year before, so his son, Claude—who's sort of a dumber, less sophisticated version of him—becomes their guide through the western world. He takes up with Ralph, starts to take the boy hunting; ultimately, the great hunt becomes about a mountain lion, which the two of them have spotted near the ranch, even though there haven't been any mountain lions in the area for decades. When Ralph gets told by his uncle Claude that they can share in the pursuit of the mountain lion, he, for a second, fantasizes that he might be the one to kill her. It's a great moment of imaginary triumph, one that kicks us into this passage:

> For a few minutes his joy was immediate and unspoiled, and then it was smashed and he remembered again what he had said to Molly in the tunnel, for through the quiet—all other noises were suspended for this new sound—came the roaring of the car, tearing along the road with the cut-out open, and he could see it, a scarlet Model A roadster with the top down as it appeared and disappeared in the lacy sarvis berry that grew along the bank.

This seems so cinematic to me, the activeness and the complete momentum of the roadster appearing and disappearing. It's such a modern perspective on detail in fiction. The car is there, and the car is vanishing, and that's how we know something is actually moving, that the place is a real place. It designates time and space in one swift gesture. We all participate in primitive ways of thinking about time and space, ways that are really childlike and peekaboo. *Is the thing gone? Is the thing here?* That's what drew me to the passage initially.

But when I went back and looked over the whole thing a second time, I realized the incredible complexity of this passage, this single sentence. There's the flicker of the roadster against the daintiness of the lace, that butch/femme combination. And then the fact that time exists in multiples. There's the time of the train moving. The time of the berries growing. And the time of the roadster, moving and then disappearing down the road. It's exacting, vivid, and real in a way that just seems very post-painting—post-literary, even. She allows so much unknow-ingness, too. I didn't bother looking up what a sarvis berry was, but somehow that detail adds to the reality of the moment.

If you've read the book, you know that, just as the train is about to go into the tunnel, Ralph says to his sister, "Tell me all the dirty words you know." That interaction is the beginning of the end of their relationship, which you sense here: The moment starts with this kid's great joy, which is then smashed by the offstage revelation of what he's just said to Molly as they go into the tunnel. Stafford never describes it, but I imagine a look of horror on her face. It just perfumes the whole last quarter of the book, this feeling that her brother is dirty. And he feels enormously guilty himself. He's just discovering sex, and he wants to know what his sister knows. What this hot car is about, by the way, is that the girl Ralph has a crush on has a boyfriend who has a roadster. The flickering road-ster, it's like sex *and* guilt. Just waves of it.

It's so emotionally true: the high of joy, and then suddenly that shitty, dirty feeling, and then quiet. It pairs pleasure and shame, interior and exterior, nature and the machinic. And suddenly, along comes the girl that he loves in a car, and it's like he's being betrayed or robbed of his future love even, all so swiftly, in one sentence. It seems incredible that she did so much at once, like a scene from a movie. That filmic quality is probably not an accident: In 1947, when she published this, every writer and every consciousness was completely imbued with the cinematic. You couldn't look at the world anymore without looking at it like a movie. And yet text is the higher movie, somehow: Here, multi-ple times are collapsed into one in a way that would be hard for any film to accomplish so fluidly.

Part of what's so exciting, too, is the consciousness of the writer who made this. We're talking about a female writer describing male joy, after all (even paired with a kind of sexual violence). The violence of his guilt, the sweetness of the loss of his innocence—all of it comes from a woman writer constructing a man. That's part of what's beautiful, and sensitive, and quickening about this passage, too. We're used to drag in literature, but by and large, when I read male characters written by women in conventional fiction, I still feel just this weighty burden of trying to prove that you're in a male body and you know it. *This must be what a man feels like when he sweats*, and so on. Likewise, I was just read-ing a novel-in-process by a friend of mine, and there was something about the woman going to the toilet that he felt like he needed to de-scribe, and it was written in a way that would just never be female. There's such lightness in this passage. Stafford just gets the feelings of the man, and it's a testament to how we're all pretty gender fluid. That's part of what great fiction is, really: transcending gender by anyone.

It's funny to think I just stumbled on this book by chance. I must have been escaping from something much more heavy—I love the tur-gid pace of an academic book, if it's a topic I really care about, about once a year. I think I probably escaped to Jean Stafford from something like that, and I didn't expect much of her. I thought, *Oh, this is just good old-fashioned fiction, I'll try that for a change.* So often you're just reacting to the last book you read, and you want something that's a little bit of an antidote to that. I've found that if I live a more programmatic life where I'm reading the books that I'm *supposed* to read—if I'm accom-plishing all my little chores of reading what everybody else is reading—I stop having time to read in a way that's rich and multiple.

I loved college, and I hated college, because for the first time in my life, my reading was being organized in some external way. I was sup-posed to read *these* books now. It created a procrastination and an un-willingness about reading in me, and I experience the same thing now. If I've got to read a book for a purpose, I start to read other sub-books around it almost out of rebellion, and those sub-books often are the most wild ones. I'd sooner read the books I found on a table on Avenue A last night than the latest thing everyone else is reading.

I never go all the way and read real mass-market crap, but I'll read things that seem middle-of-the-road or conservative just as a reaction to whatever I've been reading. Right now, Thomas Bernhard is who I'm excited by, and I've been resisting Thomas Bernhard for about ten years. As soon as somebody's in the air, I just feel like—no. I mean, I don't know when I will ever read Karl Ove Knausgaard. I may never get to that guy for a variety of reasons, but mostly because I'm *supposed* to read him. I need to read perversely. Reading is a space that is absolutely mine, that always was mine, and I'm always reclaiming it. As writers, we just need so much time to lie around, and waste time, and dream, and just be private, and flow. You can't tell me what to think. You can't tell me what to look at. You can't tell me what to know.

I always like reclaiming that perverse pleasure—even reclaiming it from myself. When I was a kid growing up in Catholic school, it was one kind of thing that I was sneaking under my desk. And now, when I'm supposed to be some kind of literary queer, I still want to read something else. As soon as I know who I am, I don't want to be that person, you know? Part of it is the constant destruction and construction of the self. The texts aren't changing, but we are—and I think that changing lens is the thing that I'm alive in.

Used bookstores seem like the place to browse most widely now. The commercial marketplaces are just so chosen. As much as all of us want our books out on the table, the fact there even *is* a table just pisses me off. What I love to do is go into a bookstore right near Café Mogador on St. Mark's Place. I think it's called Eastside Books. I can't even remember the name of it, but it's been there forever, and you always go in there looking for something, but you always come out with something else.

With all that's going on in the abstract web, and with social media, I feel like the grottiness of the used bookstore is more important than ever before. Used bookstores were where I discovered avant-garde literature, even more so than in my college classes. You just picked shit up, and you're like, what is this? I think the hand-eye connection is unseverable for passionate readers.

For me, the Internet is more of a writing place than a reading place. I just really don't enjoy reading on my computer. For a few years around 1999, 2000, I had a loft in Times Square, and it was the best space I had ever had as a person living in Manhattan or in New York. And I remember the moment when I was working on some piece on my computer—and suddenly, I realized that here I was, at last, finally, in this wonderful, beautiful space, and I had turned my back to it in order to inhabit the crappy, abstract space of the computer. The computer managed to take that all away. So I'm always carrying a portable printer around. I'm always printing shit out.

Part of what we love about Europe now is what a world of bookstores it is, especially because our country, in so many ways, is becoming the opposite of that. If I had any money, I would give it to the libraries. That's something I really feel strongly about. How many writers have I met who found some weird thing in the library, and it changed their lives? Those places have to exist.

I want to be in praise of the happy accident. It wasn't even a bookstore where I found Jean Stafford. It was a thrift store, and that's what's so amazing—finding books in the wrong places. When I'm finished with a book, I often like to put them on a bench of a café outside. It could just wind up in a dumpster, but somebody could find it, you know? I believe in the wrong reader, in the wrong book. We're just bodies moving in space and just accidentally you sometimes pick something up . . . just because you like a book's title, or its cover, or because it just happens to be nearby. You could stay in some guesthouse anywhere in the world, and there's three books there, and one of them changed your life. I love to be an agent of that. You never know what's going to happen when you leave a book someplace.

The Brain is just the weight of God—
For—Heft them—Pound for Pound—
And they will differ—if they do—
As Syllable from Sound—

        —EMILY DICKINSON,
"The Brain—is wider than the Sky—"

MARILYNNE ROBINSON

The Brain Is Larger
Than the Sea

ONE OF THE things I love about Emily Dickinson is the way that, every time I read her poetry, I feel as though I'm encountering it for the first time. It has this reserve of meaning that seems to open very slowly over a long series of readings. Part of that is due to the extreme compression of her poems, which strip away everything inessential, greatly magnifying the potency of each individual word. She puts an extraordinary pressure on language by her parsimoniousness. But she not only restricted her language very narrowly—apparently, she restricted her life very narrowly, too. Out of this came a body of poetry that really has no equivalent in American literature.

I'm drawn to that movement toward essentials, away from all secondary definitions, all extraneous props and ornaments. People always ask me why I often write about characters who have no name, and no place, and no money, and no anything else. Well, it's in those circumstances that you can get real definitions of things and people and experience. Dickinson lived that out.

"The Brain—is wider than the Sky—," one of my favorite Dickinson poems, is an instance where she achieves that sense of enormous scope in just a few short lines. It's about the expansiveness of the mind, our incredible, anomalous ability to take on what is vast, abstract, and intu-ited. It celebrates our brain's ability to relativize immensity in our favor, the fact that we can comprehend things that are totally out of scale with us.

Each of the poem's three stanzas pits the human mind—Dickinson uses the word "brain," but I translate that into "mind"—against vastness of a different sort. The first stanza focuses on the sky, which, she says, the brain can swallow with room to spare (for "you beside," Dickinson writes—the self is also included in the capacities of the mind). It's a trope of her Puritan tradition to be amazed by the human ability to under-stand the workings of the sky: the movements of the stars, the relative size and distance of the planets, cosmic measurements human beings worked out long, long ago. Our brains are large enough to contain and contemplate those faraway distances, using the stars' alignment to do real-world things like navigate tiny ships across the sea—the topic of the second stanza. The brain, Dickinson says, is large enough to contain the oceans, too. She likens it to a great sponge, big and absorbent enough to pull all the world's waters in.

In the final stanza, Dickinson suggests that our gift of comprehen-sion is unlike, but also deeply like, God himself:

The Brain is just the weight of God—
For—Heft them—Pound for Pound—
And they will differ—if they do—
As Syllable from Sound—

For the first time, here, the scale does not tip our way—the brain is "*just*" the weight of God, a relationship between seeming equals. It's interesting that she uses weight here, when, in fact, she's talking about two things that really cannot be weighed. How strange that she would talk about God pound for pound, that heft would be relevant to the circumstance. It's completely outside any conception of God that she could have been reading.

But the incomparability is her point. In order to assert a likeness between the brain and God, even to suggest how they might be compared, you have to move into language that is not appropriate to either one of them. If there is a difference, it's the difference between utterance—"syllable," which is us in the metaphor—and the *capacity* for utterance, sound. The end of the poem turns to this mystery—what other word could you use?—of a likeness that is absolute, and at the same time conditioned by the fact of our mortality. In four or five words she raises this metaphysical question of inexhaustible interest.

This final formulation puts a tremendous emphasis on human utterance, sanctifying it. It recalls "In the beginning was the word" in its suggestion that our language is somehow akin to God's own creative power.

The theologies that are built around language are really onto something, I think. It's extraordinary how language behaves like another huge mind, one that we can delve into at need. Think how much any individual mind, any brain, is enlarged by what we can know through books and through literature—places, people, ideas that we would never otherwise experience, things much larger than anyone could contain in his or her own person. People crave this. You go way back into antiquity and everybody's memorizing Homer, everybody's memorizing *The Epic of Gilgamesh*; works of literature like that build the cultural mind and make it capacious. Most of us are not the creators of those things, but we possess ourselves of them—or they possess *us* of *them*. And each successive work of literature expands the possibilities of our language, deepening our expressive capacity.

That experience instills a certain awe. This awe is the explicit subject of "The Brain—is wider than the Sky—," but other works on different topics still serve the same function: They remind us how miraculous our potential really is. In almost every major literature there are works that make you love being human, and make you love and revere the humanity of other people. That is the great potential of any art.

Viewed this way, our language—and especially literature, that special, potent case—has incredible power. I'm very struck by something that I read from a seventeenth-century English writer, one who's quoted by Jonathan Edwards. He talks about how whatever we say lives after us, that we continue to exist so long as any word we say exists in a living mind. And that there should be two judgments: one when we die, and one when the full impact of our lives has played itself out. That is, when every word that we've said, for good or ill, basically ceases to be active.

We're not in the habit of thinking of ourselves as people of influence in this way. We don't think that, if we say something cruel and destructive now, it can go down generations in terms of its consequences. But it strikes me that that's true—and the thought makes me experience certain fear and trembling about our political life at the moment. When we speak, we should ask ourselves: How will this ultimately play out? What will be the moral consequence of the fact that so many people have resorted to such crude, cruel language? We know it won't be neutral. We know it won't evaporate. It'll be in people's minds for generations.

Coming across this idea as eloquently expressed as it was by this writer really made me stop, and think, and recognize the obvious truth of what he says—as if I'd known it before, but never feeling it so sharply as when he articulated it well. Which is a strange thing: Often, when I see a new idea I really love, my response to it feels like recognition. Even though exactly my pleasure in it is the fact that I hadn't thought of it before. There's a way in which aesthetics and ideas seem to appeal to a kind of foreknowledge. And you should bring that expectation to what you read. I imagine that people who don't like to read poetry, for example, don't come to poems assuming that they'll find there something that, in some mysterious sense, they do already know. But it happens all the time. I spend a lot of time thinking about the mind, but I could not have articulated its vastness without the help of Emily Dickinson, even though I recognize what she says as something that I would wish to be able to say myself.

I have this experience of recognition, not just in response to others' ideas, but on the order of a single word. It happens, in my own writing, in those moments when you know there's a perfect word, even though you have not written it yet. You cast about for it, and over time, some obscure word will come to you—your mind knows it's there. Often, it's a word with such an extraordinary precision that you wonder how it survived. You think, *This must have come down from early modern English or Anglo-Saxon—how did it come to birth? How did it survive? Who was it that needed this word first and coined it?* It's amazing. You wonder how many people have had any use for it over the last 300 years, but there it is.

Writing should always be exploratory. There shouldn't be the assumption that you know ahead of time what you want to express. When you enter into the dance with language, you'll begin to find that there's something before, or behind, or more absolute than the thing that you thought you wanted to express. And as you work, other kinds of meaning emerge than what you might have expected. It's like wrestling with the angel: On the one hand you feel the constraints of what can be said, but on the other hand you feel the infinite potential. There's nothing more interesting than language and the problem of trying to bend it to your will, which you can never quite do. You can only find what it contains, which is always a surprise.

To Slay the Folks and Cleanse the Land
And Leave the World a Reeking Roastie
High Purpose of the Gallant Band
And Six Were Kids and One a Ghostie.

—R. A. LAFFERTY, *The Reefs of Earth*

NEIL GAIMAN

Random Joy

WHEN I WAS twelve or thirteen, I had an experience that changed the way I perceived literature. It happened when I picked up a copy of R. A. Lafferty's *The Reefs of Earth* in cheap Ace paperback in some English secondhand shop. It was an American edition, and I have no idea to this day where it came from or how it got there. But it completely turned things inside out for me.

I remember reading the book the first time, and noticing that the chapter titles were slightly odd—they felt like nice, solid chapter titles that describe what's in the chapter. Then, at some point I went back to reread the table of contents, and I realized: It's a poem. It's a glorious poem. It was as if a giant light had gone on and angels, really grubby angels, had come down from the sky tooting on mouth organs and combs with tissue paper over them, to proclaim that there are no rules. It was the moment I realized—*Oh my god, you can do anything in literature*. No matter what anybody tells you about writing, you can do whatever the fuck you want.

I love the fact that I can remember it. I can actually quote all sixteen chapter titles from memory:

1. To Slay the Folks and Cleanse the Land
2. And Leave the World a Reeking Roastie
3. High Purpose of the Gallant Band
4. And Six Were Kids and One a Ghostie.
5. A Child's a Monster Still Uncurled
6. The World's a Trap, and None Can Quit It—
7. The "Strife Dulanty" with the World
8. Was Mostly That They Didn't Fit It. . . .

You read that, you go, "You're having too much fun." But it's so easy as an author to forget about fun, to forget about joy. To forget about glorious, redundant curlicues that only exist because—well, why the fuck *wouldn't* you do that? Because you can. You should be able to have joy in making the words. You do it for the same reason that God created the duck-billed platypus. A Hemingway God would not build the duck-billed platypus. It is too ridiculous, and too redundant, and too unlikely. But it makes so much more interesting a world having duck-billed platypuses everywhere.

There are no rules. Only: Can you do this with confidence? Can you do it with aplomb? Can you do it with style? Can you do it with joy? If you can, you could write a short story that's an essay on sixteenth-century mapmaking, and everything would go, "Oh my god, what a delightful short story." It's because you enjoy yourself. You can put things in rhyme, you can create footnotes, sometimes I even just have my characters talk in iambic pentameter—you do it all because you want to. More than anything else, I just love random fucking joy. Doing things because you can. Taking pleasure in it. The joy of being an author is the joy of feeling I can do anything. While it's me and my piece of paper, I'm God.

Not that there will be joy every day, every sentence, and in every everything you do. It doesn't work like that. If you're writing something as long as a novel, you're going to write on the good days, and you're going to write on the bad. You're going to write on the days that you've got a migraine and your wife left you. You're going to write on the days when you sit down light and happy of heart, and every word drips from your pen or from your fingertips like liquid diamond glinting in the sunlight. You look up, and you somehow did 5,000 words of perfect wonderfulness that day.

But an interesting thing happens when, three or four drafts down the line, you're reading the galleys. You've been sent the proofs to read, and you're proofreading. You know intellectually that some of these pages were written on glorious days. Some of them were written on terrible days. Some of them were written on days when, as far as you were concerned, you had the worst, most appalling writer's block in the world, and you were just putting down any old nonsense to try to get something down. And some of them were put down on magic days. The truth is, you can't tell. It all reads like you. It's all part of the same book.

It shouldn't be that way. It would be wonderful if you went, "Ah, here is a fantastic page. Here is a terrible page." But once you've got a little time, that's not really detectable. And it's because of all of the work that you did. It's all the wall that you built by taking the word and putting it in, and taking another one, and taking another one.

I answered a question recently online. Somebody said something like, "What do you do when you get stuck in the middle of a novel, and you know where the plot is meant to go, but you're in a place where you can't see your way from here to there?" My answer was incredibly simple: You make stuff up. That made a few people grumpy—acting as if I was making fun of them, or I was keeping the truth from them somehow. But I wanted to go back and say, "You made the whole thing up. You made up the beginning. You made up the end. Right now you're a roadrunner running from mesa to mesa across the air on a bridge of stuff that you'd made up. All that happened is you stopped, and you looked down, and you realized there's nothing underneath you. Look back up at that mesa, and start running again."

One of the things I think people really respond to in fiction—as, perhaps, in life—is just knowing you're in safe hands. Feeling like you know that the person doing the thing knows what they're doing, and is enjoying it. Also, it's all made up. All of the things that are considered rules are rules until you break them. They're only rules until you throw them out because you don't need them anymore.

Lafferty was the only author I ever had the confidence to write to. I would have been nineteen or twenty, and I found an address in some who's who of authors in my local library. *I could write to him*, I realized, and I did. Somehow, the letter—having gone from place to place, forwarded from wherever he was living in the 1960s to his home in the 1970s—eventually made it to him. And three months later, I got a reply. And for a little while in there I corresponded with Lafferty.

I sent him a derivative story, a Lafferty-ish story. He wrote back and was polite about it. He answered lots of questions. Mostly it was just that thing when you're a nineteen-, twenty-, twenty-one-year-old and you're full of dreams, and somebody finally seems to be taking you seriously and treating you like an adult. At that age, mostly what you need is to be taken seriously, because that's where the confidence comes from.

Suddenly, I had a very real sense that writers were real people. Up until that point, they'd seemed more like magical ghosts. But, suddenly, I had a writer I loved who was writing to me. It gave me a wonderful feeling: *Well, I might be a writer, too.*

The interesting thing was that the words in Lafferty's letters read like Lafferty. I started to realize that style is not an affectation—it's the stuff that you can't help doing. I remember running into a quote once years ago from Jerry Garcia of the Grateful Dead, where he said, "Style is the stuff you got wrong." Because if you took him out, the person, everything would be played beautifully and perfectly—the falling away from perfection is what we recognize, and that makes style. It's a fascinating quote, but when I went to Google it, all I was ever able to find was me saying it quoted in interviews. (Perhaps he never said it at all.) But there's definitely that feeling that, at the end of the day, style is the stuff you can't help doing.

My sympathies lie with writing professors, but I think they are a terrible thing. (I include myself in their number.) The biggest problem is that writing professors get prescriptive. What you're trying to do with a young, unformed writer is, a lot of the time, like trying to teach a small child that there are things to eat other than peanut butter and jelly sandwiches. The writing student turns up. They've *read* nothing but peanut butter and jelly sandwiches, they want to *write* peanut butter and jelly sandwiches. And now you, as a professor, are going, "Okay, eat some of this Chinese food over here. Good, now eat this curry. Now let's examine salads." Somebody goes, "But peanut butter and jelly!" And you go, "Well, yeah—but no, not right now. Let's talk about all of the other things. Let's talk about Ethiopian food."

The trouble is that, fairly often, the love and the joy go away. The reason they wanted to be a writer was because they loved peanut butter and jelly sandwiches. All they really take away from their course is that they used to love peanut butter and jelly sandwiches, and now they've been told that's a bad thing. They had to eat all these things they didn't really enjoy, and the whole thing now tastes like spinach, and they're done.

That's why it's important to read so widely when you're younger. I think your receptors are open at a right age to so much, and you don't necessarily even understand at that point where all of your influences are coming from, or what they can mean, nor should you. They compost down anyway, good influences, no matter how old you are. It's like when you put the scraps onto your compost heap: eggshells, and it's half-eaten turnips, and it's apple cores, and the like. A year later, it's black mulch that you can grow stuff in. And influences, good ones, are that too. Trying to figure out what's influenced you is as difficult as taking the black mulch, and saying this used to be half an apple.

Some years ago, I was talking about a short story that I'd done a long, long time ago—and somebody asked if they could read it. I went and found my old notebooks, and pulled them down, and started reading the stuff that I was writing when I was eighteen, nineteen, twenty. (About when I was reading—and writing to—Lafferty.) The truth is, if somebody showed that story to me now, and said, "Does this person have a future as a writer?" I would think, "No, probably not." There's no evidence of any potential. The stuff reads like the novel openings and terrible short stories of a nineteen-year-old with nothing to say, but who is desperate to talk.

I wanted to be a writer, and I didn't have anything to write about. I was kind of judging myself against all of the prodigies. Anyone from Chatterton to Samuel R. Delany, these are people who had their first novels published when they were nineteen. I had nothing to say. That's okay. You're not actually expected to have new and original things to say. Somewhere in there I actually looked around and I had things to say.

A good writer I know—Brian Vaughan, who did *Y: The Last Man*, and now does lots of wonderful television—tells the story of meeting me when he was a young writer and couldn't get published. He turned up at one of my signings, and when he stopped to talk with me, he just basically outlined his problem. I listened. "Look," I said. "Normally the advice that I give people is: Just write. But, in your case, the advice that I give you is *live*. Stop worrying about writing, and go and do shit. Go get your heart broken. Get a job or two. Knock around. Have things happen—because you don't have anything to write about yet, and you need that. You're a good enough writer, and you have the ability, but you don't have anything to say yet."

He said he went off and did that, and everything worked. He came to me years on. He said, "Did you give that advice to everybody?" I said, "No, almost nobody." Quite possibly he was the only person I've ever given that particular piece of advice to: Just live. Sometimes, that's necessary too.

Acknowledgments

Most books are the product of willful isolation, created by many hours of prolonged solitude. This one was never like that. It's been a deeply collaborative project from the beginning, and I've been lucky to work with so many talented people along the way.

I owe a major debt to the publicists and editors, agents and assistants—too many to name here—who helped convince authors to contribute to this project. Thank you for blocking out time from crowded schedules, for facilitating phone calls to private offices and hotels on the road. This book would not exist without your work.

Thank you to my editors at *The Atlantic*—to Spencer Kornhaber, who took a chance on my pitch for an unorthodox weekly column, and subsequently to Ashley Fetters and Sophie Gilbert for shepherding many of these pieces into public life.

To Debbie Kahkejian, loyal reader: Thank you for reminding me weekly that this work matters.

To Doug McLean: Thank you for embarking on this creative partnership with me, for lending your vision to this project, for the late nights you spend planning and sketching and perfecting. Our work together has been a mainstay now for years; I consider it a great privilege, and a pleasure.

To my amazing editor, Sam Raim: Thank you for seeing the potential for this book from the beginning, for knowing intuitively what it needed at every turn, and for taking on the enormous logistical task of making it more than an idea. You simply made everything so much better.

To my agent, Ellen Levine, who enthusiastically took on a book project with unique challenges and complexities: I could not ask for a better reader and advocate. Thank you.

To my wife, Rachel: The seed of this project, like so much of what I do, sprang directly from our conversations. Thank you for encouraging me, always, to think bigger but also to follow through.

Finally, I'm deeply grateful to my author contributors: You took time away from your own projects to open up about your private memories, to find language for the workings of the mind, to let me look over your shoulder while you write. Thank you, too, for sharing these cherished texts. There is a human impulse to guard what is precious and keep it to oneself—but you have generously, freely shared what you most value. I'm a better, wiser, more productive person as a result, and I suspect—as this book makes its way into the world—that I won't be the only one.